MARKETING IN AND FOR A SUSTAINABLE SOCIETY

REVIEW OF MARKETING RESEARCH

Series Editor: Naresh K. Malhotra

REVIEW OF MARKETING RESEARCH   VOLUME 13

MARKETING IN AND FOR A SUSTAINABLE SOCIETY

EDITED BY

NARESH K. MALHOTRA

Georgia Institute of Technology,
Atlanta, GA, USA

United Kingdom – North America – Japan
India – Malaysia – China

Emerald Group Publishing Limited
Howard House, Wagon Lane, Bingley BD16 1WA, UK

First edition 2016

British Library Cataloguing in Publication Data
A catalogue record for this book is available from the British Library

ISBN: 978-1-78635-282-8
ISSN: 1548-6435 (Series)

Printed and bound by CPI Group (UK) Ltd, Croydon, CR0 4YY

ISOQAR certified
Management System,
awarded to Emerald
for adherence to
Environmental
standard
ISO 14001:2004.

Certificate Number 1985
ISO 14001

INVESTOR IN PEOPLE

CONTENTS

LIST OF CONTRIBUTORS

Panayiota J. Alevizou	Management School, University of Sheffield, Sheffield, UK
Nikhilesh Dholakia	College of Business Administration, University of Rhode Island, Kingston, RI, USA
O. C. Ferrell	Jack C. Massey Graduate School of Business, Belmont University, Nashville, TN, USA
Tracy L. Gonzalez-Padron	Department of Marketing, Strategy, and International Business, University of Colorado Colorado Springs, Colorado Springs, CO, USA
G. Tomas M. Hult	Eli Broad Graduate School of Management, Michigan State University, East Lansing, MI, USA
Bipul Kumar	Marketing Department, Indian Institute of Management, Indore, India
Matthew B. Lunde	College of Business, University of Wyoming, Laramie, WY, USA
Diane M. Martin	School of Business, Aalto University, Helsinki, Finland
Seonaidh McDonald	Aberdeen Business School, Robert Gordon University, Aberdeen, UK
Jakki J. Mohr	School of Business Administration and Institute on Ecosystems, University of Montana, Missoula, MT, USA
Caroline J. Oates	Management School, University of Sheffield, Sheffield, UK

Mark Peterson   College of Business, University of
                         Wyoming, Laramie, WY, USA

Linda L. Price   Eller College of Management, University of
                         Arizona, Tucson, AZ, USA

Aric Rindfleisch   College of Business, University of Illinois
                         at Urbana—Champaign, Champaign,
                         IL, USA

Terhi Väistö   School of Business, Aalto University,
                         Helsinki, Finland

Rajan Varadarajan   Department of Marketing, Texas A&M
                         University, College Station, TX, USA

EDITORIAL ADVISORY BOARD

AD HOC REVIEWERS

In addition to members of the Editorial Review Board, Review of Marketing Research makes use of several ad hoc reviewers. The following individuals reviewed submissions for Volume 13.

James Agarwal
University of Calgary

Justin Angle
University of Montana

Victoria L. Crittenden
Babson College

S. Tamer Cavusgil
Georgia State University

Patrick L. Murphy
Notre Dame

Robert Nason
Michigan State University

Can Uslay
Rutgers University

Richard J. Varey
Waikato Management School

INTRODUCTION

OVERVIEW

Review of Marketing Research, now in its 13th volume, is a publication covering the important areas of marketing research with a more comprehensive state-of-the-art orientation. The papers in this publication review the literature in a particular area, offer a critical commentary, develop an innovative framework, and discuss future developments, as well as present specific empirical studies. The first 12 volumes have featured some of the top researchers and scholars in our discipline who have reviewed an array of important topics. The response to the first 12 volumes has been truly gratifying and we look forward to the impact of the 13th volume with great anticipation.

PUBLICATION MISSION

The purpose of this series is to provide current, comprehensive, state-of-the-art articles in *Review of Marketing Research*. Wide ranging paradigmatic or theoretical, or substantive agendas are appropriate for this publication. This includes a wide range of theoretical perspectives, paradigms, data (qualitative, survey, experimental, ethnographic, secondary, etc.), and topics related to the study and explanation of marketing-related phenomenon. We reflect an eclectic mixture of theory, data, and research methods that is indicative of a publication driven by important theoretical and substantive problems. We seek studies that make important theoretical, substantive, empirical, methodological, measurement, and modeling contributions. Any topic that fits under the broad area of "marketing research" is relevant. In short, our mission is to publish the best reviews in the discipline.

Thus, this publication bridges the gap left by current marketing research publications. Current marketing research publications such as the *Journal of Marketing Research* (USA), *International Journal of Marketing Research* (UK), and *International Journal of Research in Marketing* (Europe) publish academic articles with a major constraint on the length. In contrast, *Review of Marketing Research* will publish much longer articles that are not only theoretically rigorous but also more expository, with a focus on implementing new marketing research concepts and procedures. This will also serve to distinguish this publication from *Marketing Research* magazine published by the American Marketing Association (AMA).

Articles in *Review of Marketing Research* should address the following issues:

- Critically review the existing literature
- Summarize what we know about the subject — key findings
- Present the main theories and frameworks
- Review and give an exposition of key methodologies
- Identify the gaps in literature
- Present empirical studies (for empirical papers only)
- Discuss emerging trends and issues
- Focus on international developments
- Suggest directions for future theory development and testing
- Recommend guidelines for implementing new procedures and concepts.

ARTICLES IN THIS VOLUME

This special issue focuses on *Marketing in and for a Sustainable Society*.

Varadarajan argues that growth in a sustainability requires that organizations while striving for a larger market footprint must also concurrently strive for a smaller environmental footprint. He presents a conceptual framework delineating a number of environmental and organizational factors that undergird greater levels of organizational responsiveness to environmental sustainability. Consumers, corporations, and the government at various levels all play a role and share responsibility for environmental sustainability. The role of the government is critical in that firms and consumers are likely to either embrace environmentally sustainable behaviors, or may find it necessary to engage in environmentally unsustainable behaviors.

In spite of business progress in environmental sustainability, global climate change metrics remain discouraging and progress is lagging behind global needs. Mohr, Price, and Rindfleisch articulate four explanations for the lack of meaningful progress in environmental sustainability. They discuss two theoretical streams (assemblage theory and resilience theory) that harmonize ecological and human domains. They integrate these theories to present a mid-range theory, biomimicry, to bridge the gap between these higher-level theories and practical managerial decisions. Finally, they offer implications and ideas for future research based on their integrated theoretical framework.

Stakeholder marketing assumes that paying attention to multiple stakeholders will increase positive impacts and decrease negative impacts on the various stakeholders of the firm and will result in increased customer satisfaction, innovation, and reputation. Gonzalez-Padron, Hult, and Ferrell investigate the incorporation of stakeholder issues in marketing strategy to explain firm performance. They find a positive relationship between overall stakeholder responsiveness and marketing outcomes, and thereby build a case for stakeholder marketing as a foundation for marketing strategy.

Overconsumption and degradation of resources have led to a focus on sustainability as a megatrend that is influencing how firms compete. Peterson and Lunde review important developments regarding such a focus in the scholarly, practitioner and consumer domains. While a turn toward sustainability can be identified across these domains, much remains to be done to realize a sustainable world where the lifestyles of future generations are not compromised due to degradation of resources. They advocate a turn to sustainable business practices as a path forward.

McDonald, Oates, and Alevizou discuss the ways in which sustainable consumption has been conceptualized within marketing. They question the norm of using the individual as a unit of analysis, arguing that individuals rarely act in a way that is acontextual and that consumption takes place as households or communities. Further, they highlight inconsistency of consumer behavior in conducting sustainability research. They examine the norms that have been inherited from positivist social science traditions and discuss the effects of positivism on research designs. They conclude that in order to make advances in sustainability research, we need alternative frames, terms, units of analysis, and methodologies.

Kumar and Dholakia contend that pro-sustainability behaviors are complex and multidimensional. Sustainability goals can be achieved only when firms, consumers, and other institutions such as governments move in cohesive and complementary ways. Thus, pro-sustainability behaviors need to be aligned across institutions and individuals. They review the literature on sustainability, behavioral change, environmentalism, and other related fields, and propose a comprehensive macromarketing framework to foster and diffuse pro-sustainability behaviors.

Martin and Väistö examine the attitude-behavior gap in sustainable consumption proposing a reconsideration of the primacy of cognitive-rational aspects of consumer purchase behavior to include a focus on the importance of fun. They argue that greater focus on consumer experience in sustainable consumption offers potential for additional strategies to bridge the gap. Research in sustainability should examine the linkages of hedonic, aesthetic, and cognitive aspect of consumption. As an illustrative case study, Martin and Väistö look at the electric vehicle marketing strategy in the United States as a possible approach to bridge the attitude-behavior gap in sustainable consumption.

It is hoped that collectively the papers in this volume will substantially aid our efforts to understand, model, and make predictions about both the firm and the consumer in the area of sustainability and provide fertile areas for future research. The *Review of Marketing Research* continues its mission of systematically analyzing and presenting accumulated knowledge in the field of marketing as well as influencing future research by identifying areas that merit the attention of researchers.

Naresh K. Malhotra
Editor

SUSTAINABILITY AND MARKETING: CONCURRENT PURSUIT OF A SMALLER ENVIRONMENTAL FOOTPRINT AND A LARGER MARKET FOOTPRINT

Rajan Varadarajan

ABSTRACT

Purpose — *The purpose of this paper is to present a conceptual frame-work that provides insights into major environmental and organizational forces underlying greater levels of organizational responsiveness to the environmental sustainability imperative by a growing number of firms, worldwide.*

Methodology/approach — *The paper is conceptual in its focus, and the proposed framework builds on extant literature from multiple literature streams.*

Marketing In and For a Sustainable Society
Review of Marketing Research, Volume 13, 1–27
ISSN: 1548-6435/doi:10.1108/S1548-643520160000013009

Findings — *Societal progress toward environmental sustainability is a shared responsibility of consumers, corporations, and the government at various levels. A potential avenue for societal progress toward environmental sustainability is fostering a macroenvironment that is conducive to the elimination of consumption certain products, reduction in consumption certain other products, and redirection of consumption of still other products from ecologically more harmful to ecologically less harmful substitute products (and relatedly, demand elimination, demand reduction, and demand redirection).*

Research and practical implications — *An implication for corporate sustainability responsibility is that firms while planning and formulating strategies for increasing their market footprint must also concurrently plan and formulate strategies for decreasing their environmental footprint. An implication for government sustainability responsibility is that even under conditions of high levels of commitment by a large and growing number of firms and consumers to engage in environmentally sustainable behaviors, in the absence of supporting infrastructure for engaging in such behavior, they may find it necessary to engage in environmentally unsustainable behaviors.*

Originality/value — *Issues relating to environmental sustainability have been the focus of a large body of recent research in a number of academic disciplines including marketing. A cursory examination of numerous articles published in scholarly journals on issues pertaining to environmental sustainability, and in the business press pertaining to the myriad environmental sustainability initiatives of firms worldwide is indicative of its growing importance.*

Keywords: Environmental sustainability and marketing; corporate sustainability responsibility; consumption elimination, reduction and redirection; demand elimination, reduction and redirection

INTRODUCTION

Today, managing a company's environmental footprint is less and less limited to the environmental department. Increasingly, it is the domain of procurement, finance, facilities, fleets, legal, operations, real estate, supply chain, marketing, investor relations, even human resources. Growing numbers of us are recycling, telecommuting, rethinking business travel, turning off lights, rooting out waste, and generally being more conscious of the impacts of the things we do at work. In some companies, such activities are tied to managers' and executives' performance evaluations and compensation. Increasingly, these efforts are directed by someone in the C-suite. (Joel Makower and editors of GreenBiz.com, 2011)

In recent years, issues relating to environmental sustainability (hereafter, sustainability) have steadily risen in importance as principal concerns of consumer groups and individual consumers, for-profit and not-for-profit organizations, governments and nongovernmental organizations (NGOs), public interest groups and other stakeholder groups, and researchers in a number of academic disciplines. Across industries worldwide, there seems to be an increasing awareness among a growing number of firms of the importance of greater organizational responsiveness to the sustainability imperative. Relatedly, there also seems to be a greater awareness that organizational responsiveness to the sustainability imperative can be a win-win proposition (i.e., good for the environment and good for the firm). For instance, a global survey of executives by the MIT *Sloan Management Review* and the Boston Consulting Group (Haanaes et al., 2011) reports that executives perceive the following as among the *potential benefits* to firms of addressing sustainability related issues: (1) reduced costs due to energy efficiency, (2) reduced costs due to material or waste efficiencies, (3) increased employee productivity, (4) access to new markets, (5) improved brand reputation, (6) increased competitive advantage, (7) increased margins or market share due to sustainability positioning, (8) better innovation of product/service offerings, (9) better innovation of business models and processes, (10) improved regulatory compliance, (11) reduced risk, (12) improved perception of how well the company is managed, (13) enhanced investor/stakeholder relations, and (14) improved ability to attract and retain top talent.

Paralleling the growing awareness of the environmental sustainability imperative, there have been a number of recent additions to the marketing lexicon such as *anti-consumption, collaborative consumption, conscious consumption, constrained consumption, de-consumption, green consumption, mindful consumption, reduced consumption, responsible consumption, shared consumption, sustainable consumption, virtuous consumption,* and *wise consumption* (see Grinstein & Nisan, 2009; Kotler, 2011; Peattie & Peattie, 2009; Prothero et al., 2011; Sheth, Sethia, & Srinivas, 2011; Varey, 2011). Other related additions include *conspicuous nonconsumption* and *conspicuous consumption of ecologically less harmful substitute products* (e.g., celebrities arriving for the Oscar Awards gala in fuel-efficient hybrid cars as opposed to in gas guzzling stretch limousines).

In a seminal article published more than a half century ago, Ansoff (1957) distinguished between four broad growth avenues available to firms:

- *Market penetration*: Increasing sales or achieving greater penetration of a firm's *present* product offerings in its *present* served markets
- *Market development*: Developing *new* markets for a firm's *present* product offerings
- *Product development*: Developing *new* products for a firm's *present* served markets
- *Diversification*: Entering *new* product-markets that are either *related* or *unrelated* to a firm's present product offerings and markets served

All else being equal, a firm's organic growth (as opposed to growth through acquisitions) in any of these growth arenas will entail a net increase in the amounts of various renewable and nonrenewable resources used during the life cycle (extraction of raw materials, production, distribution, consumption/use, and postconsumption/postuse disposal stages) of each of the firm's product offerings. However, in a sustainability oriented macroenvironment, while planning for growth, firms must strategically plan to achieve significant reductions in their environmental footprints, not merely in the context of their present scale and scope of operations, but their future scale and scope of operations. The following vignettes provide additional insights into this issue.

> Unilever, an Anglo-Dutch consumer products multinational, aspires to double the size of its business while reducing its environmental impact. By the year 2020, the company aspires to add more than one billion new customers to its customer base, halve the environmental impact of its products, and source 100% of agricultural raw materials sustainably. According to its CEO, Unilever does not believe that there is a conflict between sustainability and profitable growth. He notes that there are billions of people around the world who deserve the better quality of life which its products such as soap, shampoo, and tea can provide, and the daily act of making and selling these products drives economic and social progress (Polman, 2011).

> Procter and Gamble (P&G), a US-based consumer products multinational, aspires to add 548,000 new customers a day over a five-year period (548,000 new customers a day × 365 days × 5 years = about one billion new customers over a five-year time horizon). Key to achieving the goal is cultivating new customers (competitors' customers and nonusers) in less developed countries where the firm currently has a smaller market footprint compared to some of its global competitors such as Unilever and Colgate-Palmolive (Wayne, 2009). At the same time, P&G has also committed to reducing its use of petroleum-derived materials by 25% and its packaging by 20%, and ensuring that 30% of the power for its operations is sourced from renewable energy by 2020. The company's long-term goal is to power its plants with 100% renewable energy, to

make its packaging from 100% renewable materials, and to send zero waste to landfill. According to a former CEO of P&G, the firm does not view environmental responsibility separately from the business, and that its long-term sustainability vision transcends its business and financial goals (Marketing Week, 2010).

Against this backdrop, this paper presents a conceptual framework delineating a number of forces underlying increased levels of organizational responsiveness to the environmental sustainability imperative by an increasing number of firms, worldwide. Societal progress toward environmental sustainability calls for significant progress in the realms of corporate sustainability responsibility, consumer sustainability responsibility, and government sustainability responsibility. In this context, forces that are likely to predispose businesses and consumers to engage in environmentally sustainable and unsustainable behaviors are discussed.

SUSTAINABILITY AND MARKETING: A LITERATURE OVERVIEW

One of the most widely cited definitions of *sustainable development* is "development that meets the needs of the present without compromising the ability of future generations to meet their own needs" (World Commission on Environment and Development, 1987, p. 8). Varey (2010) points out that sustainable development entails being responsive to ecological and moral imperatives, requiring equity among the present inhabitants of the earth and future inhabitants. In a review of the diverse and contested meanings of sustainable development, Williams and Millington (2004) note that the continuum of thought on sustainable development spans from those seeking to alter the demand side at one end to those seeking to alter the resource side at the other end.

Meeting the various needs of humanity entails use of both renewable and nonrenewable resources. In this regard, Godfray et al. (2010) note that while the *principle of sustainability* implies the use of renewable resources at rates that do not exceed the capacity of Earth to replenish them, by definition, dependency on nonrenewable resources is unsustainable, even if necessary as part of a trajectory toward sustainability in the short term. In a related vein, Ehrenfeld (2005) notes that *reducing unsustainability* is not the same as *creating sustainability*, and one is not simply the converse of the other. He further notes that, for the most part, the actions of firms fall in the realm of *slowing unsustainability* rather than *creating sustainability*. Illustrative of slowing unsustainability is a firm incorporating modifications in its product offerings so that they use less of various nonrenewable resources over the life cycle (i.e., resource extraction, manufacturing, distribution, use and disposal), or substituting less abundantly available nonrenewable resources with more abundantly available nonrenewable resources. Illustrative of creating sustainability is a firm in water-intensive businesses (e.g., carbonated beverages, fruit-based beverages, and bottled water) committing resources with the goal of achieving water neutrality (particularly, in countries that are water impoverished) by replenishing the Earth with as much water as it uses through initiatives such as rainwater harvesting.

A large body of literature published under the rubrics of sustainable consumption behaviors/sustainability and consumer behavior (Goldstein, Cialdini, & Griskevicius, 2008; Luchs, Naylor, Irwin, & Raghunathan, 2010), sustainable marketing/sustainable marketing practices (Sharma, Iyer, Mehrotra, & Krishnan, 2010; Van Dam & Apeldoorn, 1996; Varey, 2011), and environmental marketing/enviropreneurial marketing/green marketing (Menon & Menon, 1997; Varadarajan, 1992), and demarketing (Grinstein & Nisan, 2009; Kotler, 2011) provide valuable insights into issues at the nexus of sustainability and marketing. For instance, consumers' sustainability related attitudes, behaviors, beliefs, concerns, emotions, knowledge, and values have been the focus of a large body of prior research. Within this body of literature, a number of studies have focused on the gap between consumers' espoused attitudes toward sustainability related issues and behavior (i.e., purchase of/ownership of/use of ecologically less harmful substitute products), as well as mechanisms for bridging the gap. Kronrod, Grinstein, and Wathieu (2012) point out that persuading consumers to engage in environmentally responsible behaviors poses a challenge in light of the fact that beneficiary may not always be the consumer who engages in pro-environmental behavior, but other consumers, the society at large or the planet Earth. Illustrative of the attitude-behavior gap in reference to sustainability enhancing products is the following. A 2008 survey of 6,000 global consumers found that 87% of the respondents believed that it was their duty to contribute to a better environment, and 55% indicated that even in a recession they would pay more for a brand if it supported a cause in which they believed (Kauffeld, Malhotra, & Higgins, 2009). However, Green Works, an environment-friendly line of cleaning products that was introduced by the Clorox Company in 2008, experienced a decline in annual sales from over $100 million to less than

$60 million in the aftermath of a recession in the United States (see Clifford & Martin, 2011).

Goldstein et al. (2008) report that appeals employing descriptive norms are more effective in motivating consumers to engage in pro-environmental behaviors compared to appeals solely focused on environmental conservation. They further note that normative appeals that describe group behaviors which occurred in a setting that most closely matched the immediate situational circumstances of individuals are most effective. In a research report, Ogilvy & Mather, an advertising agency with a worldwide presence, proposes a number of solutions for bridging the green gap including the following (see Bennett & Williams, 2010): (1) *making it personal* (asking not what the consumer can do for sustainability, but asking what sustainability can do for them, and then showing them); (2) *creating better defaults* (if green is the default, people don't have to decide to be green); (3) *innovating* (high-performing sustainable choices are key for mass adoption); (4) *making it tangible* (sustainability is harder to follow when consumers can't see the trail); and (5) *making it easy to navigate* (addressing eco-suspicion and eco-confusion with truth, transparency, and a clear road map).

Extant literature also provides valuable insights into the theoretical underpinnings of research focused on consumer-related sustainability issues (e.g., *attitudes and behaviors of consumers*), and business-related sustainability issues (e.g., *behaviors of firms*). Schultz and Holbrook (1999) explore the relevance of the tragedy of commons (Hardin, 1968) as a theoretical lens for the study of environmental issues in marketing. Polonsky, Vocino, Grau, Garma, and Ferdous (2012) use theory of reasoned action (Ajzen & Fishbein, 1980) to study the effect of consumers' general environmental knowledge and carbon-related environmental knowledge on their attitudes toward the environment, general pro-environmental behaviors and carbon offset-related behaviors. Moons and De Pelsmacker (2012) build on the theory of planned behavior (Ajzen, 1991) to study the role of emotions on the electric car usage intentions of consumers. Drawing on multiple literature streams, Gyene (2012) provides a review of theory and research on pro-sustainability attitude and behavior. In reference to sustainability related issues in an organizational context, Hunt (2011) provides an exposition of the resource advantage theory, and Connelly, Ketchen, and Slater (2011) review the potential relevance of nine organizational theories (transaction cost economics, agency theory, institutional theory, organizational ecology, resource dependence theory, resource-based view of the firm, upper echelons theory, social network theory, and signaling theory).

Managing demand for a firm's product offerings is among the principal tasks of the marketing function in organizations. Managing demand *often* entails the pursuit of marketing strategies with the objective of increasing demand for a product (e.g., increasing the number of customers, frequency of purchase, and quantity purchased on each purchase occasion/frequency of consumption and quantity consumed on each consumption occasion). However, managing demand in the context of the sustainability imperative may entail pursuit of marketing strategies with the objective of lowering demand (i.e., demand reduction through consumption reduction) for the product. For instance, electric utility companies extensively employ marketing programs with the objective of encouraging customers to consume less of the product (e.g., marketing programs designed to promote energy conservation). In other instances, entities other than firms engaged in the manufacturing and marketing of a product play a major role in the design and implementation of marketing programs with the goal of either eliminating demand (i.e., demand elimination through consumption elimination) or lowering demand for the product (i.e., demand reduction through consumption reduction). Cases in point include the role of the government and not-for-profit organizations in their attempts to lower demand for products whose consumption may be harmful to individuals and society at large (e.g., cigarettes and alcohol).

In a 1971 article, Kotler and Levy (1971) advanced the concept of demarketing in the context of marketing practice and scholarly research. In a recent article, Kotler (2011) highlighted the growing importance of demarketing from the standpoint of environmental sustainability. *Sustainability oriented demarketing* can be conceptualized as the use of marketing tools and techniques to effect changes in consumers' attitudes, knowledge, social norms, and values, and thereby behavior to promote either cessation of consumption of a product, or reduction in the amount of consumption of a product, or redirection of consumption (i.e., from an ecologically more harmful to an ecologically less harmful substitute) of a product (see Varadarajan, 2014). Varey (2011) conceptualizes "*sustainable society logic for marketing*" as a form of marketing in which consumption is brought into harmony with the carrying capacity of the ecosystem, and whose purpose is sustaining as opposed to consuming the world.

A conceptual framework that sheds insights into major drivers of organizational responsiveness to the sustainability imperative is presented in the next section. The proposed framework complements frameworks and models advanced in the literature. For instance, Chabowski, Mena, and Gonzalez-Padron (2011) propose a framework for research on sustainability with sustainability *focus* (internal and external), *emphasis* (social and environmental), and *intent* (legal, ethical, and discretionary) as principal dimensions. Hansen, Große-Dunker, and Reichwald (2009) propose the sustainability innovation cube as a framework for structuring the *sustainability effects of innovations*. Here, the authors distinguish between three effects along the target dimension (ecological effects, social effects, and economic effects — effects that respectively correspond to the planet, people and profit dimensions of the triple bottom line), three types of innovation (business model, product-service system, and technological), and three life cycle stages of a product (manufacture, use, and end-of-life). Varadarajan (2016) presents a framework for sustainable innovations that distinguishes between three broad *sustainable innovation types* (resource use reduction innovations, resource use elimination innovations, and resource use substitution innovations) and five *sustainable innovation opportunity stages* (upstream supply chain, production, downstream supply chain, use or consumption, and postuse or postconsumption).

ORGANIZATIONAL RESPONSIVENESS TO THE SUSTAINABILITY IMPERATIVE: A CONCEPTUAL FRAMEWORK

Fig. 1 presents a conceptual framework delineating *internal organizational forces* (Box 1) and *external forces* (Boxes 2—10) as impacting on *organizational responsiveness to the sustainability imperative* (Box A). Organizational responsiveness to the sustainability imperative is conceptualized as encompassing an organization's sustainability goals, areas of emphasis, and resource commitments, and manifesting as *sustainability oriented behaviors*. Some of the sustainability oriented behaviors of a firm are internally focused (e.g., resource use reduction, resource use elimination, and resource substitution focused innovations) and others are externally focused (i.e., directed at consumers, customers, competitors, upstream suppliers, etc.). Given the embeddedness of organizations in an external environment (comprised of dimensions such as cultural, economic, legal, market, political, regulatory, social, and technological environment), to varying degrees, the internal organizational forces are influenced and shaped by various external forces such as those delineated in Boxes 1—10 in Fig. 1. However, in the interests of simplicity of exposition, the effect of various external forces on internal organizational forces is not shown in the figure. The external forces delineated in the

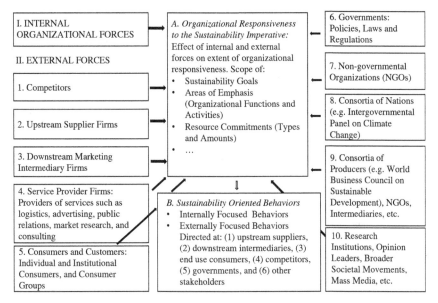

Fig. 1. Organizational Responsiveness to the Sustainability Imperative: Conceptual Framework.

figure are *representative* of forces comprising the immediate industry environment (e.g., upstream supplier firms, downstream intermediary firms, customers and consumers) and the macro-environment (e.g., governments, nongovernmental organizations, and consortia of nations). The proposed framework is intended to a broad overview of external forces impacting on the movement of organizations *in general* (regardless of their size, industry they are part of, countries in which their major operations are based, etc.) in the direction of greater responsiveness to the sustainability imperative. Within industries and across industries, there will be differences between firms in respect of the degree or extent to which they are proactively and reactively responsive to the sustainability imperative. Factors such as firm characteristics, industry characteristics, competitors' characteristics, customers' characteristics, suppliers' characteristics and country characteristics underlying differences between firms in their extent of responsiveness to the sustainability imperative are outside the scope of the proposed framework. A discussion of the major elements of the proposed framework follows.

Internal Organizational Forces

Prior research sheds insights into firm characteristics underlying organizational responsiveness to the sustainability imperative. For instance, a study distinguishing between high and low sustainability firms reports that the former evidence higher levels of leadership commitment, employee engagement, external engagement, knowledge on issues pertaining to sustainability, and integration of sustainability considerations into basic business decisions (Eccles, Perkins, & Serafeim, 2012). In reference to role of firm size and industry type, (1) a higher proportion of firms with a workforce of over 10,000 employees were found to be sustainability embracers compared to firms with a workforce of less than 1,000 employees (34% vs. 9%) and (2) a higher proportion of firms in the goods sector were found to be sustainability embracers compared to firms in the services sector (30% vs. 23%) (Haanaes et al., 2011).

External Forces

As shown in Fig. 1, at one level, global and national level forces such as the environmental sustainability related goals and protocols agreed to by consortia of nations, and the sustainability related policies, laws, and regulations of governments are major drivers of organizational responsiveness to the sustainability imperative. At another level, external forces comprising the more immediate surroundings of the firm such as customers, competitors, upstream suppliers, and downstream marketing intermediaries are major drivers of organizational responsiveness to the sustainability imperative. As an external force, specific government policies, regulations, and laws often mandate greater levels of organizational responsiveness to the sustainability imperative. Case in point would be a regulation requiring manufacturers to design auxiliary products for use over a longer life span than the frequency with which they may introduce innovative, next generation core products (products with more features, better quality, etc.). Illustrative of the above would be a regulation requiring the design of cell phone chargers so that consumers do not have to buy a new cell phone charger each time they upgrade to newer models of cell phones with new and/or more features, or switch from one cell phone service provider to another.

Sustainability Oriented Behaviors

In Fig. 1 (Box B), the sustainability related behaviors of firms are broadly classified as internally focused and externally focused. Internally focused behaviors include behaviors relating to a firm's operations efficiency focused actions (e.g., actions undertaken with the goal of reducing the amount of energy and water used in operations, and reducing waste and emissions from operations), and strategy development-related activities. Illustrative of internally focused actions by producers is sustainability initiatives with goals such as unplugging individual facilities (manufacturing plants) from the public power grid and public water grid, and shipping zero waste to landfills. Externally focused behaviors refer to behaviors of the firm directed at entities external to the firm such as customers, competitors, upstream suppliers, and downstream intermediaries. They include behaviors relating to marketing strategy implementation (e.g., influencing and shaping the sustainability related behaviors of consumers), marketing program implementation (e.g., providers of utility services such as telephone and electricity, and financial services such as mutual funds and credit cards encouraging their customers to go paperless — i.e., to sign up for monthly statements that can be accessed online, in place of statements printed on paper that are mailed to them), and monitoring sustainability compliance by upstream suppliers and downstream intermediaries.

Surveys of global firms provide valuable insights into a number of internally focused and externally focused sustainability related behaviors of firms. Based on a global survey of senior executives, a 2008 briefing paper on sustainability across borders reports the following as among the top three strategic sustainability related priorities of multinational corporations (MNCs): (1) improving energy efficiency; (2) reducing greenhouse-gas emissions, waste, water, and polluting effluents; (3) reducing the environmental impact of products; (4) developing new products/services to reduce societal or environmental risk; (5) modifying existing products/services to reduce societal or environmental risk; (6) implementing stronger controls over suppliers on environmental standards; (7) implementing stronger controls over suppliers on workers' rights standards; (8) improving the local environment around operating facilities; and (9) working with governments to promote sustainable development in the countries where they operate (Economist Intelligence Unit, 2008). Although delineation of some of the above behaviors as internally focused and others as externally focused may be debatable, within reason, behaviors 1–5 listed above can be viewed as *primarily* internally focused, and behaviors 6–9 as *primarily* externally focused. A global survey by McKinsey and Company (*McKinsey Quarterly*, 2011) reports the following as the *major sustainability related areas of emphasis* of firms: (1) reducing energy use in operations, (2) reducing waste from operations, (3) reducing emissions from operations, (4) reducing water use in operations, (5) responding to regulatory constraints or opportunities, (6) mitigating operational risk related to climate change, (7) committing R&D resources to sustainable products, (8) improving employee retention and/or motivation related to sustainability activities, (9) managing portfolio to capture trends in sustainability, (10) managing corporate reputation for sustainability, (11) leveraging sustainability of existing products to reach new customers or markets, (12) achieving higher prices or greater market share from sustainable products, and (13) managing impact of products throughout the value chain. Here again, within reason, behaviors 1–8 listed above can be viewed as *primarily* internally focused, and behaviors 9–12 as *primarily* externally focused. The scope of last of the behaviors listed above (managing impact of products throughout the value chain – upstream supply chain, production, downstream supply chain, sales, and service) spans both internal and external focused behaviors.

An externally focused action that a growing number of producers and marketing intermediaries seem to be adopting in recent years is performing sustainability audits of their upstream suppliers. That is, producers conducting environmental sustainability audits of their upstream suppliers, who in turn, conduct sustainability audits of their suppliers, and marketing intermediaries conducting environmental sustainability audits of their upstream suppliers (i.e., producers of products). In effect, the business system seems to be evolving toward a *virtuous cycle of environmental sustainability audits*.

While on one hand, various entities are delineated in Fig. 1 as external forces influencing organizational responsiveness to the sustainability imperative, they are also the entities with which the focal firm is likely to cooperate and collaborate in order to achieve its sustainability goals. For instance, upstream suppliers, downstream marketing intermediaries (intermediate customers), and end-use customers (particularly, in business-to-business markets) are not only external forces that are likely to influence the focal firm in the direction of greater responsiveness to the sustainability imperative, but are also the most logical entities for the focal firm to cooperate with in areas such as innovating for sustainability and implementing sustainability programs. As may be noted, consortia of producers (e.g.,

World Business Council on Sustainable Development) are shown in Fig. 1 as an external influence on the focal firm. However, the focal firm may also a member of the consortia of producers collaborating and cooperating on sustainability related initiatives. This implies that the focal firm also plays a role in influencing the sustainability initiatives of the consortia.

While the framework (Fig. 1) is presented in reference to producer firms (as might be noted, marketing intermediaries are delineated in the figure as an external force), it can be adapted to gain insights into major forces impacting the responsiveness of marketing intermediary firms to the sustainability imperative. Illustrative of internally focused actions in the context of marketing intermediary-type organizations is a major US-based retail chain lowering the amount of diesel fuel used in its truck fleet for shipping products from its warehouses to retail outlets by installing auxiliary power units to either heat or cool the driver's cabin during long and mandatory rest stops, instead of running the truck's engine (Diamond, 2009). Illustrative of externally focused actions is a major US-based retail chain exercising its buying power to force manufacturers of liquid detergent to transition to liquid detergent in concentrated form. Also illustrative of externally focused actions by a retailer is providing preferential shelf display for eco-friendly versions of products (e.g., end of aisle display and eye level display of compact fluorescent bulbs), and selling eco-friendly versions of products at lower profit margins.

DISCUSSION

Toward Sustainability: Corporate Sustainability Responsibility, Consumer Sustainability Responsibility, and Government Sustainability Responsibility

Of the world's 100 largest economic entities, 63 are corporations, not countries. Great power creates great expectations: society increasingly holds global businesses accountable as the only institutions strong enough to meet the huge long-term challenges facing our planet. Coming to grips with them is more than a corporate responsibility. It's essential for corporate survival. (Werbach, 2009)

There is a widespread view, particularly among environmentalists and liberals, that big businesses are environmentally destructive, greedy, evil and driven by short-term profits. I know — because I used to share that view.

But today I have more nuanced feelings. ...

The embrace of environmental concerns by chief executives has accelerated recently for several reasons. Lower consumption of environmental resources saves money in the short run. Maintaining sustainable resource levels and not polluting saves money in the long run. And a clean image – one attained by, say, avoiding oil spills and other environmental disasters – reduces criticism from employees, consumers and government.

What's my evidence for this? Here are a few examples involving three corporations – Wal-Mart, Coca-Cola and Chevron – that many critics of business love to hate, in my opinion, unjustly. (Diamond, 2009)

The proposed framework (Fig. 1) provides an overview of certain environmental and organizational forces that are likely to predispose an increasingly larger number of firms to be increasingly responsive to the sustainability imperative (i.e., demonstrate corporate sustainability responsibility). However, corporate sustainability responsibility, consumer sustainability responsibility, and government sustainability responsibility are intertwined. Cooperation and collaboration among the three key entities – producers of goods and services, consumers of goods and services, and the government – is crucial from the standpoint of societal progress toward the achievement of sustainability related goals such as reductions in greenhouse-gas emissions and energy intensity per unit of GDP. Consider, for instance, *consumption elimination, consumption reduction*, and *consumption redirection* (from ecologically more harmful to less harmful substitute products) as behaviors (and *demand elimination, demand reduction*, and *demand redirection*, respectively, as associated outcomes) for facilitating societal progress toward sustainability. On one hand, some percent of consumers and businesses, on their own volition, are likely to engage in *sustainability enhancing* behaviors in the realm of renewable resources, and *unsustainability alleviating* behaviors in the realm of nonrenewable resources. However, public policy actions by the government are also crucial for fostering sustainability enhancing and unsustainability alleviating behaviors among consumers and businesses.

Corporate social responsibility (CSR) refers to the "firm's consideration of, and response to, issues beyond the narrow economic, technical, and legal requirements of the firms" (Davis, 1973, p. 312). Myriad issues relating to CSR have been the focus of a large body of research in marketing (Luo & Bhattacharya, 2006; Rangan, Chase, & Karim, 2012), management (Barnett & Salomon, 2012; Wang & Bansal, 2012), and other disciplines. A key element of corporate social responsibility is *corporate sustainability responsibility*. For instance, drawing on extant literature, Wang and Bansal (2012) list the following as among the CSR activities of firms: (1) developing products that have social and environmental features, (2) adopting production methods that reduce environmental impacts, (3) employing human resource systems that care for employees and nurture labor relationships, (4) investing in infrastructure development for local communities, and (5) pursuing philanthropic activities. They measure a firm's extent of involvement in CSR by classifying the CSR activities of firms into the following categories: Activities pertaining to (1) the environment (e.g., using biodegradable materials for packing shipments), (2) products and production (e.g., producing products using recycled materials), (3) community (e.g., giving a percent of the firm's profits back to the community), (4) employee relations (e.g., building a work environment that is free of harassment and discrimination), and (5) other stakeholders (e.g., supporting charitable organizations, locally and internationally).

From the standpoint of societal progress toward environmental sustainability, in addition to progress in the realm of corporate sustainability responsibility, progress in the realms of *consumer sustainability responsibility* and *government sustainability responsibility* is also crucial. For instance, in reference to the *role of consumers in the government being able to achieve its targets* for reduced energy consumption, McDonald, Oates Alevizou, Young, and Hwang (2012) highlight the importance of consumers engaging in more sustainable waste management practices and lifestyles with fewer environmental consequences. In reference to *the role of the government in creating macro environmental market conditions that are conducive for consumers and businesses to be able to engage in sustainable consumption behaviors*, Jackson (2009) points out that in the absence of the government enacting effective policies, consumers are likely to be severely limited in the extent to which they can act on their prosustainability attitudes. In a similar vein, Thøgersen (2005) points out that a number of barriers to sustainable consumption behavior are rooted in the impact of public policy actions such as the availability and quality of public transportation. While effective public policy actions are crucial for *creating* conditions that are conducive for consumers and businesses to engage in sustainable behaviors such as consumption elimination, reduction, and redirection, ineffective and/or inadequate public policy actions can lead to conditions that *necessitate* consumers and businesses to engage in unsustainable behaviors. Fig. 2 sheds additional insights into this issue. As shown in the first two columns, the behaviors of businesses and consumers, on their own volition, can either foster or impede societal progress toward sustainability in the domain of renewable resources, and either alleviate or accentuate unsustainability in the domain of nonrenewable resources. The last two columns highlight the impact of public policy actions versus inactions and ineffective

Behaviors of Businesses and Consumers (→) Resource Domain (↓)	A. Behaviors of Businesses on their Own Volition[a]	B. Behaviors of Consumers on their Own Volition[a]	C. Effects of Public Policy Actions on Behaviors of Businesses[b]	D. Effects of Public Policy Actions on Behaviors of Consumers[b]
1. Renewable Resources	A1. Fostering Sustainability Vs. Impeding Sustainability	B1. Fostering Sustainability Vs. Impeding Sustainability	C1. Fostering Sustainability Vs. Impeding Sustainability	D1. Fostering Sustainability Vs. Impeding Sustainability
2. Nonrenewable Resources	A2. Alleviating Unsustainability Vs. Accentuating Unsustainability	B2. Alleviating Unsustainability Vs. Accentuating Unsustainability	C2. Alleviating Unsustainability Vs. Accentuating Unsustainability	D2. Alleviating Unsustainability Vs. Accentuating Unsustainability

Fig. 2. Fostering versus Impeding Sustainability and Alleviating versus Accentuating Unsustainability. *Notes*: [a]In the domain of renewable resources, certain behaviors or actions of businesses and consumers (on their own volition) are likely to foster societal progress toward sustainability. Other behaviors are likely to impede societal progress toward sustainability (cells A1 and B1). Likewise, in the domain of nonrenewable resources, while certain behaviors or actions of businesses and consumers are likely to contribute toward alleviating unsustainability, other behaviors are likely to accentuate unsustainability (cells A2 and B2). [b]Impact of public policy actions (or dearth of public policy actions and ineffective public policy actions) on the behaviors of businesses and consumers in the domains of renewable resources (cells C1 and D1) and nonrenewable resources (cells C2 and D2).

actions on the behaviors of businesses and consumers. Thus, in the domain of renewable resources, the impact of public policy actions (inactions and ineffective actions) on the behaviors of businesses and consumers can foster (impede) societal progress toward sustainability. Similarly, in the domain of nonrenewable resources, the impact of public policy actions (inactions and ineffective actions) on the behaviors of businesses and consumers can alleviate (accentuate) unsustainability.

Toward Sustainability: Consumption Elimination, Consumption Reduction, and Consumption Redirection

Identifying and leveraging product-market opportunities for consumption elimination, reduction, and redirection and thereby facilitating societal progress toward sustainability are issues of concern to for-profit organizations (i.e., concurrent pursuit of a larger market footprint and a smaller environmental footprint), as well as governments at various levels, and not-for-profit organizations. Varadarajan (2014) highlights the role of the government in creating macroenvironmental conditions that are conducive for elimination of consumption of a class of products (*intrinsically zero demand products*), reduction in consumption of a second class of products (*intrinsically lower demand products*), and redirection of consumption from ecologically more harmful to ecologically less harmful substitute products of a third class of products. Table 1 provides illustrative examples of consumption elimination, consumption reduction, and consumption redirection (and relatedly, demand elimination, demand reduction, and demand redirection) enabled by technology and innovation, and facilitated by public policy actions.

All else being equal, businesses are likely to be more predisposed toward identifying and leveraging product-market opportunities for consumption/demand redirection (from ecologically more harmful to ecologically less harmful substitute products; e.g., from tungsten filament light bulbs to compact fluorescent light bulbs), relative to product-market opportunities for consumption elimination and consumption reduction. To the extent the focus at the firm level is on product-market opportunities for consumption/demand elimination and consumption/demand reduction, it is likely to be in the realms of ingredient products (i.e., demand elimination or demand reduction for an ingredient product; e.g., phosphate-free detergent) and complementary products (i.e., demand elimination or demand reduction for a complementary product; e.g., cold-water formulation of detergents that eliminate electricity used for heating water used in washing machines, and single rinse formulations of detergents that reduce the amount of water used in washing machines). This brings to fore the interdependencies between consumption elimination, reduction, and redirection (and relatedly, demand elimination, reduction, and redirection). For instance, in the context of *established end-use consumer products, demand redirection* innovations (innovations that result in demand redirection from an ecologically more harmful to an ecologically less harmful substitute product) can result in *demand reduction* effects and/or *demand elimination* effects for complementary products in business-to-consumer (B2C) markets and ingredient products in business-to-business (B2B) markets. The following examples and Fig. 3 shed additional insights into this issue:

> It's estimated that about three-quarters of the energy use and greenhouse-gas emissions from washing a load of laundry come from heating the water. In 2005, using enzymes

Table 1. Toward Sustainability: Consumption Elimination, Reduction, and Redirection.

	Consumption Elimination → Demand Elimination[a,b]	Consumption Reduction → Demand Reduction[a,b]	Consumption Redirection → Demand Redirection[a,b,c]
Technology and innovation[d]	*Demand elimination for complementary products*: Vacuum cleaners that do not require use of disposable bags. Coffee makers that do not require use of disposable filters.	*Product integration*: Impact of smart phone on the demand for erstwhile standalone products integrated into it (e.g., digital cameras).	*Product reformulation*: From traditional formulations of detergents to phosphate free, single rinse, cold water, and concentrated formulations.
Government policies, laws, and regulations[e]	*Phase out of ingredients harmful to the environment*: Phase out of ozone-destroying fluorocarbon gases in most aerosol products.	*Ancillary product standardization*: Standardization of cell phone charger across competing brands and models. *Demand reduction for complementary products*: Higher corporate average fuel economy (CAFE) standards for automobiles.	From incandescent light bulbs to compact fluorescent light bulbs. From travel by privately owned vehicles to public transportation through levy of higher toll prices during peak hours. From disposable plastic bags to reusable cloth bags at grocery stores through imposition of mandatory charge on plastic bags.
Government public policy actions: infrastructure deficiencies alleviation[f]	Intrinsically Zero demand (IZD) products	Intrinsically Lower demand (ILD) products	From ecologically more harmful to less harmful substitute (EMHS) products

[a]The *framework* is applicable in the context of both business-to-business (**B2B**) markets and business-to-consumer (**B2C**) markets. The *scope* of product-market opportunities for consumption elimination, reduction, and redirection in the context of innovation, regulation, etc. are far more numerous than the illustrative examples presented.

[b]A consequence of successful *consumption* elimination/reduction/redirection for a product is *demand* elimination/reduction/redirection for the product. A consequence of successful demand elimination, reduction or redirection efforts for products in B2C markets is *reduction in demand* for ingredient products in B2B markets.

[c]Consumption redirection from ecologically more harmful substitute (**EMHS**) products to ecologically less harmful substitute (**ELHS**) products.

[d]Product and process innovations.

[e]Government regulations, as well as laws, policies, programs, and initiatives.

[f]See Varadarajan (2014) for a discussion on the potential for *consumption elimination* of specific IZD products, *consumption reduction* of specific ILD products, and *consumption redirection* from specific ecologically more harmful to ecologically less harmful substitute products through public policy actions.

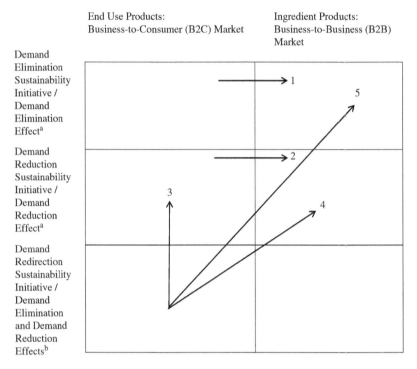

Fig. 3. Sustainability Initiatives by Businesses: Interdependencies between Demand Elimination, Demand Reduction, and Demand Redirection. *Notes*: [a]Link 1 (2) denotes a demand elimination sustainability initiative (demand reduction sustainability initiative) for an end use product in the B2C market resulting in a demand elimination effect (demand reduction effect) for an ingredient product in the B2B market. [b]Links 3, 4 and 5 denote a demand redirection sustainability initiative resulting in a demand reduction effect for a complementary product in the B2C market, a demand reduction effect for an ingredient product in the B2B market, and a demand elimination effect for an ingredient product in the B2B market, respectively.

and surfactants that work better in cold water, P&G introduced a new formulation of its Tide brand detergent – Tide Coldwater. In the aftermath of a number of other detergent manufacturers also introducing similar formulations of detergents, the percent of laundry loads washed in cold water in the United States is estimated to have risen from about 30% in 2005 to close to 40% in 2011(Martin & Rosenthal, 2011).

In 2009, Walmart transitioned to selling only concentrated liquid laundry detergent. The company estimates that as a result of the transition, its customers will save more than 400 million gallons of water, 95 million pounds of plastic resin, 125 million pounds of cardboard, and 520,000 gallons of diesel fuel over three years (Rosenbloom & Barbaro, 2009).

The first example is illustrative of demand redirection from an ecologically more harmful (EMH) to an ecologically less harmful (ELH) substitute product in the B2C market resulting in demand reduction for a complementary product in the B2C market (i.e., energy used by households for heating water used in washing machines). Link # 3 in Fig. 3 serves to highlight such interdependencies. The second example is illustrative of demand redirection from an EMH to an ELH substitute product in the B2C market resulting in demand reduction (e.g., reduction in the amount of plastics and cardboard used for packaging, and diesel used for transportation) for ingredient products in the upstream B2B market. Link # 4 in Fig. 3 serves to highlight such interdependencies. A number of demand redirection oriented innovations in the B2C market from EMH to ELH substitute products entail discontinuation of use of ingredients that are harmful to the environment (e.g., phosphates in detergents). Such innovations result in demand elimination in the B2B market for the ingredients eliminated from the consumer product. Link # 5 in Fig. 3 serves to highlight such interdependencies. Demand reduction and demand elimination for end-use consumer products in the B2C market will inevitably result in demand reduction and demand elimination for ingredient products in the B2B market, respectively. Link # 1 and link # 2 in Fig. 3, respectively, serve to highlight such interdependencies. For instance, greater levels of sustainability awareness manifesting as a shift toward shared consumption or collaborative consumption (e.g., renting as opposed to owning) will result in demand reduction for the end-use product in the B2C market and demand reduction for ingredient products in the B2B market (link # 2 in Fig. 3).

Toward Sustainability: Fostering Facilitating Forces and Mitigating Impeding Forces

Suchman (1995, p. 574) defines organizational legitimacy as "a generalized perception or assumption that the actions of a firm are desirable, proper, or appropriate within some socially constructed system of norms, values, beliefs, and definitions." As shown in Fig. 1, in a sustainability oriented macroenvironment, organizational legitimacy considerations can be expected to orient an increasing number of firms, worldwide, in the direction of increased levels of investments in sustainability initiatives with the objective of substantially reducing the environmental degradation effects of their activities. As noted in earlier sections, the findings reported in various global surveys of multinational firms (e.g., *Economist* Intelligence Unit, 2008; Haanaes et al., 2011; *McKinsey Quarterly*, 2011) are indicative of greater responsiveness to the sustainability imperative by a growing number of firms, worldwide. A cursory examination of the scope and content of the corporate sustainability reporting initiatives of firms is also indicative greater responsiveness to the sustainability imperative by a growing number of firms, worldwide.

Notwithstanding such positive developments and indications, the prospect of prevalence of forces analogous to centripetal forces (forces attracting toward the center) and centrifugal forces (forces pulling away from the center) must be borne in mind. On the one hand, as shown in the proposed framework (Fig. 1), a number of forces are likely to move an increasing number of businesses and consumers toward greater levels of environmentally sustainable behaviors. However, as shown in the last two columns of Fig. 2 (i.e., consequences of public policy inactions, inadequate actions, and ineffective actions), certain other forces are likely to move businesses and consumers toward environmentally unsustainable behaviors. On the one hand, it is conceivable that in a sustainability oriented macroenvironment, a greater number of firms will demonstrate higher levels of organizational commitment to significantly lowering their environmental footprint, even as they aspire to increase their market footprint. On the one hand, the rate of growth in demand for a firm's product offerings outpacing its rate of progress on the sustainability front is within the realm of possibilities. In addition to at the individual firm level, at more macrolevels such as the industry level and the national level, the rate of growth in demand for various goods and services and the attendant increase in demand for various renewable and nonrenewable resources outpacing the rate of progress on the sustainability front is within the realm of possibilities.

On the one hand, certain sustainability oriented business model innovations enable consumers to derive the benefits of a product without actually owning the product (i.e., collaborative consumption/shared consumption). To the extent these business models make greater inroads in a number of product-market arenas, this may facilitate societal progress toward sustainability. On the other hand, in for-profit organizations, a principal responsibility of the marketing function is generating revenue by stimulating demand for the firm's product offerings. In their attempts to stimulate greater demand for their product offerings, businesses pursue marketing strategies to (1) broaden their customer base (increasing the size of the customer base) through actions such as acquisition of new customers in presently served markets, new market segments and new geographic markets; (2) broaden, deepen, and strengthen their relationship with present customers; and (3) stimulate increased amounts of consumption by uncovering and leveraging potential opportunities for promoting new uses for the product, and new times, new occasions, and new places for use/consumption of the product. Aided by analysis of customers' buying patterns such as recency of purchase, frequency of purchase and monetary value of purchase, firms explore potential avenues for increasing customer lifetime value by increasing the frequency of purchase (consumption), quantity purchased (consumed) during each purchase occasion (consumption occasion), and/or the average monetary value of the purchase. In today's prototypical large firm (a multinational, multibusiness firm with each business being comprised of multiple products), such marketing effort is likely to be multipronged. That is, focused toward increasing the size of the customer base, frequency of purchase (consumption), and average purchase amount (consumption amount) for a multiplicity of products in a multiplicity of markets, as well as cross-selling of products (i.e., marketing to a firm's current customers of one of its product offerings other product offerings of the firm).

Paralleling the above actions of firms, the general thrust of the managerial implications section of a number of journal articles in marketing tends to be on marketing actions that would enable firms to broaden (increase) their customer base, and increase the lifetime value of their customers by increasing the frequency of purchase (consumption) and/or the average purchase quantity bought (consumed) during each purchase occasion. That is, offering guideposts to managers for increasing the size of their customer base, frequency of purchase (consumption), average purchase (consumption) amount, etc. Table 2 provides additional insights into forces analogous to centripetal forces (forces attracting toward the center) and centrifugal forces (forces pulling away from the center), that are likely to move businesses and consumers toward and away from environmentally sustainable behaviors. Broadening the scope of the strategic toolkit from strategies for market development and market expansion to strategies for market development, market expansion and *market contraction* calls for a change in mindset and outlook.

Table 2.   Toward Sustainability: Fostering Facilitating Forces and
Mitigating Impeding Forces.

Forces Facilitating Progress toward Sustainability[a]	Forces Impeding Progress toward Sustainability[a]
Green technology based innovations-driven economic growth and job creation	Demand stimulation and consumption-driven economic growth and job creation[b]
Adoption of sustainable business practices	Persistence of unsustainable business practices
Adoption of sustainable consumption behaviors	Persistence of unsustainable consumption behaviors
Resource conserving product, process, and business model innovations	Consumer demand for innovations enabled new-to-the-world products without regard to their sustainability consequences
	Strategy of planned obsolescence[c]
	Inevitability of technological obsolescence
Public policy actions	Public policy inactions, ineffective actions, and inadequate actions

[a]Analogous to *centripetal forces* (forces pulling toward the center), and *centrifugal forces* (forces pulling away from the center).
[b]Kotler (2006, p. 157) notes: "Marketing is the discipline responsible for job creation. Our success in demand creation results in job creation. If we slow down demand creation, we slow down job creation and, therefore, incomes."
[c]It's conceivable that during an earlier era, decision-makers in organizations could have afforded to be largely oblivious to the environmental sustainability consequences of pursuing a strategy of planned obsolescence. However, in a sustainability oriented macroenvironment, this may be untenable.

REFERENCES

Ajzen, I. (1991). The theory of planned behavior. *Organizational Behavior and Human Decision Processes, 50,* 179–211.
Ajzen, I., & Fishbein, M. (1980). *Understanding attitudes and predicting social behavior.* Englewood Cliffs, NJ: Prentice-Hall.
Ansoff, H. I. (1957). Strategies for diversification. *Harvard Business Review, 30*(September–October), 113–124.
Barnett, M. L., & Salomon, R. M. (2012). Does it pay to be really good? Addressing the shape of the relationship between social and financial performance. *Strategic Management Journal, 33,* 1304–1320.
Bennett, G., & Williams, F. (2010). *Mainstream green: Mainstream green: Moving sustainability from niche to normal.* Ogilvy & Mather Red Paper.
Chabowski, B. R., Mena, J. A., & Gonzalez-Padron, T. L. (2011). The structure of sustainability research in marketing, 1958–2008: A basis for future research opportunities. *Journal of the Academy of Marketing Science, 39*(February), 55–70.

Clifford, S., & Martin, A. (2011). As shoppers reduce spending, 'Green' Loses Allure. *New York Times*, April 22, p. B1, New York Edition.

Connelly, B. L., Ketchen, D. J., Jr., & Slater, S. F. (2011). Toward a "Theoretical Toolbox" for sustainability research in marketing. *Journal of the Academy of Marketing Science, 39*(February), 86–100.

Davis, K. (1973). The case for and against business assumption of social responsibilities. *Academy of Management Journal, 16*(2), 312–323.

Diamond, J. (2009). Will big business save the Earth. *New York Times*, December 6.

Eccles, R. G., Perkins, K. M., & Serafeim, G. (2012). How to become a sustainable company. *MIT Sloan Management Review, 53*(4), 43–50.

Economist Intelligence Unit. (2008). Sustainability across borders. *Economist Intelligence Unit.* Briefing Paper Sponsored by SAS. Retrieved from http://www.eiu.com/report_dl.asp?mode=fi&fi=123934397.PDF

Ehrenfeld, J. R. (2005). The roots of sustainability. *MIT Sloan Management Review, 46*(Winter), 23–25.

Godfray, H. C. J., Beddington, J. R., Crute, I. R., Haddad, L., Lawrence, D., Muir, J. J., ... Toulmin, C. (2010). Food security: The challenge of feeding 9 billion people. *Science, 327*(February), 812–818.

Goldstein, N. J., Cialdini, R. B., & Griskevicius, V. (2008). A room with a viewpoint: Using social norms to motivate environmental conservation in hotels. *Journal of Consumer Research, 35*(October), 472–482.

Grinstein, A., & Nisan, U. (2009). Demarketing, minorities and national achievement. *Journal of Marketing, 73*(March), 105–122.

Gyene, G. (2012). Changing current course: The psychology of adopting or rejecting sustainability solutions. Theory and research on pro-sustainability attitude and behavior. In M. Meimeth & J. D. Robertson (Eds.), *Sustainable development — How to bridge the knowledge-action gap* (pp. 117–167). Germany: Nomos.

Haanaes, K., Balagopal, B., Arthur, D., Kong, M. T., Velken, I., Kruschwitz, N., & Hopkins, M. S. (2011). First look: The second annual sustainability and innovation survey. *MIT Sloan Management Review, 52*(2), 77–83.

Hansen, E. G., Große-Dunker, F., & Reichwald, R. (2009). Sustainability innovation cube: A framework to evaluate sustainability-oriented innovations. *International Journal of Innovation Management, 13*(December), 683–713.

Hardin, G. (1968). The tragedy of the commons. *Science, 162*, 1243–1248.

Hunt, S. D. (2011). Sustainable marketing, equity, and economic growth: A resource-advantage, economic freedom approach. *Journal of the Academy of Marketing Science, 39*(February), 7–20.

Jackson, T. (2009). *Prosperity without growth*. London: The Sustainable Development Commission.

Kauffeld, R., Malhotra, A., & Higgins, S. (2009). Green is a strategy. *strategy + business*, December 21.

Kotler, P. (2006). Ethical lapses of marketing. In J. S. Sheth & R. Sisodia (Eds.), *Does marketing need reform?* (pp. 153–157). Armonk, NY: M. E. Sharpe.

Kotler, P. (2011). Reinventing marketing to manage the environmental imperative. *Journal of Marketing, 75*(July), 132–136.

Kotler, P., & Levy, S. J. (1971). Demarketing, yes demarketing. *Harvard Business Review, 49*(November–December), 74–80.

Kronrod, A., Grinstein, A., & Wathieu, L. (2012). Go Green! Should environmental message be so assertive? *Journal of Marketing*, 76(January), 95–102.

Luchs, M. G., Naylor, R. W., Irwin, J. R., & Raghunathan, R. (2010). The sustainability liability: Potential negative effects of ethicality on product preference. *Journal of Marketing*, 74(September), 18–31.

Luo, X., & Bhattacharya, C. B. (2006). Corporate social responsibility, customer satisfaction and market value. *Journal of Marketing*, 70(October), 1–18.

Makower, Joel and the Editors of GreenBiz.Com. (2011). *State of green business 2011*. GreenBiz Group. Retrieved from http://www.greenbiz.com/

Marketing Week. (2010). P&G to take sustainability message to brand campaigns. *Marketing Week*, September 29. Retrieved from http://www.marketingweek.com/2010/09/29/pg-to-take-sustainability-message-to-brand-campaigns/

Martin, A., & Rosenthal, E. (2011). Cold-water detergents get a chilly reception. *New York Times*, September 17, p. B1, New York Edition.

McDonald, S., Oates, C. J., Alevizou, P. J., Young, C. W., & Hwang, K. (2012). Individual strategies for sustainable consumption. *Journal of Marketing Management*, 28(3–4), 445–468.

McKinsey Quarterly. (2011). The business of sustainability: McKinsey global survey results. *McKinsey Quarterly, October*. Retrieved from http://www.mckinsey.com/business-functions/sustainability-and-resource-productivity/our-insights/the-business-of-sustainability-mckinsey-global-survey-results

Menon, A., & Menon, A. (1997). Enviropreneurial marketing strategy: The emergence of corporate environmentalism as market strategy. *Journal of Marketing*, 61(1), 51–67.

Moons, I., & De Pelsmacker, P. (2012). Emotions as determinants of electric car usage. *Journal of Marketing Management*, 28(3–4), 195–237.

Peattie, K., & Peattie, S. (2009). Social marketing: A pathway to consumption reduction? *Journal of Business Research*, 62, 260–268.

Polman, P. (2011, March). *Message from our CEO*. Unilever Company Website. Retrieved from http://www.unilever.com/sustainability/introduction/ceo/index.aspx

Polonsky, M. J., Vocino, A., Grau, S. L., Garma, R., & Ferdous, A. S. (2012). The impact of general and carbon-related environmental knowledge on attitudes and behavior of US consumers. *Journal of Marketing Management*, 28(3–4), 238–263.

Prothero, A., Dobscha, S., Freund, J., Kilbourne, w. E., Luchs, M. G., Ozanne, L. K., & Thøgersen, J. (2011). Sustainable consumption: Opportunities for consumer research and public policy. *Journal of Public Policy & Marketing*, 30(Spring), 31–38.

Rangan, K., Chase, L. A., & Karim, S. (2012). *Why every company needs a CSR strategy and how to build it*. HBS Working Paper No. 12-088.

Rosenbloom, S., & Barbaro, M. (2009). Environmental sustainability, now at Wal-Mart. *New York Times*, February 5. Retrieved from http://www.nytimes.com/2009/01/25/business/worldbusiness/25iht-25walmart.19647095.html?scp = 2&sq = Rosenbloom%20and%20Barbaro%20January%202009&st = cse

Schultz, C. J., & Holbrook, M. B. (1999). Marketing and the tragedy of commons: Synthesis, commentary, and analysis for action. *Journal of Public Policy and Marketing*, 18(Fall), 218–229.

Sharma, A., Iyer, G. R., Mehrotra, A., & Krishnan, R. (2010). Sustainability and business-to-business marketing: A framework and applications. *Industrial Marketing Management*, 39, 330–341.

Sheth, J. N., Sethia, N. K., & Srinivas, S. (2011). Mindful consumption: A customer-centric approach to sustainability. *Journal of the Academy of Marketing Science*, 39(February), 21–39.

Suchman, M. C. (1995). Managing legitimacy: Strategic and institutional approaches. *Academy of Management Review*, *20*(3), 571–610.

Thøgersen, J. (2005). How may consumer policy empower consumers for sustainable lifestyles. *Journal of Consumer Policy*, *28*(July), 143–178.

Van Dam, Y. K., & Apeldoorn, P. A. C. (1996). Sustainable marketing. *Journal of Macromarketing*, *16*(Fall), 45–56.

Varadarajan, R. (1992). Marketing's contribution to strategy: The view from a different looking glass. *Journal of the Academy of Marketing Science*, *20*(Fall), 335–343.

Varadarajan, R. (2014). Toward sustainability: Public policy, global social innovations for base-of-the-pyramid markets, and demarketing for a better world. *Journal of International Marketing*, *22*(2), 1–20.

Varadarajan, R. (2016). Innovating for sustainability: A framework for sustainable innovations and a model of sustainable innovations orientation. *Journal of the Academy of Marketing Science*, *44*.

Varey, R. J. (2010). Marketing means and ends for a sustainable society: A welfare agenda for transformative change. *Journal of Macromarketing*, *30*(2), 112–126.

Varey, R. J. (2011). A sustainable society logic for marketing. *Social Business*, *1*(1), 69–83.

Wang, T., & Bansal, P. (2012). Social responsibility in new ventures: Profiting from a long-term orientation. *Strategic Management Journal*, *33*, 1135–1153.

Wayne, L. (2009). P&G sees the world as its client. *New York Times*, December 12.

Werbach, A. (2009). *Strategy for sustainability: A business manifesto*. Cambridge, MA: Harvard Business Press.

Williams, C., & Millington, A. C. (2004). The diverse and contested meanings of sustainable development. *The Geographical Journal*, *170*, 99–104.

World Commission on Environment and Development. (1987). *Our common future*. Oxford: Oxford University Press.

MARKETING'S QUEST FOR ENVIRONMENTAL SUSTAINABILITY: PERSISTENT CHALLENGES AND NEW PERSPECTIVES

Jakki J. Mohr, Linda L. Price and Aric Rindfleisch

ABSTRACT

Purpose — *The purpose of this chapter is fivefold. First, it highlights that, despite apparent progress, business in general, and marketing in particular, has made little impact upon environmental sustainability. Second, it offers four explanations for the persistent challenges that contribute to this lack of meaningful progress. Third, it presents two theoretical lenses (i.e., assemblage theory and socio-ecological systems theory) for viewing environmental sustainability from new perspectives. Fourth, it offers a mid-range theory, biomimicry, to bridge the gap between these higher-level theories and managerial decisions on the ground. Finally, it offers implications and ideas for future research based on these persistent challenges and new perspectives.*

Marketing In and For a Sustainable Society
Review of Marketing Research, Volume 13, 29–59
Copyright © 2016 by Emerald Group Publishing Limited
All rights of reproduction in any form reserved
ISSN: 1548-6435/doi:10.1108/S1548-643520160000013010

Methodology/approach − *Our paper is theoretical in focus. We offer a conceptual analysis of persistent challenges facing business efforts in environmental sustainability and suggest useful lenses to integrate marketing decisions more closely with our natural environment.*

Findings − *We present biomimicry as an actionable framework that seeks inspiration from nature and also explicitly grounds marketing decisions in the natural world.*

Practical Implications − *Our paper draws attention to the challenges facing firms seeking to achieve better performance in environmental sustainability. In addition, it offers a set of fresh theoretical perspectives as well as future issues for scholarly research in this domain.*

Originality/value − *Our work is designed to be provocative; it articulates reasons why business efforts in environmental sustainability do not scale to meaningful impact upon our planet and explores theoretical lenses by which those efforts could be more impactful.*

Keywords: Sustainability; biomimicry; assemblage theory; socio-ecological systems theory; marketing strategy; resources and capabilities

The natural environment has no voice of its own. (Etzion, 2007)

We live on a planet with finite resources. The global rise of industrialized economies over the course of the 20th century has severely depleted many of these resources (such as ozone and water), and has begun to threaten our long-term survival by expanding our carbon footprint. For example, the concentration of CO_2 in our atmosphere recently reached 400 parts-per-million (ppm), which is more than 100 ppm higher than our pre-industrial atmosphere. At its present rate of increase (2.5 ppm per year), our atmosphere will surpass 600 ppm by the end of the 21st century and increase our planet's temperature by 3−5 °C (IPCC, 2014). Likewise, over the past century, sea levels rose nearly 20 cm and the rate is accelerating. Rising sea levels not only will dislocate millions of people in coastal locations due to erosion and flooding, but also will lead to salinization of aquifers and soils, and a loss of habitats for fish, birds, and plants (IPCC, 2014). Thus, the quest for environmental sustainability is one of the most critical challenges of the 21st century (McKibben, 2011).

Over the past 20 years, a growing number of firms have begun to recognize this threat to our planet; thus, environmental sustainability has become a strategic priority for many firms, including WalMart, Nestle, and Unilever to name just a few (Whan, 2015). In order to realize their sustainability objectives, many firms have sought to innovate their marketing activities, such as developing more environmentally-friendly products and redesigning their processes to reduce waste (Nidumolu, Prahalad, & Rangaswami, 2009; Shrivastava, 1995). These sustainability initiatives typically seek to minimize material and energy usage and create products with smaller environmental footprints (cf., KPMG, 2012; Makower, 2014; Shrivastava & Hart, 1995). Based on its position between the upstream side of the supply chain and downstream connection to customers, marketing plays a prominent role in many of these sustainability initiatives. In addition, sustainability efforts are commonly leveraged as a marketing tool and also receive substantial attention from the business press. For example, WalMart is on track to realize its highly publicized goals of zero-waste, utilizing 100% renewable energy and eliminating 20 million metric tons of greenhouse gas (GHG) emissions from its global supply chain (WalMart Highlights Progress in 2015, 2015). Similarly, since 2011, Nike has bragged about its 3% reduction in carbon emissions (Nike, 2015).

Thus, at first glance, it appears that firms are making good progress in terms of realizing their sustainability goals. Unfortunately (for both firms and the environment), this progress is largely illusory. According to the State of Green Business Report (Makower, 2014), "corporate environmental progress seems to have stalled" (p. 3), as "metrics of environmental performance show little or no progress in recent years" (p. 45). Similarly, the MIT/BCG Sustainability and Innovation Report (Goh, Haanaes, Kiron, Kruschwitz, & Reeves, 2013) showed that although sustainability appears to be gaining traction across several industries, many North American companies encounter difficulty translating sustainability demands into marketing-related outcomes. Both of these reports suggest that although most firms are highly interested in environmental sustainability, this quest is extremely challenging. Indeed, according to Kotler (2011), there is a clear and widening gap between current marketing capabilities and the global imperative for sustainability.

In this chapter, we present four inter-related arguments why firms' sustainability efforts are falling short of environmental needs: (1) *insufficiency of existing theoretical lens* from which to view the problem of sustainability;

(2) *insignificance* in terms of the magnitude of the change these efforts are making; (3) *incompatibility* between the logic of marketing and the logic of sustainability; and (4) *incommensurability* between the changes made by individual firms versus the scalability of those changes. We elaborate on these persistent challenges in the next section.

After exploring these challenges, we identify two possible theoretical perspectives and paths forward. These perspectives are grounded in assemblage theory and socio-ecological systems theory. Both of these theories offer the potential to integrate the human environment of business with the physical environment found in the natural world. However, both theories operate at a level of abstraction that makes it difficult for managers to put them into practice. Hence, we offer a mid-range theory to bridge the gap: biomimicry (Benyus, 1997). This perspective offers a lens and a decision-making framework to integrate marketing decisions with the natural world and increases the potential for marketers to improve the impact of their sustainability efforts. Finally, we summarize our thesis and identify a set of intriguing directions for both marketing practice and academic inquiry. Our research not only examines the four challenges marketers face in pursuing their quest for sustainability but also offers ideas for possible paths forward.

POSSIBLE EXPLANATIONS FOR LACK OF MEANINGFUL PROGRESS IN ENVIRONMENTAL SUSTAINABILITY

The manner in which firms typically approach their quest for sustainability is depicted in Fig. 1. As shown in this figure, firms traditionally view the environment as a source of natural resources from which inputs can be sourced, processed into finished products, distributed, sold, and then used and disposed of. Although this chain of activities often results in substantial waste, pollution, and natural resource depletion, concern for these "externalities" received little consideration until recently. Today, increased environmental awareness and changing customer demands result in firms paying closer attention to the environmental impact of their business activities. For example, a growing number of firms are seeking renewable and recyclable resources as product inputs. In addition, many companies are manufacturing these products using more energy- and resource-efficient processes. Moreover, most firms are also seeking ways to minimize the by-products

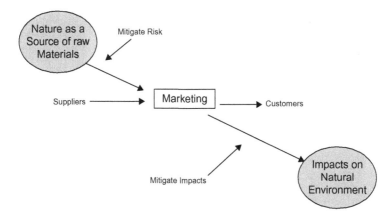

Fig. 1. Marketing's Relationship with the Natural Environment.

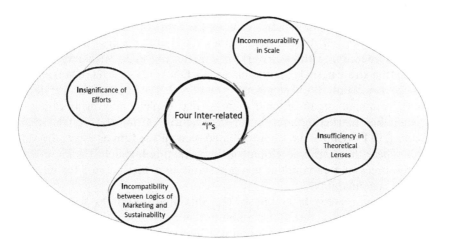

Fig. 2. Reasons for Stalled Progress on Environmental Sustainability Efforts.

and waste associated with their manufacturing operations (cf. McDonough & Braungart, 2002a).

As noted earlier, despite the increased focus on these environmental initiatives, our planet's health continues to decline. Fig. 2 identifies four inter-related reasons that might explain this state of affairs.

Insufficiency of Existing Theoretical Lenses

A natural-resource-based-view of the firm must integrate 'the voice of the environment'.
(Hart, 1995)

A firm's long-term growth and profitability are related to its ability to achieve a sustainable (i.e., something that can be maintained over the long term) competitive advantage (Day, 1994). Although the strategy and marketing literatures offer many different perspectives about how such an advantage is attained, the dominant theoretical lens is resource-capability theory (Barney, 1991; Day, 1994). According to this perspective, firms achieve long-run profitability by acquiring resources and developing capabilities that competitors find difficult to imitate. For example, Honda's long-term success has been attributed to its superior capability in developing highly reliable motor engines across a wide array of product offerings (Prahalad & Hamel, 1990).

Theoretical developments in marketing with respect to sustainability rely heavily on this resource-based view of the firm. For example, Crittenden, Crittenden, Ferrell, Ferrell, and Pinney (2011) offer a resource-based framework identifying three drivers to strategically align sustainability with marketing strategies: (1) an organization's DNA; (2) its level of stakeholder involvement; and (3) its managerial practices. Likewise, in their overview of nine prominent organizational theories that explain how firms engage in sustainable marketing and business practices, Connelly, Ketchen, and Slater (2011) identify the resource-based view of the firm as especially valuable. These theoretical developments in marketing highlight the importance of resources and capabilities in understanding a firm's quest for environmental sustainability.

However, given its emphasis on obtaining resources for achieving growth and profits, resource-capability theory largely fails to consider the impact of a firm's actions upon the natural environment. From this perspective, the natural environment is a resource to be extracted for corporate gain. According to Hart (1995), resource-capability theory "systematically ignores the constraints imposed by the biophysical (natural) environment" (p. 986). This conflict between the constraints of the natural world versus marketing imperatives for growth is further amplified by the emergence of dynamic capability theory, which places increased emphasis on firms' need to obtain new resources and update their capabilities in response to changes in their operating environment (Day, 2011; Teece, Pisano, & Shuen, 1997). Unfortunately, the cumulative impact of traditional business practice upon our ecosystem has made natural resources increasingly difficult and more costly to acquire (KPMG, 2012; Winston, 2014a).

In recognition of resource-capability theory's insufficient focus on the natural world, Hart (1995) developed the natural-resource-based view of the firm. This theoretical lens is based on the premise that "strategy and competitive advantage in the coming years will be rooted in capabilities that facilitate environmentally sustainable economic activity" (Hart, 1995, p. 991). Specifically, this theory suggests that firms can achieve competitive advantage by engaging in pollution prevention, product stewardship, and sustainable development. Since its publication, Hart's theory has garnered over 4,000 citations and has attracted substantial managerial attention. Unfortunately, its actual impact on sustainability is questionable. According to a recent review of this theory, "empirical research on product stewardship or sustainable development strategies" is still quite scarce due to the small number of firms pursuing these approaches (Hart & Dowell, 2011).

This lack of progress in sustainability may be due, in part, to the paradoxical voices in this broader theory. While one branch of resource-capability spurs managers to churn their resource base in search of more dynamic capabilities, the other urges them to achieve competitive advantage by conserving their resources. Moreover, as we discuss subsequently, the fundamental logic of marketing is based on growth and profit. Although a growing number of firms are adopting expanded performance metrics (such as the triple bottom line) that account for their environmental impacts, the profit motive still drives corporate strategy in general, and marketing activities in particular (Kotler, 2011). Thus, resource-capability theory appears to present an insufficient (and perhaps even incoherent) lens for achieving meaningful progress in environmental sustainability efforts.

Insignificance: Tweaking at the Margins

… being less unsustainable is still not sustainable. (Spowers, 2013)

Another problem with many sustainability initiatives is their subordinate role to traditional economic criteria of growth and profitability (Borland & Lindgreen, 2013; Kilbourne, McDonagh, & Prothero, 1997; Milne & Gray, 2013). Marketing messages about sustainability, often focused on their strategic fit with and ability to facilitate corporate objectives, are often couched in the rhetoric of the triple bottom line (TBL): economic profit, environmental profit, and social profit. For example, a recent *Harvard Business Review* spotlight on practical sustainability – "Sustainability a CFO can Love" – showcases how corporate sustainability initiatives have helped drive growth, efficiency, and profitability while contributing to society and the environment (Kuehn & McIntire, 2014, p. 66). For example, Marks & Spencer is commended for initiating a "shwopping" program that encourages customers to bring a piece of clothing they no longer want to the store and get a discount coupon on their next purchase. Kuehn and McIntire proudly conclude, "Everyone wins" (p. 70).

Unfortunately, when shoppers are prompted to shed old clothes and acquire new ones, the environment doesn't win. In fact, this example points to the inherent paradox of a sustainability initiative that feeds on promoting increased levels of consumption. Efficiency drives and competitive moves dressed in the trappings of sustainability fail to challenge "business as usual" (Henriques & Richardson, 2013; Milne & Gray, 2013; Unruh & Ettenson, 2010). As a result, "good" marketing practices – say, recycling fast food packaging – get confused with creating a just and sustainable world (Hawken, 2010; Milne & Gray, 2013). Wilk (2010) posits that "the concept of 'sustainable consumption' has been a bit of jargon that allows science to say one thing and the public to hear another" (p. 10). Thus, consumption-oriented sustainability initiatives highlight the tension underlying marketing efforts and messages about sustainability.

Without addressing the fundamental motive of marketing (i.e., to sell more stuff), current efforts in sustainability result in mere tweaking at the margins. Any meaningful movement toward sustainability requires widespread questioning of consumer culture (Borland & Lindgreen, 2013; Scott, Martin, & Schouten, 2014; Shrivastava, 1995; Wilk, 2010). This type of questioning is tantamount to an existential threat to marketing itself (Rindfleisch & Burroughs, 2004). Indeed, adherence to traditional marketing objectives is a frequently invoked reason why most corporate sustainability initiatives have had little or no substantive impact on ecological sustainability (Archel, Fernández, & Larrinaga, 2008; Laine, 2010; Moneva, Archel, & Correa, 2006).

Borland and Lindgreen (2013) reason that what's missing from both the business and marketing strategy literature is "how to couple the science of ecological sustainability with the needs of commercial industry and human materialism" (p. 179). This lack of connection between human needs and the nature of the biophysical world is "dangerous and destructive" (Borland & Lindgreen, 2013, p. 176). As a result, tweaking "business as usual" won't work. Meaningful progress in sustainability initiatives requires, among other things, breaking down the artificial separation of humans and nature as well as promoting discontinuous change and creative destruction within the constraints of natural ecosystems (Borland & Lindgreen, 2013; Hart & Milstein, 2003; McDonough & Braungart, 2002b; Young & Tilley, 2006). Unfortunately, the incompatibility between the logics of marketing and sustainability makes this imperative quite difficult to achieve.

Incompatibility between the Logic of Marketing and the Logic of Sustainability

Francis Bacon's injunction 'Nature, to be commanded, must be obeyed' was not an intimation of humility and even less a counsel of meekness. It was an act of defiance. (Bauman, 2004)

Contemporary marketing theory (as well as business theory in general) exhibits a strong belief that knowledge of the laws of nature allows us to conquer our physical world. Although nature is recognized as a force to reckon with, humans are viewed as superior. As noted by Bauman (2004), "the world is manageable and demands to be managed, in as far as it has been remade to the measure of human comprehension" (p. 19).

Over the past three centuries, we have seen an increasing separation of the logic of human progress versus the logic of nature. Biologists describe this divergence as the "arrogance of humanism" (Gladwin, Kennelly, & Krause, 1995, p. 875). For example, the rise of cities, modern architecture, plumbing, and industrialization served to separate people from their waste — literally flushing it out — blind to its reverberating effects on the natural world (Hawkins, 2007). Mining represents a quintessential illustration of these divergent logics (Mumford & Copeland, 1961). Rather than a natural continuity of death and rebirth according to natural laws, mining is perpetually destructive through its "meticulous and merciless dissociation between the target product and everything else that stands in the way of its arrival," including burning forests, removing and disposing of layer after layer of soil and producing "irreversible and irrevocable" waste (Bauman, 2004, p. 21). Unfortunately, the logic of human progress (i.e., business in general and marketing in particular) often runs counter to the goals and logics of nature. As noted in the prior section, efforts to attain greater environmental sustainability are often compromised by the predominant business motives of cost reduction, competiveness, legitimation, and risk mitigation (Bansal & Roth, 2000; Etzion, 2007; Haddock-Fraser & Tourelle, 2010; Shrivastava, 1995).

The title of a best-selling book, *Green to Gold: How Smart Companies Use Environmental Strategy to Innovate, Create Value, and Build Competitive Advantage* (Esty & Winston, 2009), is illustrative of the essential disconnect between the logics of marketing versus nature. Esty and Winston (2009) suggest that pursuing an environmental strategy can give a firm a competitive edge and enhance its profitability. However, given its inherent focus on increasing consumption and purchase activity, marketing requires firms to acquire growing stocks of resources and energy to turn these materials into finished products. At best, environmental strategies based on traditional goals are limited in scope and at worst, they are a chimera. Without questioning underlying goals and assumptions, the logic of business is inherently at odds with the logic of nature. Nature and its methods are fundamentally grounded in the logic of complex adaptive systems, yet business struggles mightily to adopt a systems-oriented perspective (Dickson, 1992). Thus, our ability to integrate human progress with nature is a considerable challenge for our industrial economy (Fergus & Rowney, 2005; Gladwin et al., 1995; Habermas, 1990).

To address this inherent disconnect, a number of scholars are beginning to suggest that firms look to nature as not just a resource provider but also a source for inspiration (Lusch & Spohrer, 2012; Mars, Bronstein, & Lusch, 2012; Sagarin, 2012). This stimulating perspective posits that rather than trying to be superior to nature, firms could improve how they do business by mimicking biological ecosystems. Although this approach focuses on looking to nature for achieving business goals such as enhanced innovation and profits, it stops short of questioning fundamental business assumptions (Hutchins, 2012). Without questioning these assumptions, even efforts to emulate nature can take a firm's sustainability efforts down the wrong path by focusing on enhancing consumption rather than reducing this ecologically taxing value system.

In sum, although acknowledging that natural systems might offer useful insights for marketing managers and others, the impact of this approach in terms of solving large-scale environmental challenges such as global warming is largely incremental. Both "greening" strategies as well as the use of nature as a metaphor are steps in the right direction. However, these approaches will likely have little impact in terms of reintegrating the logics of marketing versus nature. In essence, we need to confront this dilemma at a larger scale.

Incommensurability in Scale

Taking some action has to be better than doing nothing. (Anderies, Folke, Walker, & Ostrom, 2013)

Another possible reason for marketing's lack of meaningful progress in its quest for sustainability is related to problems of scale and level of organization (Anderies et al., 2013). Although there is a broad belief that actions by individual firms and consumers can drive change and address global sustainability challenges, this belief has been called into question. Empirical evidence (Pizer, Morgenstern, & Shih, 2011; Rivera & De Leon, 2004) and theoretical perspectives (Prakash & Potoski, 2007; Segerson & Miceli, 1998) suggest that voluntary efforts toward sustainability have had little overall effect, and suffer from the problem of the commons (Gordon, 1954, 1991; Ostrom, 1990). For instance, when incentive structures privilege what is good for the individual firm over what is good for the planet, overuse of unregulated resources is a natural by-product. These effects are then amplified and propagated across multiple players, resulting in even greater unsustainability of the system as a whole. Indeed, "a cumulative series of small changes, each individually reversible, may 'flip the system' into another, possibly undesirable domain where it will tend to remain" (Gallopín, 2006, p. 299; cf. Gunderson & Holling, 2002; Holling, 1986). Hence, as noted by Anderies et al. (2013), "it is insufficient and even dangerous to assume that individual [firm] actions will aggregate up to generate system-level sustainability" (p. 2).

Therefore, in order to realize their quest for sustainability, firms need to focus not only on their individual actions but also on broader system-level concerns. Because "it is highly unlikely that uncoordinated actions of actors will scale up in a nice predictable way" (Anderies et al., 2013, p. 10), understanding the system as a whole requires a much broader perspective. Hence, theories that offer a systems-oriented lens are crucial. As a starting point, our next section examines two different theoretical approaches that offer this shift in perspective.

NEW THEORETICAL LENSES INTEGRATING SUSTAINABILITY AND THE NATURAL ENVIRONMENT

In addition to seeking financial gains, companies must actively seek harmony with the natural environment.... One of the primary stakeholders must be nature, both in the regions where it [the business] operates and globally. (Shrivastava & Hart, 1995)

In this section, we examine two different theoretical lenses that explicitly couple business and nature. Assemblage theory and socio-ecological systems theory combine both the logic of nature and that of human-based organizations. As such, these two theories have the potential to reconcile some of the sustainability challenges noted earlier. However, these theories also have some drawbacks. Table 1 provides an overview of these theoretical approaches with a summary of their relative strengths and weaknesses.

Assemblage Theory as a Lens for Sustainability

Inspired largely by the work of the French philosopher Gilles Deleuze, assemblage theory presents a systems-level perspective that has been usefully applied to a number of fields including marketing, management, and political science (Bennett, 2010; Canniford & Bajde, 2015; Connolly, 2005; Coole & Frost, 2010; DeLanda, 2006; Deleuze & Guattari, 1987; Hicky-Moody & Malins, 2007; Latour, 2005; Scott et al., 2014; Sellar, 2009). According to this perspective, any entity (from as small as a molecule to as large as the planet) can be understood as a set of inter-related components that assemble into a broader whole (Bennett, 2010; Coole & Frost, 2010; DeLanda, 2006; Deleuze & Guattari, 1987). Moreover, assemblage theory views the environment as made up of fluid, contingent layers of components. This theory conceives the world "as a process that unfolds through changing assemblages of humans, other species, technologies, and institutions" (Ogden et al., 2013, p. 341). Hence, from an assemblage theory perspective, marketing and nature are inextricably bound.

Assemblage theory investigates the world as constituted from diverse kinds and scales of interacting components, whose relations are "always uncertain, open to change and never final" (Canniford & Bajde, 2015, p. 2; cf. Pierides & Woodman, 2012, p. 671). The relations among these components are contingent upon one another and constituted in a web made up of "humans and nonhumans; animals, vegetables, and mineral; nature, culture and technology" (Bennett, 2005, p. 445). Moreover, each component of a broader system has the capacity to reassemble and reconfigure into new entities (DeLanda, 2006; Latour, 2005; Sassen, 2006), particularly "when one part comes into contact with another part with which it can interact" (Sellar, 2009, p. 69). Hence, from an assemblage theory perspective, the apparent disconnect between the human and the natural worlds can be easily bridged, and new configurations and capacities can emerge. As a result, business can be brought in harmony with nature. For example,

Table 1. Theoretical Lenses that Explicitly Incorporate Natural (Ecological) and Human (Business) Spheres.

	What	Strengths	Limitations
Assemblage theory	Assemblages are comprised of individual components of a system that can be mixed-and-matched such that different assemblages exhibit different capacities. Social formations are assemblages of other complex configurations, which in turn play roles in other, more extended configurations. Rather than being designed to do one thing, assemblages are characterized by their fluidity, exchangeability, and multiple functionalities.	• Explicitly recognizes humans' inescapable embeddedness in both social and natural contexts • Offers insights about how human connections to the environment can affect behavior • Views nature as an integral part of – and as important as – human systems • Directly addresses scale issues and articulation of lower-order processes and higher-order impacts	• Few concrete applications • Relative role of humans *vis a vis* nature is unclear/underappreciated • May underestimate the role of structural forces in constraining change • Indefiniteness and indeterminacy make it difficult to explain properties and behaviors of systems
Social-ecological systems (SES): Resilience, vulnerability, and adaptive capacity	SES's include both human and biophysical subsystems in mutual interaction Resilience, vulnerability, and adaptive capacity capture key processes in the interaction of ecological and social subsystems	• Can be specified at any scale • Explicitly addresses the dynamic interplay of social and ecological components	• Collaboration between natural and social scientists is extremely challenging • Trading off ecological and human outcomes requires economic valuation of ecosystem services, which is extremely challenging • Operates at a level of abstraction that makes it difficult to operationalize

a building in Amsterdam known as "The Edge" achieves harmony between business and nature by reconfiguring traditional offices into flexible workspaces that can support more office workers using a less resource-intensive footprint (Bloomberg, 2015).

Assemblage theory appears useful for addressing the incompatibility between the logic of business versus the logic of nature through its focus on recognizing "humans' inescapable embeddedness" in our natural environment (Gabrielson & Parady, 2010, p. 376). For marketers, this approach suggests a shift in thinking to "grasp entire systems and their entanglements of matter and meaning" (Scott et al., 2014, p. 289). More broadly, this theory offers three key ideas for helping marketers address the challenges of insufficiency, incompatibility, insignificance, and incommensurability.

First, assemblage theory emphasizes that we are embedded in the world as part of broader system. This shifts marketers' (and consumers') perspectives from "the indifferent stuff of a world 'out there', articulated through notions of 'land', 'nature' or 'environment', to the intimate fabric of corporeality that includes and redistributes the 'in here' of human being" (Whatmore, 2006, p. 602). One implication of this shift is the notion that reducing consumption might best be achieved by highlighting embodied connections to our environments (Gorman-Murray & Lane, 2012). For example, research suggests that gardening connects people to their love of nature and, in turn, motivates water collection and recycling behavior (Allon & Sofoulis, 2006). In this case, collaborating and being embedded with nature helps people appreciate their capabilities and dependencies in relation to this broader assemblage.

Second, assemblage theory also introduces an understanding of agency that emphasizes the complex, symbiotic relationship of humans and nature, in which neither has mastery over the other (Bendle, 2002). Neither the agency of humans nor nature is deterministic in its own right; they are both intertwined and interdependent (Gorman-Murray & Lane, 2012). One implication of this interdependency is that sustainability initiatives should tease out the component parts of assemblages and treat them all as having actor roles in conjunction with other components (Bennett, 2004, 2010; Latour, 2005). Hence, structures, surroundings, contexts, and environments are more than passive backgrounds; instead, they should be viewed as "spirited actants" within a common ecology (Bennett, 2005, p. 455; Srnicek, 2010; Whatmore, 2006). For example, when organizations introduce new packaging to reduce waste, they need to consider how interactive capacities across the full assemblage of human and nonhuman actors are altered — from how the packaging itself is sourced and produced, to how well it works in the product's conveyer belt, to whether it is reused and recycled after delivery. A sturdier shoe box may require more natural materials to produce but work better in the production process for the product and also have a longer useful life because of its increased likelihood of being reused.

Third, assemblage thinking provides a reconceptualization of scale such that a higher-order component (such as a firm) is itself an assemblage of interacting lower-order components (such as its marketing initiatives) (Perey, 2014). Thus, this theory helps firms recognize that sustainability is a multiscalar problem (Perey, 2014; Stead & Stead, 2013; Stoddart, Tindall, & Greenfield, 2012). From this perspective, sustainability initiatives should attend to how relations among lower-order assemblages affect and are affected by higher-order assemblages — "how the 'local' articulates with and is transformed by economic globalization and global climate change" (Ogden et al., 2013, p. 341). For example, coffee cultivation has shaped global economies, tropical mountain ecosystems, and local socio-environmental relations at the edges of the global market economy (Ogden et al., 2013). Ogden et al. (2013) state that in Papua, New Guinea (PNG), coffee harvesters earn only about 15¢ U.S. per hour for picking specialty coffee that sells for over $12.00 per pound at Starbucks (p. 343). This substantial profit margin creates a global economic structure that increases coffee production in PNG while also fueling poverty and environmental degradation.

Despite its strengths, assemblage theory also has some limitations. First, this perspective is currently an abstract and rather loosely organized theory that is rather difficult to put into practice. Concrete applications, especially at the intersection of marketing and sustainability, are rare (Canniford & Bajde, 2015; Scott et al., 2014). Second, although its emphasis on distributed agency is a welcome alternative to the usual narrative of man over nature, it may underappreciate the role of motivated human actors — including consumers, marketers, and policy makers — to alter and realign relations within assemblages (Price & Epp, 2015). Third, assemblage theory places considerable emphasis on the role of diversity, dynamism, and instability. Thus, this lens may downplay the role of more deterministic structural mechanisms such as organizational inertia and routines that constrain and shape marketing thought and practice (Price & Epp, 2015). Finally, this theory's indefiniteness and indeterminacy make it difficult to explain specific properties and behaviors of systems (Little, 2012): "This poses a very hard problem for explanation. How are we to explain the properties and behavior of systems if there is so much contingency in its parts and the ways in which they interact?" As described later, we believe a more mid-range (e.g., applied) theory such as biomimicry could be useful in overcoming these limitations.

Socio-Ecological Systems Theory

A second theoretical lens that explicitly integrates the natural (i.e., environmental) and social (i.e., marketing) is socio-ecological systems (SES) theory (Berkes, Colding, & Folke, 2003; Berkes & Folke, 1998; Boyd & Folke, 2011). An SES is defined as a system that includes human and biophysical (i.e., "natural") subsystems in mutual interaction (Gallopín, 1991). Thus, this perspective bears some resemblance to assemblage theory by recognizing the close relationship between humans and natural systems (Turner et al., 2003). Similar to assemblage theory, this perspective suggests that a system "can be specified for any scale from the local community and its surrounding environment to the global system constituted by the whole of humankind and the ecosphere" (Gallopín, 2006, p. 294). The "social" or human component of SES includes all actors that affect, and are affected by, the relevant natural/ecological landscape, and can include policy makers, NGOs and nonprofits, businesses, and other stakeholders. This approach explicitly argues that meaningful progress on the environmental front requires the simultaneous consideration of ecological and social components and recognizes the dynamic interplay between them (Carpenter, Brock, & Hanson, 1999; Gallopín, 2006). According to this perspective, a society's material artifacts (such as the products that firms market) are inherently dependent upon the availability of renewable resources and the capacity of our biosphere to generate and sustain these resources. In addition, social structures (such as firms) are also part of our biosphere, and are ultimately dependent on its functioning, while also shaping its form. Consequently, markets are deeply nested within and cannot be decoupled from ecological systems (Boyd & Folke, 2011).

Given the tight connection between the social and the ecological, this theoretical lens pays close attention to the vulnerability, resilience, and adaptive ability of SES (cf. Turner, 2010). Vulnerability refers to "a susceptibility to harm, a potential for change or transformation of a system when confronted with a perturbation" (Gallopín, 2006, p. 294). From an SES perspective, vulnerability arises from exposure to "perturbations" (disturbances, shocks, hazards), a system's sensitivity to those perturbations, and its capacity to adapt to them (Adger, 2006; Smit & Wandel, 2006). When a firm attends to vulnerabilities arising from the natural environment, it can better anticipate how it might need to adapt in the future, leading to resilience.

Resilience refers to a system's capacity to sustain a shock and continue to function, and more generally, cope with change in its current environment (Walker et al., 2006; Walker, Holling, Carpenter, & Kinzig, 2004; Walker & Salt, 2006). The concept of resilience emerged from ecological sciences to address persistence and change in ecosystems and evolved to include a system's capacity to respond, self-organize, and adapt (Folke et al., 2002, 2010; Walker, Abel, Anderies, & Ryan, 2009). This capacity to respond and adapt to change can help a social entity, such as a firm, react more effectively to "unknown change and hidden fragilities and to find innovative new mechanisms for dealing with transformative change" (Anderies et al., 2013, p. 11).

Adaptive capacity refers to the capacity of any system to maintain (or increase) the quality of life of its individual members when operating in a changing environment (Gallopín, Gutman, & Maletta, 1989; Smit & Wandel, 2006). Adaptability is important in helping an organism adapt to changes in its environment.

Vulnerability, resilience, and adaptability are different manifestations of more general processes of response to changes in the relationship between organisms and their external environment. As such, SES provides a general theory of change and transformation, and can help managers better understand how a system interacts within a changing environment.

Like assemblage theory, the SES perspective also presents a number of limitations. First, although this theory recognizes the close coupling between social and ecological systems, the explicit nature of this coupling remains somewhat unclear. Second, although SES theory implies that large-scale problems such as environmental sustainability should be understood via collaborative efforts between social and natural scientists (Gallopín, 2006), these types of collaborations are fraught with difficulty (Alberti et al., 2011; Liu et al., 2007). Third, for this theory to be useful, it must not only explicitly couple the human system with the environmental, but also acknowledge the implicit tradeoffs between the two (Turner, 2010). According to Turner (2010), coupled human-natural systems axiomatically involve tradeoffs among environmental services and human outcomes. Firms seeking to put this theory into practice face the daunting challenge of sacrificing either short-term profits or long-term survival (Bockstael, Freeman, Kopp, Portney, & Smith, 2000; Smith, 1996). The notion of placing a valuation on ecosystem services (also known as "natural capital") offers a potential solution to this dilemma. However, placing a dollar amount on something as widespread and essential as fresh air or clean water presents a considerable challenge for any particular firm (Hawken, Lovins, & Lovins, 1999; Odum & Odum, 2000). Finally, as with assemblage theory, SES operates at a level of abstraction that makes it difficult to put into practice.

In order to overcome some of the limitations of these two broader theoretical frameworks while retaining their strengths, the next section explores a more tractable conceptual framework: biomimicry. We posit biomimicry as a mid-range theory that facilitates an integration between marketing and nature to help firms address the four persistent challenges identified earlier.

BIOMIMICRY: A FRAMEWORK FOR INTEGRATING MARKETING AND NATURE

> Sustainability requires different organizational cultures and processes...[that] emphasize harmonious co-existence with the natural world, view humans as part of the natural world, and acknowledge the rights of nature to exist. Only when environmental considerations [nature] are integrated into day-to-day operations can an organization approach sustainability. (Shrivastava & Hart, 1995)

Biomimicry provides a set of concepts and tools for helping business, education, government, and other human actors look to the natural world for solutions to various types of problems. Conceptually, rather than viewing the "human" (for our purposes, marketing) domain as something that is separate from nature, biomimicry views human activity as an inherent component of nature. The term "biomimicry" means, quite literally, mimicking or emulating ideas from the natural world. Popularized by Benyus (1997), "bios" means life and "mimesis" means to imitate. Therefore, biomimicry is the conscious seeking of inspiration and innovation — the search for finding new and better ways to do things — through understanding nature and the principles of biology. In addition, biomimicry also offers a set of tools and processes for invoking nature's insights to solve human challenges. This process heavily engages biologists, who work hand-in-hand with engineers, architects, and product designers, to find sustainable innovations to solve a wide array of problems.

A growing number of businesses are using biomimicry to sustainably innovate in many marketing domains, including product development, packaging, and distribution. For example, one firm mimicked the molecular structure in feathers to design a radically new fabric to cool athletes in hot climates. Likewise, PAX Scientific used the unique three-dimensional spiral shapes found in the shells of mollusks to develop propellers for fans that dramatically reduce the friction and energy requirements compared to traditional fan designs. As seen from these examples, nature's design principles can offer innovative thinking that is in harmony with the natural world.

In addition to helping firms develop more innovative and environmentally-friendly new products, biomimicry also offers a potential response to the sustainability challenges outlined earlier. First, rather than "tweaking at the margins" or simply "greening" business as usual, biomimicry can help firms fundamentally rethink the underlying premise of their business. For example, after using biomimicry in its product development process to design its line of carpet tiles patterned after a forest floor, InterfaceFlor moved to deeply embed the philosophy of harmony with nature into the very core of its business. In a radical departure from a traditional business model, the company decided to explicitly uncouple revenue from product sales. Rather than selling products, it provides "flooring as a service" to its industrial customers. Questioning consumption as the basis of its business model has allowed InterfaceFlor to minimize the amount of materials customers need (e.g., replacing only worn areas of carpeting). Moreover, this approach also allows it to control its complete material supply chain to ensure that all environmentally related activities and processes are in harmony with nature. Most recently, this company's deeply embedded philosophy has led to even more ambitious nature-based goals: not only to be in harmony with nature, but also to identify ways to become "restorative" to nature through its business practices (Interface.com, 2015).

Second, rather than viewing nature as a stock of inputs or as something to be dominated, biomimicry privileges the voice of nature as a source of genius. By "quieting the human cleverness" (cf. Benyus, 1997), this framework allows firms to become aware of the genius in nature. By looking toward nature as a source of inspiration, biomimicry can help resolve the incompatibility between marketing and sustainability. A biomimicry-based solution begins by framing a problem in terms of "how would nature do this?" Biologists create a taxonomy of nature-based solutions that a firm's design team then evaluates for viability. Traditionally, a company might start its sustainability process by identifying where a product's carbon footprint is heaviest. In contrast, biomimicry might offer new insights about radical redesigns to completely eliminate the source of the problem, rather than to merely "minimize" it. For example, in designing the Eastgate

Center in Harare, Zimbabwe, biomimicry-inspired architects looked to nature to understand how termite mounds in the area were able to maintain a constant ambient air temperature despite the wide fluctuations between hot days and cool desert nights. By understanding the ways termites tunnel to create airflow, they were able to design the building to mitigate 90% of the need for any air conditioning at all.

Third, guided by a set of "life principles," biomimicry offers firms the opportunity to scale sustainability efforts up or down − from ingredients to processing, from packaging to distribution, and to networks, supply chains, and entire ecosystems. In this way, a biomimicry lens can include the sourcing of materials, the manufacturing process, the distribution process, etc. This type of systems perspective allows biomimicry to deliver one of the key conceptual lessons of both assemblage theory and SES theory in a more accessible manner. In addition, this systems-oriented perspective also considers feedback loops that can help firms identify unintended consequences and address them proactively. For example, although minimizing packaging is often a goal of traditional sustainability efforts, packaging redesign has ripple effects downstream with respect to shipping, storing, shelving at the retailer, as well as post-consumer recycling. By reconceptualizing packaging as a nature-based problem (i.e., "how does nature contain fluids or protect fragile organisms?"), new solutions can be surfaced.

The marketing function is uniquely qualified to bring biomimicry thinking into the organization. First, the biomimicry process is often leveraged for innovation in product design, making marketing a logical entry point. Second, because of its focus on solving customers' problems in ways that create value, say in energy utilization or functionality, biomimicry offers marketing stronger value propositions and positioning of its products. Third, as part of their market orientation and customer focus, marketers are trained to consider a multiplicity of sources during information gathering and concept development. Consequently, asking marketers to expand their listening capabilities to including "listening to nature" would be complementary. From there, marketing managers could invite others in the organization to also listen to nature as a source of creativity and inspiration. Companies find that nature-based workshops can create new team dynamics, especially in offering a new lens for those parts of an organization that might not be particularly good at listening to outside perspectives and needs.

In summary, biomimicry offers the potential to integrate marketing processes in ways that are consistent with the natural world. By grounding its decisions explicitly in the natural world, business success is coupled with environmental impacts – one cannot be successful at the expense of the other.

CONCLUDING THOUGHTS AND
FUTURE DIRECTIONS

Environmental sustainability presents marketing scholars and practitioners with a paradox. Although both academics and marketing managers widely acknowledge the serious environmental concerns facing the planet, they have had considerable difficulty channeling this concern into meaningful action. In this chapter, we propose that the root of this difficulty is neither a lack of motivation nor effort on the part of individual actors or firms; rather, this difficulty arises from persistent challenges that marketers face. Specifically, we suggest that four inter-related factors explain the limited impact of marketers' sustainability efforts. First, progress in environmental sustainability has been limited by insufficient theoretical lenses. Second, the insignificance of marketers' sustainability efforts can be traced back to environmental strategies that merely "tweak at the margins" while maintaining business as usual. Third, the inherent incompatibility between the logic of marketing (focused on revenue growth by selling products and defining competitive advantage in terms of profitability) and the logic of nature (in which humans and their creations are inextricably linked into the ecology of the environment) poses a potentially intractable divide. Finally, incommensurability in terms of scale suggests that individual marketers' efforts at sustainability may not scale up in a logical way, and indeed, may have unintended consequences.

Solving these four challenges is a formidable task that requires radical changes in marketing thought and practice. As a stepping-stone toward identifying these changes, we outlined two alternative theoretical lenses that transcend the divide between nature and marketing: assemblage theory and SES theory. Both theoretical perspectives offer an explicit coupling of the natural and human spheres and highlight the absolute necessity of a systems perspective. Nonetheless, few practical applications of these theoretical lenses exist and more research is needed to translate them from theoretical abstractions to marketing practice. Therefore, we also illustrate how the explicit coupling of nature and marketing decisions can be enacted through biomimicry, a pragmatic, mid-range lens that offers substantial promise to help confront the four challenges of insignificance, incommensurability, insufficiency, and incompatibility.

Biomimicry offers a specific methodology that explicitly integrates a nature-based perspective into marketing decision-making. Specifically, we advocate that marketers should systematically use the tools and principles of biomimicry to engage nature as a vital stakeholder. Marketers pride themselves on their ability to listen to human voices, and work with various types of data to garner customer insights (Day, 1994). They are perfectly positioned to engage nature as a stakeholder. Using biomimicry, marketers can add to their tool-kit by incorporating new skills for listening to nature and develop "radical collaborations" with biologists and ecologists to answer "what would nature do?" in response to today's profound environmental challenges.

Some organizations have already fruitfully employed biomimicry for product innovation, but more work is needed to expand nature's voice across the full spectrum of marketing decisions. Nature's principles and the methodology of biomimicry can shift marketers' perspective of the natural world and how they approach sustainability. Currently, marketers and other organizational actors rarely receive training on environmental sustainability and they have little to no exposure to biology and ecology. As a result, little is known about the science of sustainability and most marketing decisions fail to account for the complex dynamics between human and environmental systems (Clark, 2007; Clark & Munn, 1986; Turner, 2010). Research questions along these lines might explore how companies build an ecological capacity, as well as the extent to which nature and the value of ecosystem services are explicitly addressed in marketing decision-making. For example, when decisions about product innovation or resource inputs *explicitly* address ecological considerations, do environmental sustainability metrics show differential improvement? How can the worlds of nature and humans be integrated through productive collaborations between marketers and others to give voice to nature in organizational decisions (cf. Pascale, Millemann, & Gioja, 2000)?

When marketing and nature are viewed as inextricably linked, new perspectives and insights for research and practice arise. Fig. 3 invites readers to envision marketing and nature in harmony — bound together in processes and outcomes. Nidumolu, Ellison, Whalen, and Billman (2014) note that the earth's natural commons — the atmosphere, natural resources, and biological ecosystems — provide enormous value to both business and society. However, much of that value is being destroyed through the suboptimal ways in which marketers and firms interact with these complex and

Fig. 3. Interlocking Connection between Marketing and Nature.

fragile systems. As this figure shows, nature is not merely a source of resources and raw materials (a link in a distribution channel), nor just an input to be managed. Instead, the natural world is an essential ecosystem that is inherently valuable by itself (Hawken et al., 1999). From this perspective, nature's "nonhuman actors," such as fauna, forests, and floodplains, have consequential agency. By ignoring the value and agency of nature, marketers will continue to grapple with environmental sustainability because they view nature as a resource to be managed.

As noted by Turner (2010, p. 571), "The environment constitutes the subsystem providing services required for the maintenance of humankind, regardless of our awareness of, or the lack of economic value placed on, them." He goes on to state that "sustainability science examines the relationships between environmental services (ecosystem services) and human outcomes to uncover qualities that make SESs less vulnerable or more resilient to perturbations and disturbances." This depiction of sustainability as a nature-directed stakeholder, rather than a firm-directed imperative, runs counter to the approach most marketing efforts adopt in their sustainability quest.

Moreover, when nature and marketing are truly coupled, engagement with other stakeholders shifts from a trade-off mentality to mutuality. As Fig. 3 shows, with this systems perspective agency is redistributed, and raw materials, customers, ecosystem services and partnerships with NGOs, society and government are framed differently. For example, how marketers think about partnerships is broadened when nature is considered a vibrant force in the business/natural environment nexus (Nidumolu et al., 2014). Radical collaboration requires business to rethink the role of environmental NGOs and the potential for new processes and insights by partnering with what previously might have been considered "the enemy" (Tercek & Adams, 2013). Customers, too, are brought in to the collaboration with attention to how to align them more closely with nature. Relational marketing can be directed to managing a mutuality of relationships among customers, nature and the firm rather than framing these as tradeoffs. Research questions in this area might address the extent to which companies are partnered with nature-based NGOs in their sustainability efforts and whether firms that exhibit more radical collaboration perform better on sustainability metrics.

At its heart, sustainability requires that marketers first understand nature as a stakeholder and then creatively apply this knowledge to guide their environmental sustainability efforts. When nature is viewed as a legitimate stakeholder, it becomes not a thing to be "managed and controlled," but instead, an actor that should be listened to and respected. For example, incorporating the "voice of nature" in organizational decision-making can help transcend the incompatibility between the logic of business versus the logic of nature. Unfortunately, most firms seek to tame nature rather than listen to it. Thus, new skills and capabilities need to be cultivated. Research in this area might address how marketers can develop additional listening skills to include "the voice of the environment" (Allenby, 1991; Fiksel, 1993) in organizational decision-making, and its relative influence and impacts on firm outcomes.

The next frontier of value creation needs to address ways to preserve and protect the natural commons (Nidumolu et al., 2014; Winston, 2014b). Firms on the forefront of sustainability are asking not just how to be more environmentally sustainable, but how their practices can actually be "restorative" to the environment. For example, Hawken (2010) states, "We have the capacity and ability to create a remarkably different economy, one that can restore ecosystems and protect the environment while bringing forth innovation, prosperity, meaningful work, and true security" (p. 2). In a restorative economy, marketing success and viability are determined by the ability to integrate with or replicate ecological systems in the means of production and distribution. Two examples of companies attempting to meet this higher standard of more than just sustainable, but actually restorative, practices are InterfaceFlor (previously mentioned) and Kingfisher. Kingfisher, a large European home-improvement retailer strives to help people build homes that generate more energy than they use, a restorative business model that it calls "Net Positive" (Winston, 2014b). What motivates companies and what their trajectory looks like as they move in their sustainability journey to a philosophy of restoration are intriguing questions for future research.

Connecting organizational actions to the workings of natural systems — or the harmonizing of marketing and nature for planetary well-being — will require sea changes in organizational practices and institutional frameworks. Viable ways of giving nature agency and voice within organizations offer a crucial first step. As noted earlier, biomimicry may provide a pathway toward acquiring requisite skills and capabilities through its useful approaches for giving nature an active voice in marketing decisions. Biomimicry offers the potential to be part of a bigger solution to planetary woes; however, it is just a starting point rather than a final answer. Despite the many case studies of companies leveraging this methodology (cf. Harman, 2013), biomimicry lacks systematic inquiry. In particular, the barriers and success factors companies face in using this framework to achieve sustainability outcomes have not been systematically studied. If biomimicry is to achieve its full potential as a valuable protocol to explicitly couple business with nature, solid theoretical development and empirical grounding is vital. More research is needed to understand how biomimicry can facilitate business-nature collaborations and how to build these skills within organizations.

ACKNOWLEDGMENTS

The first author thanks the University of Montana for funding her sabbatical to pursue this research and feedback from research presentations at the University of Montana, University of Arizona, University of Illinois, University of Stockholm, University of Wyoming, and Montana State University. In addition, helpful comments by Justin Angle and Naresh Malhotra have improved this chapter.

REFERENCES

Adger, W. N. (2006). Vulnerability. *Global Environmental Change*, *16*(3), 268–281. doi:10.1016/j.gloenvcha.2006.02.006

Alberti, M., Asbjornsen, H., Baker, L. A., Brozovic, N., Drinkwater, L. E., Drzyzga, S. A., ... Urquhart, G. (2011). Research on coupled human and natural systems (CHANS): Approach, challenges, and strategies. *Bulletin of the Ecological Society of America*, *92*, 218–228.

Allenby, B. R. (1991). Design for environment: A tool whose time has come. *SSA Journal*, *12*(9), 5–9.

Allon, F., & Sofoulis, Z. (2006). Everyday water: Cultures in transition. *Australian Geographer*, *37*(1), 45−55.

Anderies, J. M., Folke, C., Walker, B., & Ostrom, E. (2013). Aligning key concepts for global change policy: Robustness, resilience, and sustainability. *Ecology and Society*, *18*(2), 8.

Archel, P., Fernández, M., & Larrinaga, C. (2008). The organizational and operational boundaries of triple bottom line reporting: A survey. *Environmental Management*, *41*, 1/106−117.

Bansal, P., & Roth, K. (2000). Why companies go green: A model of ecological responsiveness. *Academy of Management Journal*, *43*(4), 717−736.

Barney, J. (1991). Firm resources and sustained competitive advantage. *Journal of Management*, *17*, 99−120.

Bauman, Z. (2004). *Work, consumerism and the new poor*. Maidenhead: McGraw-Hill Education.

Bendle, M. F. (2002). Teleportation, cyborgs and the posthuman ideology. *Social Semiotics*, *12*(1), 45−62.

Bennett, J. (2004). The force of things: Steps toward an ecology of matter. *Political Theory*, *32*(3), 347−372.

Bennett, J. (2005). The agency of assemblages and the North American Blackout. *Public Culture*, *17*(3), 445.

Bennett, J. (2010). *Vibrant matter: A political ecology of things*. Durham, NC: Duke University Press.

Benyus, J. M. (1997). *Biomimicry*. New York, NY: William Morrow.

Berkes, F., Colding, J., & Folke, C. (2003). *Navigating social-ecological systems: Building resilience for complexity and change*. Cambridge, UK: Cambridge University Press.

Berkes, F., & Folke, C. (1998). *Linking social and ecological systems for resilience and sustainability: Management practices and social mechanisms for building resilience*. Cambridge, UK: Cambridge University Press.

Bloomberg. (2015). See the world's greenest office building: The Edge. *Bloomberg*, September 23. Retrieved from http://www.bloomberg.com/news/videos/2015-09-23/see-the-world-s-greenest-office-building-the-edge. Accessed on January 5.

Bockstael, N. E., Freeman, A. M., Kopp, R. J., Portney, P. R., & Smith, V. K. (2000). On measuring economic values for nature. *Environmental Science & Technology*, *34*(8), 1384−1389. doi:10.1021/es9906731

Borland, H., & Lindgreen, A. (2013). Sustainability, epistemology, ecocentric business, and marketing strategy: Ideology, reality, and vision. *Journal of Business Ethics*, *117*(1), 173−187.

Boyd, E., & Folke, C. (Eds.). (2011). *Adapting institutions: Governance, complexity and social-ecological resilience*. Cambridge, UK: Cambridge University Press.

Canniford, R., & Bajde, D. (2015). *Assembling consumption: Researching actors, networks and markets*. New York, NY: Routledge Press.

Carpenter, S. R., Brock, W. A., & Hanson, P. C. (1999). *Ecological and social dynamics in simple models of ecosystem management*. Social Systems Research Institute, University of Wisconsin.

Clark, W. C. (2007). Sustainability science: A room of its own. *Proceedings of the National Academy of Sciences*, *104*(6), 1737−1738. doi:10.1073/pnas.0611291104

Clark, W. C., & Munn, R. E. (1986). *The sustainable development of the biosphere*. Cambridge, UK: Cambridge University Press.

Connelly, B. L., Ketchen, D. J. Jr, & Slater, S. F. (2011). Toward a "theoretical toolbox" for sustainability research in marketing. *Journal of the Academy of Marketing Science, 39*(1), 86−100.

Connolly, W. E. (2005). *Pluralism.* Durham, NC: Duke University Press.

Coole, D., & Frost, S. (Eds.). (2010). *New materialisms: Ontology, agency and politics.* Durham, NC: Duke University Press.

Crittenden, V. L., Crittenden, W. F., Ferrell, L. K., Ferrell, O. C., & Pinney, C. C. (2011). Market-oriented sustainability: A conceptual framework and propositions. *Journal of the Academy of Marketing Science, 39*(1), 71−85.

Day, G. S. (1994). The capabilities of market-driven organizations. *Journal of Marketing, 58*(October), 37−52.

Day, G. S. (2011). Closing the marketing capabilities gap. *Journal of Marketing, 75,* 183−195.

DeLanda, M. (2006). *A new philosophy of society.* New York, NY: Continuum International.

Deleuze, G., & Guattari, F. (1987). *A thousand plateaus.* Minneapolis, MN: University of Minnesota Press.

Dickson, P. R. (1992). Toward a general theory of competitive rationality. *Journal of Marketing, 56*(January), 69−83.

Esty, D., & Winston, A. (2009). *Green to gold: How smart companies use environmental strategy to innovate, create value, and build competitive advantage.* Hoboken, NJ: John Wiley & Sons, Inc.

Etzion, D. (2007). Research on organizations and the natural environment, 1992-present: A review. *Journal of Management, 33*(4), 637−664.

Fergus, A. H. T., & Rowney, J. I. A. (2005). Sustainable development: Lost meaning and opportunity? *Journal of Business Ethics, 60*(1), 17−27.

Fiksel, J. (1993). Environment: An integrated systems approach. *Proceedings of 1993 IEEE international symposium on electronics and the environment* (pp. 126−131). doi: 10.1109/ ISEE.1993.302823.

Folke, C., Carpenter, S., Elmqvist, T., Gunderson, L., Holling, C. S., & Walker, B. (2002). Resilience and sustainable development: Building adaptive capacity in a world of transformations. *AMBIO: A Journal of the Human Environment, 31*(5), 437−440. doi:10.1579/0044-7447-31.5.437

Folke, C., Carpenter, S. R., Walker, B., Scheffer, M., Chapin, T., & Rockström, J. (2010). Resilience thinking: Integrating resilience, adaptability and transformability. *Ecology and Society, 15*(4), 20.

Gabrielson, T., & Parady, K. (2010). Corporeal citizenship: Rethinking green citizenship through the body. *Environmental Politics, 19*(3), 374−391.

Gallopín, G. C. (1991). Human dimensions of global change-linking the global and the local processes. *International Social Science Journal, 43*(4), 707−718.

Gallopín, G. C. (2006). Linkages between vulnerability, resilience, and adaptive capacity. *Global Environmental Change, 16*(3), 293−303. doi:10.1016/j.gloenvcha.2006.02.004

Gallopín, G. C., Gutman, P., & Maletta, H. (1989). Global impoverishment, sustainable development and the environment a conceptual approach. *International Social Science Journal, 121,* 375−397.

Gladwin, T. N., Kennelly, J. J., & Krause, T.-S. (1995). Shifting paradigms for sustainable development: Implications for management theory and research. *Academy of Management Review, 20*(4), 874−907.

Goh, E., Haanaes, K., Kiron, D., Kruschwitz, N., & Reeves, M. (2013). *The innovation bottom line.* MIT Sloan Management Review and The Boston Consulting Group: Winter Research Report.

Gordon, H. S. (1954). The economic theory of a common-property resource: The fishery. *Journal of Political Economy, 62*, 124–142.

Gordon, H. S. (1991). The economic theory of a common-property resource: The fishery. *Bulletin of Mathematical Biology, 53*(1–2), 231–252. doi:10.1016/S0092-8240(05)80048-5

Gorman-Murray, A., & Lane, R. (Eds.). (2012). *Material geographies of household sustainability.* Burlington, VT: Ashgate Publishing Company.

Gunderson, L. H., & Holling, C. S. (Eds.). (2002). *Panarchy: Understanding transformations in human and natural systems.* Washington, DC: Island Press.

Habermas, J. (1990). *The philosophical discourse of modernity (F. Lawrence, Trans.).* Cambridge, MA: MIT Press.

Haddock-Fraser, J. E., & Tourelle, M. (2010). Corporate motivations for environmental sustainable development: Exploring the role of consumers in stakeholder engagement. *Business Strategy and the Environment, 19*(8), 527–542.

Harman, J. (2013). *The Shark's paintbrush: Biomimicry and how nature is inspiring innovation.* Ashland, OR: White Cloud Press.

Hart, S. L. (1995). A natural-resource-based view of the firm. *Academy of Management Review, 20*, 986–1014.

Hart, S. L., & Dowell, G. (2011). A natural-resource-based view of the firm: Fifteen years after. *Journal of Management, 37*(5), 1464–1479.

Hart, S. L., & Milstein, M. B. (2003). Creating sustainable value. *The Academy of Management Executive, 17*(2), 56–67.

Hawken, P. (2010). *The ecology of commerce: A declaration of sustainability* (Rev. ed.). New York, NY: HarperBusiness.

Hawken, P., Lovins, A., & Lovins, L. H. (1999). *Natural capitalism.* Boston: Little, Brown.

Hawkins, G. (2007). Waste in Sydney: Unwelcome returns. *Proceedings of the Modern Languages Association, 122*, 348–351.

Henriques, A., & Richardson, J. (Eds.). (2013). *The triple bottom line: Does it all add up.* London: Routledge.

Hicky-Moody, A., & Malins, P. (2007). *Deleuzian encounters: Studies in contemporary social issues.* New York, NY: Palgrave MacMillan.

Holling, C. S. (1986). The resilience of terrestrial ecosystems: Local surprise and global change. *Sustainable Development of the Biosphere, 14*, 292–317.

Hutchins, G. (2012). *The nature of business: Redesigning for resilience.* Gabriola Island, BC: New Society Publishers.

Interface.com. (2015). Retrieved from http://www.interfaceflor.se/web/sustainability/mission_zero. Accessed on January 5, 2016.

IPCC. (2014). *Global carbon project.* Retrieved from http://www.globalcarbonproject.org/ http://www.ipcc.ch/

Kilbourne, W., McDonagh, P., & Prothero, A. (1997). Sustainable consumption and the quality of life: A macromarketing challenge to the dominant social paradigm. *Journal of Macromarketing, 17*, 1/4–24.

Kotler, P. (2011). Reinventing marketing to manage the environmental imperative. *Journal of Marketing, 75*(July), 132–135.

KPMG. (2012). *Expect the unexpected: Building business value in a changing world.* KPMG International. Retrieved from https://www.kpmg.com/Global/en/IssuesAndInsights/ArticlesPublications/Documents/building-business-value.pdf.

Kuehn, K., & McIntire, L. (2014). Sustainability a CFO can love. *Harvard Business Review, 92*(4), 66–74.

Laine, M. (2010). Towards sustaining the status quo: Business talk of sustainability in Finnish corporate disclosures 1987–2005. *European Accounting Review, 19*(2), 247–274.

Latour, B. (2005). *Reassembling the social: An introduction to actor-network-theory.* New York, NY: Oxford University Press.

Little, D. (2012). *Assemblage theory.* Retrieved from http://understandingsociety.blogspot. com/2012/11/assemblage-theory.html. Accessed on November 15.

Liu, J., Dietz, T., Carpenter, S. R., Alberti, M., Folke, C., Moran, E., ... Taylor, W. W. (2007). Complexity of coupled human and natural systems. *Science, 317*(5844), 1513–1516. doi:10.1126/science.1144004

Lusch, R. F., & Spohrer, J. C. (2012). Evolving service for a complex, resilient, and sustainable world. *Journal of Marketing Management, 28*(13–14), 1491–1503.

Makower, J. (2014). *State of green business 2014.* Retrieved from Greenbiz.com

Mars, M. M., Bronstein, J. L., & Lusch, R. F. (2012). The value of a metaphor: Organizations and ecosystems. *Organizational Dynamics, 41*(4), 271–280.

McDonough, W., & Braungart, M. (2002a). *Cradle to Cradle: Rethinking the way we make things.* Johnson City, NY: North Point.

McDonough, W., & Braungart, M. (2002b). Design for the triple top line: New tools for sustainable commerce. *Corporate Environmental Strategy, 9*(3), 251–258.

McKibben, B. (2011). *Earth: Making a life on a tough new planet.* New York, NY: St. Martin's Griffin.

Milne, M. J., & Gray, R. (2013). W(h)ither ecology? The triple bottom line, the global reporting initiative, and corporate sustainability reporting. *Journal of Business Ethics, 118*(1), 13–29.

Moneva, J. M., Archel, P., & Correa, C. (2006). GRI and the camouflaging of corporate unsustainability. *Accounting Forum, 30*(2).

Mumford, L., & Copeland, G. (1961). *The city in history: Its origins, its transformations, and its prospects.* New York, NY: Harcourt, Brace & World.

Nidumolu, R., Ellison, J., Whalen, J., & Billman, E. (2014). The Collaboration Imperative. *Harvard Business Review, 92*(4), 76–84.

Nidumolu, R., Prahalad, C. K., & Rangaswami, M. R. (2009). Why sustainability is now the key driver of innovation. *Harvard Business Review, 87*(September), 57–64.

Nike. (2015). *Nike's sustainability report shows company reducing environmental impact while continuing to grow.* Retrieved from http://news.nike.com/news/nike-s-sustainability-report-shows-company-reducing-environmental-impact-while-continuing-to-grow. Accessed on December 7, 2015.

Odum, H. T., & Odum, E. P. (2000). The energetic basis for valuation of ecosystem services. *Ecosystems, 3*(1), 21–23.

Ogden, L., Heynen, N., Oslender, U., West, P., Kassam, K.-A., & Robbins, P. (2013). Global assemblages, resilience, and earth stewardship in the anthropocene. *Frontiers in Ecology and the Environment, 11*(7), 341–347.

Ostrom, E. (1990). *Governing the commons: The evolution of institutions for collective action.* Cambridge, UK: Cambridge University Press.

Pascale, R. T., Millemann, M., & Gioja, L. (2000). *Surfing The Edge of Chaos: The laws of nature and the new laws of business.* New York, NY: Three Rivers Press.

Perey, R. (2014). Organizing sustainability and the problem of scale: Local, global, or fractal? *Organization and Environment, 27*(3), 215–222.

Pierides, D., & Woodman, D. (2012). Object-oriented sociology and organizing in the face of emergency: Bruno Latour, Graham Harman and the material turn. *The British Journal of Sociology, 63*(4), 662–679.

Pizer, W. A., Morgenstern, R., & Shih, J.-S. (2011). The performance of industrial sector voluntary climate programs: Climate Wise and 1605(b). *Energy Policy, 39*(12), 7907–7916. doi:10.1016/j.enpol.2011.09.040

Prahalad, C. K., & Hamel, G. (1990). The core competence of the corporation. *Harvard Business Review, 68*(3), 79–91.

Prakash, A., & Potoski, M. (2007). Collective action through voluntary environmental programs: A club theory perspective. *Policy Studies Journal, 35*(4), 773–792. doi:10.1111/j.1541-0072.2007.00247.x

Price, L. L., & Epp, A. M. (2015). The heterogeneous and open-ended project of assembling family. In R. Canniford & D. Bajde (Eds.), *Assembling consumption*. New York, NY: Routledge Press.

Rindfleisch, A., & Burroughs, J. E. (2004). Terrifying thoughts, terrible materialism? Contemplations on a terror management account of materialism and consumer behavior. *Journal of Consumer Psychology, 14*(3), 219–224.

Rivera, J., & De Leon, P. (2004). Is Greener Whiter? Voluntary environmental performance of western Ski areas. *Policy Studies Journal, 32*(3), 417–437. doi:10.1111/j.1541-0072.2004.00073.x

Sagarin, R. (2012). *Learning from the octopus: How secrets from nature can help us fight terrorist attacks, natural disasters, and disease*. New York, NY: Basic Books.

Sassen, S. (2006). *Territory, authority, rights: From medieval to global assemblages*. Princeton, NJ: Princeton University Press.

Scott, K., Martin, D. M., & Schouten, J. W. (2014). Marketing and the new materialism. *Journal of Macromarketing, 34*(3), 282–290.

Segerson, K., & Miceli, T. J. (1998). Voluntary environmental agreements: Good or bad news for environmental protection? *Journal of Environmental Economics and Management, 36*(2), 109–130. doi:10.1006/jeem.1998.1040

Sellar, B. (2009). Assemblage theory, occupational science, and the complexity of human agency. *Journal of Occupational Science, 16*(2), 67–74.

Shrivastava, P. (1995). Environmental technologies and competitive advantage. *Strategic Management Journal, 16*, 183–200.

Shrivastava, P., & Hart, S. (1995). Creating sustainable corporations. *Business Strategy and the Environment, 4*, 154–165.

Smit, B., & Wandel, J. (2006). Adaptation, adaptive capacity and vulnerability. *Global Environmental Change, 16*(3), 282–292.

Smith, V. K. (1996). *Estimating economic values for nature: Methods for Non-market Valuation*. Cheltanham, UK: Edward Elgar Publishing.

Spowers, H. (2013). *Enigma talks: River simple in bournemouth*. Retrieved from http://eventful.com/bournemouth/events/enigma-talks-20th-february-river-simple-/E0-001-054229901-5 (see also Hugo Spowers, Riversimple – redesigning cars, redesigning business 2:23AM, the podcast, Season #1, Episode #9 – http://223am.com/2014/10/hugo-spowers/. Accessed on February 20.

Srnicek, N. (2010). Conflict networks: Collapsing the global into the local. *Journal of Critical Globalisation Studies, 2*(2), 30–64.

Stead, J. G., & Stead, W. E. (2013). The coevolution of sustainability strategic management in the global marketplace. *Organization and Environment, 26*(2), 162–183.

Stoddart, M., Tindall, D. B., & Greenfield, K. L. (2012). 'Governments have the Power?' Interpretations of climate change responsibility and solutions among Canadian environmentalists. *Organization and Environment, 25*(1), 39–58.

Teece, D. J., Pisano, G., & Shuen, A. (1997). Dynamic capabilities and strategic management. *Strategic Management Journal, 18*, 509–533.

Tercek, M., & Adams, J. (2013). *Nature's fortune: How business and society thrive by investing in nature.* New York, NY: Basic Books.

Turner, B. L. (2010). Vulnerability and resilience: Coalescing or paralleling approaches for sustainability science? *Global Environmental Change, 20*(4), 570–576. doi:10.1016/j.gloenvcha.2010.07.003

Turner, B. L., Kasperson, R. E., Matson, P. A., McCarthy, J. J., Corell, R. W., Christensen, L., & Schiller, A. (2003). A framework for vulnerability analysis in sustainability science. *Proceedings of the National Academy of Sciences, 100*(14), 8074–8079. Retrieved from http://doi.org/10.1073/pnas.1231335100

Unruh, G., & Ettenson, R. (2010). Winning in the green frenzy. *Harvard Business Review, 88*(11), 110–116.

Walker, B., Gunderson, L., Kinzig, A., Folke, C., Carpenter, S., & Schultz, L. (2006). A handful of heuristics and some propositions for understanding resilience in social-ecological systems. *Ecology and Society, 11*(1), 1–13.

Walker, B., Holling, C. S., Carpenter, S. R., & Kinzig, A. (2004). Resilience, adaptability and transformability in social-ecological systems. *Ecology and Society, 9*(2), 5.

Walker, B., & Salt, D. (2006). *Resilience thinking: Sustaining ecosystems and people in a changing world.* Washington, DC: Island Press.

Walker, B. H., Abel, N., Anderies, J. M., & Ryan, P. (2009). Resilience, adaptability, and transformability in the Goulburn-Broken Catchment, Australia. *Ecology and Society, 14*(1), 12.

WalMart Highlights Progress in 2015. (2015). *Global responsibility report.* Retrieved from http://corporate.walmart.com/_news_/news-archive/2015/04/22/walmart-highlights-progress-in-2015-global-responsibility-report. Accessed on December 7.

Whan, E. (2015, July 2). *Who are the sustainability leaders (besides Unilever)?* Retrieved from http://www.greenbiz.com/article/who-are-sustainability-leaders. Accessed on December 7.

Whatmore, S. (2006). Materialist returns: Practising cultural geography in and for a more-than-human world. *Cultural Geographies, 13*, 600–609.

Wilk, R. (2010). Consumption embedded in culture and language: Implications for finding sustainability. *Sustainability: Science, Practice, & Policy, 6*(2), 38–48.

Winston, A. (2014a). Resilience in a hotter world. *Harvard Business Review, 92*(4), 66–74.

Winston, A. (2014b). *The big pivot: Radically practical strategies for a hotter, scarcer, and more open world.* Boston, MA: Harvard Business School Press.

Young, W., & Tilley, F. (2006). Can businesses move beyond efficiency? The shift toward effectiveness and equity in the corporate sustainability debate. *Business Strategy and the Environment, 15*, 402–415.

A STAKEHOLDER MARKETING APPROACH TO SUSTAINABLE BUSINESS

Tracy L. Gonzalez-Padron, G. Tomas M. Hult and O. C. Ferrell

ABSTRACT

Purpose — *Further understanding of how stakeholder marketing explains firm performance through greater customer satisfaction, innovation, and reputation of a firm.*

Methodology/approach — *Grounded in stakeholder theory, the study provides a conceptualization of stakeholder orientation based on cultural values that is distinctive from stakeholder responsiveness and examines the relationship of stakeholder responsiveness to firm performance. The study determines the mediating role of marketing outcomes on the impact of stakeholder responsiveness on firm performance. Multiple regression analysis tests hypotheses using a data set consisting of qualitative data obtained from corporate documents and quantitative data from respected secondary sources.*

Findings — *Our findings provide support for stakeholder marketing creating a strong relationship to organizational outcomes. There exists a*

Marketing In and For a Sustainable Society
Review of Marketing Research, Volume 13, 61–101
ISSN: 1548-6435/doi:10.1108/S1548-643520160000013012

*positive relationship between stakeholder responsiveness and firm perfor-
mance through customer satisfaction, innovation, and reputation.*

Research implications – *Our definition implies that stakeholder responsiveness is acting in the best interests of the stakeholder as a responsible business. This study shows that stakeholder marketing may not always represent
socially responsible marketing. Further research could explore how and why
firms may not respond ethically and responsibly to stakeholders.*

Practical implications – *We further the discussion whether stakeholder
marketing equates to sustainability. Marketers can build on expertise of
managing customer relationship and generating customer value to
develop a stakeholder marketing approach that addresses the economic,
social, and environmental concerns of multiple stakeholders.*

Originality/value – *We further the discussion whether stakeholder
marketing equates to sustainability. Marketers can build on expertise of
managing customer relationship and generating customer value to develop
a stakeholder marketing approach that addresses the economic, social, and
environmental concerns of multiple stakeholders.*

Keywords: Marketing strategy; sustainability; stakeholder marketing;
corporate social responsibility

INTRODUCTION

Corporate social responsibility (CSR) and corporate sustainability (CS)
have converged to very similar concepts in recent years (van Marrewijk,
2003). Corporate social responsibility refers to the obligations of a business
to meet or exceed the organizational behavior expected by its stakeholders
(Maignan & Ferrell, 2004). Corporate sustainability refers to the strategic
imperative of business for "meeting the needs of the present generation
without compromising the ability of future generations to meet their own
needs" (World Commission on Environment and Development, 1987,
p. 43). Scholars offer differing views on whether CS resides within CSR,
whether CSR is a part of CS, or whether CS and CSR are interchangeable
(Montiel, 2008). In marketing literature, Chabowski, Mena, and Gonzalez-
Padron (2011) describe CSR as the social dimension in sustainability,
Cronin, Smith, Gleim, Ramirez, and Martinez (2011) describe CS in terms

of the standalone concept of green marketing, and Crittenden, Crittenden, Ferrell, Ferrell, and Pinney (2011) consider sustainability in marketing as going beyond voluntary CSR. Regardless, an integrating theme in marketing reflections on CSR and CS is a strategic focus on stakeholders as part of a responsible business that has implications for marketing strategy.

The concept of corporate sustainability relates to a need for business to optimize the economic, environmental, and social components of society. Sustainable firms view their responsibilities through a Triple Bottom Line, incorporating economic, environmental, and social responsibilities to company stakeholders (Elkington, 1998). The economic dimension of a sustainable business considers the financial impact of the organization on the surrounding community through taxes paid, on customers with sales of products, and on investors with profits earned. The environmental dimension impacts the community through stewardship of natural resources, investors by reducing energy use, employees through nontoxic manufacturing, and regulators by complying with environmental standards. Finally, the social dimension includes encouraging an inclusive approach to employees, customers and suppliers; respecting the human dignity of the workforce; and supporting community projects for addressing social issues. Attention and responding to stakeholders is "a rare management practice that aims at integrating economic, social and environmental issues" (Steurer, Langer, Konrad, & Martinuzzi, 2005, p. 275), leading to a competitive advantage.

Marketing managers are in unique positions in firms' value chains to include stakeholder concerns in strategy and to promote sustainable practices in the firm in two ways. First, a longstanding marketing focus on customer relationships can extend to multiple stakeholders and sustainability (Sheth, 2012). Building on relationship marketing constructs, Murphy et al. (2005) defines stakeholder relationship marketing as "creating, maintaining, and enhancing strong relationships with customer, employee, supplier, community, and shareholder stakeholders of a business with the goal of delivering long-term economic, social, and environmental value to all stakeholders in order to enhance sustainable business financial performance" (pp. 1050−1051). Crittenden et al. (2011) suggest that sustainability encompasses topics of consumer demand and consumption of resources that reside in the marketing domain. Second, marketing is experiencing a shift from customer exchange to a value creation paradigm encompassing all stakeholders (Sheth & Uslay, 2007). The value that consumers and other company stakeholders perceive of social and environmental activities of a firm is complex, encompassing both internal (self-centered) or external (other-oriented) evaluations (Peloza & Shang, 2011). Bhattacharya and Korschun (2008) recognize that value creation among diverse stakeholder groups can be problematic and recommend research into the processes for marketers to understand and respond appropriately to all constituents of the firm.

Recent marketing thought recommends a stakeholder marketing perspective to align with sustainable business goals. Stakeholder marketing refers to "activities within a system of social institutions and processes for facilitating and maintaining value through exchange relationships with multiple stakeholders" (Hult, Mena, Ferrell, & Ferrell, 2011, p. 57). Drawing from market orientation conceptualizations as culture and behaviors (Kohli & Jaworski, 1990; Narver & Slater, 1990), stakeholder marketing encompasses a cultural component (stakeholder orientation) and an action (stakeholder responsiveness). Stakeholder orientation refers to the extent to which a firm understands and addresses stakeholder demands in daily operations and strategic planning (Ferrell, Gonzalez-Padron, Hult, & Maignan, 2010; Maignan, Gonzalez-Padron, Hult, & Ferrell, 2011). Adoption of a stakeholder orientation provides firms with an opportunity to understand its impact on stakeholders, anticipate changing societal expectations, and use its capacity for innovation to create additional business value from superior social and environmental performance (Laszlo, Sherman, Whalen, & Ellison, 2005). A prevailing assumption in business is that a stakeholder orientation demonstrates greater corporate social responsibility (Maignan, Ferrell, & Ferrell, 2005). Greenwood (2007) questions that assumption, noting how firms may act responsibly toward stakeholders or, conversely, engage in deceptive practices under the guise of concern for stakeholders. For our purposes, stakeholder responsiveness refers to the extent to which the organization implements policies and programs seeking to increase positive impacts and reduce negative impacts on stakeholder groups (Maignan et al., 2011; Mena & Chabowski, 2015).

Responsiveness to stakeholders is a unique balancing act that requires investments toward various stakeholder constituencies because firms often do not have the resources to tackle all stakeholder groups at the needed level. Thus, questions that need addressing by marketing managers include How much investment in stakeholder responses is enough, and which stakeholders should the firm address (Berman, Wicks, Kotha, & Jones, 1999; Bundy, Shropshire, & Buchholtz, 2013; Seifert, Morris, & Bartkus, 2004)? Understanding how a firm's stakeholder orientation influences customer satisfaction, innovation, and reputation can help managers determine which stakeholder groups to incorporate in marketing strategy, prompting further conceptual or empirical examinations on the relative impact of various stakeholders on marketing activities.

Therefore, the overall goal of this research is to examine how the incorporation of stakeholder issues in corporate marketing strategy can explain firm performance. First, we explain how the incorporation of a stakeholder marketing approach affects firm performance through marketing outcomes. Second, we provide an analysis of how firm performance reacts to responsiveness to multiple stakeholders over a single stakeholder group.

THEORETICAL PERSPECTIVES

The concept of CSR evolved formally during the past 50 years with various interpretations, theoretical perspectives, and empirical methods. Many of the initial definitions for social responsibility focus on "positive duty," representing manager responsibilities to society beyond economic, technical, or legal obligations (Davis, 1960). This normative perspective persists in the CSR literature 40 years later. For example, McWilliams and Siegel (2001) define corporate social responsibility as "actions that appear to further some social good, beyond the interests of the firm and that which is required by law" (p. 117). Carroll (1979) provides a classification scheme for corporate social responsibility that is widely employed by later research (Aupperle, Carroll, & Hatfield, 1985; Wartick & Cochran, 1985). He views social responsibility of business as the obligations to meet economic, legal, ethical, and discretionary expectations that society has of an organization.

In recent decades, a focus on sustainability as a part of a social responsibility is becoming increasingly common for businesses. The term sustainability comes from a 1987 United Nations Brundtland Commission to recommend solutions to the decline of global natural resources. Their report "Our Common Future" calls for businesses, governments, and nonprofits to consider sustainable development, or "meeting the needs of the present generation without compromising the ability of future generations to meet their own needs" (World Commission on Environment and Development, 1987, p. 43). In 2000, then secretary-general of the United Nations Kofi Annan created the Global Compact for business to dialogue with stakeholders on social and environmentally responsible practices. A company affiliating with the Global Compact signals a commitment to sustainability, thereby reducing risks and gaining investor confidence (Coulmont & Berthelot, 2015; Fussler, 2004).

Sustainability is an integral part of responsible business defined as an organization that "assumes responsibility for the triple bottom line, stakeholder value, and moral dilemmas" (Laasch & Conaway, 2015, p. 27). A responsible business monitors and assesses environmental conditions, attends to stakeholder demands, and designs policies to respond to changing conditions. Firms can be responsive to environmental conditions and stakeholder demands, but without reflection or responsibility, they may act irresponsibly or unethically (Greenwood, 2007). A responsible business achieves a coexistence of a competitive advantage and above-average responsible business performance (Laasch & Conaway, 2015). We use the resource-based view and stakeholder theory as theoretical foundations to explore stakeholder marketing and sustainability.

Resource-Based View

A resource-based view (RBV) proposes that organizational performance depends on organization-specific resources and capabilities (Barney, 1991; Wernerfelt, 1984). A basic assumption of RBV is that firms are fundamentally heterogeneous in resources and capabilities, and when resources are not perfectly mobile across firms, heterogeneity can be long lasting (Barney, 1991). Resources include all assets, capabilities, organizational processes, firm attributes, information, and knowledge controlled by a firm. Hunt and Morgan (1995) position CSR and organizational ethics as an intangible resource that yields competitive advantage equal to or surpassing tangible resources. To provide a competitive advantage, resources must be (a) valuable (exploit opportunities or neutralize threats), (b) rare (not possessed by large numbers of competitors), (c) inimitable (competitors cannot obtain them through unique historical conditions, causally ambiguous links, or social complexities), and (d) nonsubstitutable (no strategically equivalent valuable resources) (Wernerfelt, 1984). According to RBV, firm resources lead to capabilities, and capabilities influence firm performance.

Applications of RBV to corporate social responsibility and sustainability assert that social responsiveness constitutes a resource or capability that leads to sustained competitive advantage (Falkenberg & Brunsæl, 2011). Chabowski et al. (2011) propose that capabilities-based resources a firm develops that relates to a stakeholder focus, sustainability emphasis, and CSR can create marketing assets leading to financial performance. A stakeholder responsiveness capability is "valuable" to a firm because it allows them to respond to its specific stakeholders' issues, and the heterogeneity of these issues makes it difficult for others to imitate responsiveness policies. Stakeholder responsiveness capability meets all three determinants of inimitability. First, responsiveness policies develop over a period of years and are difficult to acquire on the market by competitors. Second, it is difficult to identify the exact mechanisms by which the corporate responsiveness policies interact to generate value, owing to causal ambiguity. Lastly, socially complex elements such as culture and interpersonal relationships inherent in responsiveness capabilities inhibit imitation. Research provides support for the relationship of stakeholder responsiveness with financial and competitive advantages using RBV theory, including environmental socially responsible performance (Baker & Sinkula, 2005; Falkenberg & Brunsæl, 2011; Glavas & Mish, 2015).

Stakeholder Theory

A dominant theoretical perspective in corporate social responsibility research is the stakeholder concept that business has wider responsibilities than economic performance. A stakeholder is any group or individual who can affect, or be affected by, the achievement of an organization's purpose, with each of the many stakeholder groups having a unique set of expectations, needs, and values (Freeman, 1984). The first uses of stakeholder theory in social responsibility are associated with normative justifications to engage in social involvement. Normative stakeholder theory addresses the purpose of the firm and to whom management has an obligation (Parmar et al., 2010). To some extent, stakeholder theory can bridge the normative perspective with empirical instrumental investigation of managers to justify stakeholder orientation. This provides a new way to approach management.

The implication of embracing a stakeholder concept is that firms that address diverse stakeholder interests perform better than those that do not (Greenley & Foxall, 1998). Stakeholder theory argues that managers must satisfy various constituents (e.g., customers, employees, suppliers, local community organizations) that would withdraw support for the firm if important social responsibilities were unmet (Freeman, 1984). According to Clarkson (1995), the survival and profitability of the corporation depends on its ability to create and distribute wealth or value to ensure primary stakeholder commitment.

Instrumental stakeholder theory focuses on the connections between the practice of stakeholder management and achievement of corporate goals (Donaldson & Preston, 1995). Generally adopting a position that stakeholders are a means by which the firm achieves its assumed ends, instrumental stakeholder research includes a strategic approach to stakeholder management, providing direction for enhanced organizational performance (Friedman & Miles, 2006). Freeman (1984) warns that consequences of not adopting a stakeholder approach include legal action, regulation, and loss of markets. Sustainable companies develop expertise in understanding the formation of stakeholder groups, their key issues, and the potential for helping or harming the corporation.

Instrumental stakeholder theory provides a theoretical basis for predicting the nature of the relationship between the firm's stakeholder orientation and its financial performance. A number of studies show that firms perceived as socially responsible have higher financial performance (Maignan, Ferrell, & Hult, 1999; Margolis & Walsh, 2003; Orlitzky, Schmidt, & Rynes, 2003). A stakeholder marketing approach that incorporates social, environmental, and economic considerations can lead to superior financial performance (Falkenberg & Brunsæl, 2011; Murphy et al., 2005). Choi and Wang (2009) suggest that good stakeholder relations not only contribute to superior performance, but also is a key factor for a firm to recover from poor performance. However, the positive relationship with financial performance does not hold across all stakeholders or corporate response activities. For example, Seifert et al. (2004) show that community philanthropy is not related to financial performance. Likewise, Berman et al. (1999) find that relationships with many stakeholders other than employees and customers have only indirect effects on firm financial performance.

A stakeholder mismatching perspective is one explanation for why the correlation between corporate social responsibility and corporate financial performance varies among studies. The stakeholder mismatching thesis of Wood and Jones (1995) argues that effects of corporate social responsive actions vary depending on different expectations and evaluations of stakeholder groups. Programs and policies responding to market-oriented stakeholders such as customers and shareholders are more likely to influence market-based firm performance, whereas community-related philanthropic activities may not correlate directly to market-based firm performance. For many stakeholder groups, responsiveness may effect non-financial outcomes, such as corporate reputation (Brammer & Millington, 2005; Maignan et al., 2011), customer satisfaction (Luo & Bhattacharya, 2006), and innovation (McWilliams & Siegel, 2001). Based on results of their meta-analysis, Orlitzky et al. (2003) call for additional research to include well-defined stakeholder groups, precise definitions of socially responsive outcomes, and appropriate measures for performance. Likewise, stakeholder marketing scholars promote further exploration of the manner

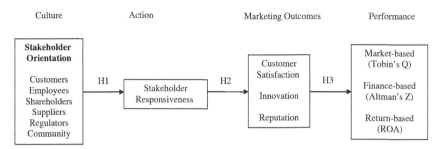

Fig. 1. Conceptual Framework.

that stakeholder groups enhance firm performance (Ferrell et al., 2010; Hult et al., 2011).

Our study adopts an instrumental stakeholder theoretical perspective to examine the marketing and financial performance outcomes of stakeholder marketing. We consider six stakeholder groups commonly included in the marketing literature – customers, employees, shareholders, suppliers, communities, and government regulatory agencies (Maignan et al., 2005, 2011; Mena & Chabowski, 2015). A conceptual framework is in Fig. 1.

HYPOTHESIS DEVELOPMENT

Stakeholder Orientation and Stakeholder Responsiveness

The concept of stakeholder orientation has been defined and operationalized in research focusing on the attitude and behavior of the organization toward various stakeholders (Greenley & Foxall, 1996, 1997; Maignan & Ferrell, 2004). There exists a parallel between market orientation and stakeholder orientation, in such that both have conceptualizations as culture and behaviors (Kohli & Jaworski, 1990; Narver & Slater, 1990). Deshpande, Farley, and Webster (1993) argue that internal processes and the organizational strategies are influenced by a deep, culture-driven characteristic of an organization allowing for the integration of strategic orientations of multiple stakeholders. Following this cultural competitive view, we adopt the definition of Ferrell et al. (2010) to define stakeholder orientation as "the organizational culture and behaviors that induce organizational members to be continuously aware of and proactively act on a variety of stakeholder issues" (p. 93).

Customer orientation centers on what is often considered the most important stakeholder for most firms, customers. Customers help establish the firm's reputation and identification. The relationship between a customer and a firm exists because of mutual expectations built on trust, good faith, and fair dealing in their interactions. In fact, there is an implied covenant of good faith and fair dealing, and performance cannot simply be a matter of the firm's own discretion. Not only is this an ethical requirement but it has been legally enforced in some states (Ferrell, 2004). Paying attention to customers improves responsiveness to other stakeholders, such as shareholders reacting in a significantly positive manner to improvements in customer service (Ogden & Watson, 1999). Consumer orientation emerged as the most important group in studies of stakeholder orientation (Greenley & Foxall, 1996).

Employee orientation refers to the development of employees and nurturing labor relations within the firm. A focus on employees is increasingly important in strategic marketing and is starting to rival customer orientation for attention among executives. Specifically, research indicates that marketing might well need to give as much attention to the strategic management of managers and employees as it does to customers (Jackson, 2001). Employees can position the organization in the minds of customers, employees, and other stakeholders. A study of the airline industry finds that labor relations has a direct effect on performance, and an indirect effect on reputation through customer experiences (Martinez & Norman, 2004).

Shareholder orientation typically refers to a form of profit orientation, but shareholders are also a primary stakeholder that can influence responsiveness to multiple stakeholders. Meeting the needs of creditors directly affects both return on assets and net profit margin (Martinez & Norman, 2004). As typical contemporary investors rarely control corporate activities, management feels it is highly questionable whether most have obligations to stakeholders. Whether or not shareholders have obligations to stakeholders, business managers have a greater obligation to educate shareholders about how corporate activities affect stakeholders (Spurgin, 2001). Research provides support that shareholders financially benefit when management meets the demands of multiple stakeholders, as change in corporate social responsibility is positively associated with growth in sales for the current and subsequent year (Ruf, Muralidhar, Brown, Janney, & Paul, 2001). Investors are looking with increasing favor on shareholder proposals asking firms to disclose and monitor their political contributions, to report on their fair employment policies, and to issue broad-based reports on sustainability (Voorhes, 2006).

Supplier orientation refers to attention toward both the needs of the supply chain and to socially responsible purchasing practices, including buying criteria relating to diversity, environmental, and labor issues. The network of relationships inherent in the supply chain has resulted in a greater likelihood that organizations shoulder more responsibility for actions of their suppliers (Phillips & Caldwell, 2005). As firms recognize social issues related to their supply chain, some seek vendors with good social policies and help them become competent or help competent vendors to become socially responsive (Drumwright, 1994). A study by Wolf (2014) supports a supplier orientation, finding firms that invest in environmental and social sustainability in their supply chains to build a reputation as a responsible business have greater success than firms responding to external stakeholder pressures do.

Regulatory orientation refers to the attention to the regulatory environment, trends, and policies. Distinctive advantages arise from partnerships with local communities or government agencies, such as reduced unfavorable litigation, reduced levels of negative publicity, and favorable regulatory policies (Harrison & St John, 1996). The influences of regulatory forces are typically a function of top management commitment and affected by the industry in which the firm operates (Banerjee, Iyer, & Kashyap, 2003). The growing regulatory concerns over the environmental impact of corporate practices have begun to influence marketing policies and practices (Menon & Menon, 1997).

Community orientation refers to the attention to social duties relating to the common good of the host community. Pulling from stewardship theory, Laczniak and Murphy (2006) argue that marketers are obligated to ensure that their marketing operations will not impose external costs on society. Community stakeholders include many nongovernmental organizations and other potential activist groups that have an interest in social issues and have the ability to mobilize public opinion (Banerjee et al., 2003). Community advocacy groups can influence corporate and marketing strategy. For example, a chemical company's plans to locate in an economically deprived Louisiana community changed in response to community opinion (Berry, 2003). Brammer and Millington (2003) suggest that community involvement activities reflect the preferences of societal stakeholders.

While specific stakeholders have varying concerns, firms should strive for responses that appeal to multiple stakeholders. Such multifaceted strategic planning toward stakeholders reaps better advantages than if, for example, only customers were targeted (Greenley & Foxall, 1998; Greenley, Hooley, Broderick, & Rudd, 2004). To examine the relationship that each stakeholder has on overall stakeholder responsiveness, we set forth the following set of hypotheses that delineate how attention to stakeholders drives the overall implementation of responsive programs and policies.

H1. Stakeholder responsiveness is affected by stakeholder orientation. Specifically:

a. Customer orientation has a positive effect on stakeholder responsiveness.
b. Employee orientation has a positive effect on stakeholder responsiveness.
c. Shareholder orientation has a positive effect on stakeholder responsiveness.
d. Supplier orientation has a positive effect on stakeholder responsiveness.
e. Regulatory orientation has a positive effect on stakeholder responsiveness.
f. Community orientation has a positive effect on stakeholder responsiveness.

Stakeholder Responsiveness and Marketing Outcomes

Stakeholder responsiveness is a critically important dimension of stakeholder marketing and the effective implementation of the basic tenets in the resource-based view. Specifically, a stakeholder orientation – marketing outcomes link lacks face validity because cultural orientations are not action in and of themselves; instead, they may lead to certain actions such as stakeholder responsiveness (cf. Ketchen, Hult, & Slater, 2007). Given this logic, the influence of responding to stakeholders on marketing outcomes, such as customer satisfaction, innovation, and reputation is a key component of marketing strategy.

Customer satisfaction is an overall evaluation based on the customer's total purchase and consumption experience with a good or service over time (Fornell, 1992). An equity approach to exchange evaluation shows that fairness from the customer's view is a strong predictor of customer satisfaction (Symanski & Henard, 2001). Not just attention to customers increases customer satisfaction. Consumers react to corporations' initiatives to address outside stakeholders in their evaluation and subsequent loyalty to the organization (Bhattacharya & Sen, 2003). For example, an increase in organizational commitment to employees improves customer satisfaction (Roca-Puig, Beltrin-Martin, Escrig-Tena, & Bou-Llusar, 2005). Overall, corporate responsiveness to stakeholders positively affects customer satisfaction (Luo & Bhattacharya, 2006).

Innovation relates to the implementation of new ideas, products, and processes (Hurley & Hult, 1998). While marketing traditionally focuses on product innovation, organizational innovation differentiates between technical innovation, referring to work activities related to products and services, and administrative innovation, referring to processes indirectly related to products and services (Damanpour, 1991). Focusing on the degree to which an organization encourages introducing new ideas and processes, Hult and Ketchen (2001) found an organization's openness to new ideas, products, or processes to be an influencing factor in developing positional advantage. There is also evidence of a relationship between market-focused firms and innovation (Day, 1994; Deshpande et al., 1993). For example, Han, Kim, and Srivastava (1998) find a positive relationship between customer orientation and innovation. This relationship extends to all stakeholder orientations. Specifically, instrumental stakeholder theory suggests that social responsibility leads to sustained competitive advantage through innovation (Bunn, Savage, & Holloway, 2002; McWilliams, Siegel, & Wright, 2006). In addition, the resource-based view perceives stakeholder responsiveness as a capability that is valuable, rare, and inimitable (Deniz-Deniz & Saa-Perez, 2003). For example, Baker and Sinkula (2005) find that a firm's capability in environmental marketing strategy development leads to new product success. Attention to multiple stakeholders also increases innovation among, for example, oil firms (Sharma & Vredenburg, 1998).

Reputation refers to a perceptual representation of a company's past actions and future prospects that describe the firm's overall appeal to all its key constituents when compared to other competitors (Fombrun, 1996, p. 72). Corporate responsiveness to stakeholders has external effects on organizational reputation through building a positive image with customers, investors, creditors, and suppliers (Orlitzky & Benjamin, 2001). In addition, Fombrun and Shanley (1990) found that publics assign higher reputations to organizations that exhibit responsibility. Sharma and Vredenburg (1998) found that stakeholder integration translates into increased goodwill that eased opposition to everyday operations and development plans of oil firms.

Theoretically and empirically, research has shown that stakeholder responsiveness results in enhanced marketing outcomes. We set forth the following hypotheses related to the marketing outcomes of customer satisfaction, innovation, and reputation to test this premise.

H2. The greater the stakeholder responsiveness,

a. the greater the customer satisfaction,
b. the more innovative the firm,
c. the more favorable is the firm's reputation.

Stakeholder Responsiveness and Performance: Marketing Outcomes as Mediators

The final element of our research model in Fig. 1 involves the marketing outcomes as mediators of the stakeholder responsiveness–performance relationships. Given that prior research has shown that marketing outcomes such as customer satisfaction, innovation, and reputation are key determinants of firm performance, we place our main emphasis on the mediating effects of these marketing outcomes on the stakeholder responsiveness–performance relationships. A key focus is on the role that the marketing outcomes play in full or partial mediation between stakeholder responsiveness on performance.

To address the mediating role of marketing outcomes, we resort to stakeholder theory. Stakeholder theory argues that companies that address diverse stakeholder interests perform better than companies that do not (Clarkson, 1995; Greenley & Foxall, 1998). Stakeholder-oriented companies develop expertise in understanding the formation of stakeholder groups, their key issues, and the potential for helping or harming the corporation. The stakeholder mismatching thesis of Wood and Jones (1995) also argues that effects of corporate social responsive actions vary depending on the expectations and evaluations of stakeholder groups. Therefore, specific stakeholder orientations may influence different marketing and performance measures (Orlitzky et al., 2003). For example, reputation relates to the values of individual evaluators, resulting in different aspects of stakeholder responsiveness influencing corporate reputation (Siltaoja, 2006).

Customer satisfaction as a mediator has implications for the economic performance of firms. One reason is that customer satisfaction has a negative impact on customer complaints and a positive impact on customer loyalty and usage behavior (Bolton, 1998; Fornell, 1992). Therefore, customer satisfaction may reduce costs related to warranties, complaints, defective goods, and field service costs. Studies find a strong relationship between customer satisfaction and Tobin's Q (as a measure of shareholder value) (Anderson, Fornell, & Mazvancheryl, 2004).

Innovation as a mediator is an important component of firm performance (Deshpande et al., 1993; Hurley & Hult, 1998). Organizational innovation in products, managerial systems, and marketing strategies can lead to successful market performance. New product research finds that firm innovativeness relates positively to firm performance (Montoya-Weiss & Calantone, 1994). The diffusion of innovations literature suggests that firms must be innovative to gain a competitive edge in order to survive (Li & Calantone, 1998). The foundation for this competitive advantage relates to a full understanding of customer needs, competitors' actions, and technological development (Calantone, Cavusgil, & Zhao, 2002). A linkage exists, therefore, between cultural orientations, innovativeness, and performance.

Reputation as a mediator involves a complex relationship with firm performance, as past financial performance is one component of a company's reputation dimension (Fombrun & Shanley, 1990). However, recent studies find that reputation influences future financial performance after controlling for past performance (Eberl & Schwaiger, 2005; Roberts & Dowling, 2002). Fombrun (1996) argued that a positive reputation could present an organization with a competitive advantage that enables the firm to charge premium prices and economize on promotional costs. For example, a positive reputation affects customers' buying intentions (Yoon, Guffey, & Kijewski, 1993), influences supplier choice (Weiss, Anderson, & MacInnis, 1999), and supports superior profit outcomes over time (Roberts & Dowling, 2002). In sum, this would lead to higher profitability for the "well reputed" firm.

A number of mechanisms influence the relationship between stakeholder responsiveness and firm performance. Understanding how and why stakeholder responsiveness increases performance requires probing the mediating roles of marketing outcomes. Support exists in stakeholder theory and the resource-based view that suggest intermediate outcomes (e.g., for marketing outcomes) affect action's (e.g., stakeholder's responsiveness) effect on bottom-line performance of firms. In the context of marketing outcomes, we hypothesize:

H3. Stakeholder responsiveness increases firm financial performance through marketing outcomes:

a. Stakeholder responsiveness → customer satisfaction → performance
b. Stakeholder responsiveness → innovation → performance
c. Stakeholder responsiveness → reputation → performance.

DATA COLLECTION

The hypothesized model testing draws from a sample of organizations representing publicly traded firms on the U.S. stock exchange. The final study sample consists of 141 firms that had complete data for all variables after merging data from different archival sources (i.e., Annual Reports, KLD STATS, Fortune's Most Admired Firms, ACSI, and Compustat). These archival sources provided data for the antecedents, the mediators, and the outcomes. The final data set includes individual firms in various industries – 30 firms (21.3%) are from durable goods (e.g., automobiles, household appliances, personal computers), 34 (24.1%) from nondurable goods (e.g., beverages, pharmaceuticals, cigarettes, apparel), 31 (22%) are services (e.g., airlines, hotels, and banking), 26 (18.4%) are retail (e.g., department stores, discount stores, supermarkets), and 20 (14.2%) provide utilities (e.g., power, telecommunications). The firms range from four to 154 years old, have total sales on average of US$38.85 billion (from $1.8 billion to $346 billion), and employ from 1,700 to 1.9 million people. Prior marketing studies of strategic orientation and stakeholder management have used a similar sample frame for empirical research (Berman et al., 1999; Hillman & Keim, 2001; Noble, Sinha, & Kumar, 2002).

MEASURES

We incorporate qualitative data obtained from corporate documents with quantitative data from secondary sources to assess the hypothesized relationships. Measures for the constructs draw from extant marketing and management research.

Stakeholder Orientation

A qualitative content analysis of corporate annual reports provided the mechanism to assess the six stakeholder orientations. The documents for coding consisted of annual reports from Mergent OnLine™ or the corporate website. Content analysis is a method for analyzing a variety of text, visual, and verbal data through reducing large quantities of content into defined categories (Harwood & Garry, 2003). Theoretically, publicly scrutinized annual reports reflect the values and positioning of the top management team, representing the values of the organization rather than the individuals (Bettman & Weitz, 1983). Therefore, through cognitive mapping techniques, the managerial mind-set expressed in annual reports can offer insights on the strategic orientations of the firm (Noble et al., 2002). Methodologically, content analysis of corporate annual reports has been used in marketing studies of customer orientation (Judd & Tims, 1991), market orientation (Noble et al., 2002), and corporate social responsibility communication (Branco & Rodrigues, 2006).

Content analysis is appropriate for this research because the use of self-reported data in many empirical studies of stakeholder issues attracts criticism regarding respondent bias and failure to address validity (Harris, 2001). Self-reporting of stakeholder issues often involve asking questions that are sensitive, embarrassing, threatening, stigmatizing, or incriminating and result in a strong bias to "answer according to the wishes of the person asking the question," distortion to avoid reporting honestly about certain behaviors, and a social desirability bias to deny socially undesirable behaviors and to admit to socially desirable ones.

We coded each corporate annual report based on established practices in the marketing literature (cf. Noble et al., 2002). This involved identifying the extent to which the organization values and prioritizes the needs of stakeholder groups. For example, statements representing a stakeholder orientation should include an action verb such as value, focus, depend, believe, consider; or express a relationship with or responsibility to a particular stakeholder. We used the computer software Atlas.ti® to organize, code, and analyze quotations from the annual reports relating to the six stakeholder orientations. Computer assisted qualitative data analysis software (CAQDAS) offers many advantages in both the qualitative and quantitative analysis of data from annual reports (Lindsay, 2004). Features of Atlas.ti include tools to manage, extract, compare, explore, and reassemble meaningful quotes from the documents through visual linking of concepts (Muhr & Friese, 2004). Use of CAQDAS software provides more rigor and traceability, thereby enhancing reliability (Lindsay, 2004). The Atlas.ti® software allows multiple coders to access documents for consistent coding of stakeholder orientations for the quantitative analysis.

Multiple independent coders for each document were trained, supervised, and provided with a codebook to establish inter-rater reliability (Noble et al., 2002; Swenson-Lepper, 2005). A master code list drew from the prior literature and an initial qualitative review of annual reports. Two independent coders conducted a manual pre-test of the coding instructions using annual reports not in the research sample. As a result, the code list, coding instructions, and coding process improved, including the decision to permit coding to occur only in a supervised environment. The raters coded each phrase reflecting orientation toward a stakeholder without assessing quality or motivation.

The documents for coding consisted of Annual Reports from Mergent OnLine™ or the corporate website. Where available, the narrative annual report was the primary coding document, supplemented by the first sections of the SEC 10-K report. In order to provide as consistent documents for coding as possible, photos, financial charts, tables, and management's discussion of the financial reports (i.e., "Notes" and/or "Changes in Accounting") were not included in the coding process. The amount of content in the original documents varied greatly, even with the removal of graphics and tables. Random assignments of coders for each documents eliminated industry or company bias and avoided pairs of coders consistently working on the same documents.

A procedure for calculating inter-rater reliability allowed the coders to identify discrepancies in classifying a sentence as representing orientation to one of the six stakeholders. While some researchers report a percentage agreement among raters, Cohen's (1960) kappa coefficient is a better standard measure of the degree of agreement existing beyond chance alone across a wide range of annotation efforts. A score of 0.8 or higher is considered a high level of agreement, whereas above 0.6 is considered substantial agreement, and above 0.4 moderate agreement (Rietveld & van Hout, 1993). The Kappa coefficient for the documents shows substantial agreement in coding orientations toward all stakeholders (0.6–0.95).

There are three ways of viewing stakeholder orientation from the data collected. First, the relative attention paid to all stakeholders derives from dividing the total counts by number of pages. Second, measures representing the attention for the specific groups include the percent of mentions per page for community, customers, employees, regulatory agencies, shareholders, and suppliers. The third measure for stakeholder orientation is the prioritization among the stakeholders by the percentage of attention allocated to each stakeholder group, calculated by dividing the stakeholder group raw count by total count of all stakeholders. Table 1 illustrates the means, minimum, and maximum of each of the stakeholder orientation fields.

Table 1. Summary Statistics for Stakeholder Orientation.

	Mentions per Page				Prioritization			
	Min	Max	Mean	sd.	Min	Max	Mean	sd.
All stakeholders	0.76	14.70	6.21	3.02				
Community orientation	0.00	4.13	1.04	1.06	.00	.58	.15	.14
Customer orientation	0.00	5.33	1.78	1.33	.00	.75	.28	.15
Employee orientation	0.03	6.79	1.56	1.22	.01	.79	.23	.13
Regulatory orientation	0.00	5.03	0.76	0.85	.00	.90	.16	.18
Shareholder orientation	0.00	3.21	0.65	0.63	.00	.41	.10	.08
Supplier orientation	0.00	3.00	0.43	0.51	.00	.43	.07	.08

Stakeholder Responsiveness

Stakeholder responsiveness refers to the extent that the organization implements policies and programs seeking to increase positive impacts and reduce negative impacts on stakeholder groups. For this study, we measure stakeholder responsiveness through the KLD social indicators provided by KLD Research & Analytics, Inc., the social investment research firm founded by Kinder, Lydenburg and Domini. KLD conducts research on the social, governance, and environmental performance of publicly traded companies for reporting to institutional investors worldwide. Through their commercial database of corporate ratings, SOCRATES, the company provides narrative accounts and ratings on over 90 indicators in seven major areas including Community, Corporate Governance, Diversity, Employee Relations, Environment, Human Rights, and Product. The KLD data is an accepted assessment of corporate social responsibility with construct validity established in empirical studies (Sharfman, 1996; Szwajkowski & Figlewicz, 1999).

Berman et al. (1999) used the KLD data to operationalize stakeholder responsiveness. Correspondingly, Mattingly and Berman (2006) argue that the KLD data represent social actions rather than outcomes. The proliferation of references to actions, policies, and programs in the KLD rating criteria further supports the data as representing responsiveness. For example, one indicator for community responsiveness is "The company has consistently given over 1.5% of trailing three year net earnings before taxes (NEBT) to charity, or has otherwise been notably generous in its giving."

There are three views of stakeholder responsiveness for this study. First, overall stakeholder responsiveness (SR AGG) involves adding strengths and subtracting concerns. Following the Greenwood (2007) distinction of responsible and irresponsible actions toward stakeholders, positive stakeholder responsiveness (Pos SR) is the sum of all of the strengths while negative stakeholder responsiveness (Neg SR) is the sum of all the concerns. The aggregated score for stakeholder responsiveness ranges from a minimum of −9.00 to a maximum of 11, with a mean score of .10. Positive stakeholder responsiveness (Pos SR) is the sum of all of the strengths and ranges from no strengths to a maximum of 18. Negative stakeholder responsiveness (Neg SR) is the sum of all the concerns ranging from no concerns to a maximum of 16. To generate scores for responsiveness to the six stakeholder groups, the 113 items in the KLD database were allocated to community, customer, employee, regulatory, shareholder, and supplier. Some items represented actions to more than one stakeholder. An overall score for responsiveness to each stakeholder group involved adding strengths and subtracting concerns. As the number of items for each stakeholder varied, the total scores were centralized.

Marketing Outcomes

Innovation reflects the implementation of new ideas, products, or processes (Hurley & Hult, 1998). While marketing traditionally focuses on product innovation, this study also includes innovative managerial processes indirectly related to products and services (Damanpour, 1991). Our measure for innovation is the sum of two items relating to innovation in the KLD database: R&D/innovation and beneficial products and services. R&D/innovation relates to the notion that a company is a leader in its industry for R&D, particularly by bringing notably innovative products to market. Beneficial products and services relate to the notion that the company derives substantial revenues from innovative remediation products, environmental services, or products that promote the efficient use of energy, or it has developed innovative products with environmental benefits.

Reputation refers to a perceptual representation of a company's past actions and future prospects that describe the firm's overall appeal to its key constituents when compared to other competitors (Fombrun, 1996). Our data source for reputation is the *Fortune* database on corporate reputations (FAMA); it has been used to measure constructs such as corporate reputation (Fombrun & Shanley, 1990), stakeholder orientation (Preston & Sapienza, 1990), corporate social responsibility (Luo & Bhattacharya, 2006), and management quality (Waddock & Graves, 1997). The FAMA index has been described as a reflection of the image that a company has in the business community (Sharfman, 1996) and has been recommended as a measure of overall business reputation instead of using single components (Szwajkowski & Figlewicz, 1999).

Customer satisfaction is an overall evaluation based on the customer's total purchase and consumption experience with a good or service over time (Fornell, 1992). An often-used measure for customer satisfaction is the American Customer Satisfaction Index (ACSI) (Fornell, Johnson, Anderson, Cha, & Everitt Bryant, 1996). The ACSI has been a reliable source of measuring customer satisfaction in the marketing literature (Anderson et al., 2004; Luo & Bhattacharya, 2006). We complement the ACSI with a RepTrak™ ranking for firms not included in the ACSI. The Reputation Institute provides a measure of the company's reputation with consumers through the Global RepTrak™ Pulse index (RepTrak™). Interviews of over 30,000 consumers in 25 countries measure the esteem, good feeling, trust, and admiration felt toward more than 750 firms. The RepTrak™ measure correlates with the ACSI measure for customer satisfaction (.61 $p < .01$). The score for customer satisfaction for the 141 sample firms ranged from 22 to 87, with a mean score of 72.

Firm Performance

We use Tobin's Q to measure market-based firm performance, following prior marketing studies (Lee & Grewal, 2004; Luo & Bhattacharya, 2006). The financial-based performance measure we adopted is Altman's Z, which forecasts the probability of a firm entering bankruptcy within a two-year period (Altman, 1968). The accounting-based performance measure we included is return on assets (ROA), representing how efficient management is at using its assets to generate earnings. For this study, Tobin's Q, Altman's Z, and ROA derive from variables available in Compustat®.

Control Variables

We include three control variables to ensure that any relationships found are not a result of other confounding variables. First, we included dummy coding for industry by using the first two codes of the Standard Industrial Classification (SIC) of each firm. Second, we included size of the firm. Size (assets) can relate to the urgency and salience of stakeholder relations with larger firms given greater public scrutiny. Size can also influence the type and level of stakeholder relations and responsiveness. Large firms may have more resources for implementing social responses, while smaller firms may be more flexible to respond to changing social issues. Third, we included firm age to address the common notion that age lends to firms' credibility and reputation-building capabilities.

RESULTS

Hypothesis 1. Stakeholder Responsiveness.

Three sets of hierarchical regression models examined the relationship of stakeholder orientation with stakeholder responsiveness (Cohen, Cohen, West, & Aiken, 2003). The first models analyze the relationship between stakeholder orientation and aggregated stakeholder responsiveness, measured by subtracting harmful actions from actions seen as positively responding to all stakeholder groups. The second and third sets of regression models consider stakeholder responsiveness to consist of two distinct components – the positive actions toward stakeholders (Positive SR) and the actions that harm stakeholders (Negative SR). We would expect that greater attention to stakeholder groups would increase favorable actions, while decreasing harmful actions. Table 2 summarizes the results of these nine regression models.

The first models analyze the relationship between stakeholder orientation and aggregated stakeholder responsiveness, with the independent variable in Model 1a as the overall stakeholder orientation (SO Total) and the orientation to specific stakeholder groups (Community, Customer, Employee, Regulatory, Shareholder, Supplier) entered as the independent variables in Model 1b.

Greater insights on the relationship between stakeholder orientation and stakeholder responsiveness are evident from the regression models with the positive stakeholder responsive actions as a dependent variable. Both Models 2a and 2b explain over 30% of the variance. Overall stakeholder orientation has a negative relationship with stakeholder orientation ($-.17$ $p < .05$), with shareholder ($-.15$ $p < .10$) and regulatory ($-.14$ $p < .05$) orientations the only significant relationships of the six stakeholder groups. Results of Model 3b show that orientation on the two secondary stakeholder groups, community ($.21$ $p < .01$) and regulatory ($.11$ $p < .10$), are

Table 2. Relationship of Stakeholder Orientation and Responsiveness.

Dependent Variable:	Aggregated Stakeholder Responsiveness			Positive Stakeholder Responsiveness			Negative Stakeholder Responsiveness		
	Stakeholder orientation mention per page		Stakeholder prioritization	Stakeholder orientation mention per page		Stakeholder prioritization	Stakeholder orientation mention per page		Stakeholder prioritization
Variable	Model 1a	Model 1b	Model 1c	Model 2a	Model 2b	Model 2c	Model 3a	Model 3b	Model 3c
SO total	−.15*			−.17**			−.01		
Customer		.04	.23**		−.04	.13		−.11	−.14*
Employee		−.06	.04		−.13	−.03		−.07	−.08
Shareholder		−.15	−.04		−.15*	−.04		.01	.01
Supplier		.06	.22**		.04	.17**		−.02	−.08
Regulatory[a]		−.22**			−.14**			.11*	
Community		−.10	.04		.06	.14		.21***	.12
Age	−.02	−.06	−.04	.08	.06	.08	.13*	.15**	.15**
Industry	.04	.01	.02	−.22***	−.21***	−.19**	−.32***	−.26***	−.26***
Size	.13	.19**	.19*	.57***	.57***	.56***	.53***	.45***	.44***
Adj R^2	.01	.04	.04	.33	.34	.34	.36	.40	.39
ΔR^2	.02	.09	.08	.03	.07	.05	.00	.06	.05
F for ΔR^2	3.06*	2.09*	2.34**	5.44**	2.36**	2.27**	.00	2.29**	2.13*

[a]Regulatory orientation was excluded from prioritization models due to multicollinearity.
***$p < .01$; **$p < .05$; *$p < .10$.

significant, and both are positively related to negative stakeholder responsiveness.

Regressing the prioritization of each stakeholder group on responsiveness explains a significant portion of variance. The amount of attention on customers (.23 p <.05) and suppliers (.22 p <.05) has a significant relationship with overall stakeholder responsiveness. Models 2c and 3c indicate how the prioritization of these two groups relates to stakeholder responsiveness. The amount of prioritization that is given to suppliers is related to positive responsiveness (.17 p <.05), while the prioritization to customers reduces negative responsiveness (−.14 p <.10).

Hypothesis 2. Marketing Outcomes.

The results of the regression analyses for the marketing outcomes are in Table 3. Overall stakeholder responsiveness has a moderate and positive relation to customer satisfaction (.24 p <.01), innovation (.26 p <.01), and reputation (.26 p <.01). Positive stakeholder responsiveness is somewhat significantly related to customer satisfaction (.17 p <.10), and harmful responses have a stronger and negative relationship with customer satisfaction (−.24 p <.05). Only positive stakeholder responsiveness is related to innovation (.42 p <.01), whereas the positive relationship of proactive responsiveness with reputation (.20 p <.05) has to consider the stronger negative relationship of harmful activities (−.25 p <.05).

Further insights on how stakeholder responsiveness relates to marketing outcomes evolve by examining the coefficients in the model that includes the measures of responsiveness to specific stakeholder groups as the independent variable. There were no significant relationships between specific stakeholder groups and customer satisfaction, although customer responsiveness has the largest coefficient for customer satisfaction (.16 p =.107). Customer (.29 p <.01), community (.43 p <.01), and employee (.15 p <.10) responsiveness has a positive relationship with innovation, while regulatory responsiveness (−.30 p <.01) has a negative relationship. These results support those scholars arguing that increasing regulation can hamper innovation. Shareholder responsiveness has the strongest positive relationship with reputation (.26 p <.01), while regulatory responsiveness has a positive and slightly significant relationship with firm reputation (.20 p <.10).

Hypothesis 3. Mediating Effects of Marketing Outcomes.

Understanding how and why stakeholder responsiveness increases performance requires probing the mediating roles of marketing outcomes on performance (cf. Baron & Kenny, 1986). Three regression models explored

Table 3.   Relationship of Stakeholder Responsiveness and Marketing Outcomes.

Variable	Customer Satisfaction			Innovation			Reputation		
	Model 1a	Model 1b	Model 1c	Model 2a	Model 2b	Model 2c	Model 3a	Model 3b	Model 3c
SR total	.24***			.26***			.26***		
Positive SR		.17*			.42***			.20**	
Negative SR		−.24**			.03			−.25**	
Customer			.16			.29***			.11
Employee			.14			.15*			.11
Shareholder			.07			.04			.26***
Supplier			−.07			−.10			−.03
Regulatory			.16			−.30***			.20*
Community			−.04			.34***			−.14
Age	−.04	−.03	−.02	.13	.09	.07	.08	.10	.14
Industry	.08	−.11	−.12	−.13	−.02	−.02	−.02	−.05	−.07
Sales (assets)	−.27***	−.22*	−.13	−.32	−.24**	−.10	.13	.18	.32***
Adj R^2	.10	.10	.10	.08	.12	.18	.07	.06	.12
ΔR^2	.06	.06	.08	.07	.12	.19	.07	.07	.14
F for ΔR^2	8.56***	4.54***	2.19**	10.19***	9.24***	5.43***	9.62***	5.01***	3.74***

***p < .01; **p < .05; *p < .10.

each hypothesized mediation relationship: regressing the mediator on the independent variable, regressing the dependent variable on the independent variable, and regressing the dependent variable on both the independent variable and the mediator. Table 3 provides the result of the first regression model used to test the previous hypothesis that examined the relationship between stakeholder responsiveness and the proposed mediator variables of marketing outcomes. For the second equation, three regression analyses examine the relationship between the marketing outcomes and financial performance (see Table 4). Since not all of the marketing outcomes have significant relationships with the performance measures, testing for mediation relationships is appropriate for customer satisfaction with Tobin's Q, reputation with Altman's Z, and innovation and reputation with ROA.

To test the third condition that stakeholder responsiveness affects performance outcomes, a series of regression analyses examined the relationship of stakeholder responsiveness on the three financial performance outcomes. Again, we tested these relationships using three measures for stakeholder responsiveness: overall stakeholder responsiveness, positive and negative aspects of responsiveness, and responsiveness to specific stakeholder groups (see Table 5).

Table 4. Results of Marketing Outcomes on Financial
Performance Outcomes.

Variable	Tobin's Q	Altman's Z	ROA
Customer satisfaction	.19**	.07	.01
Innovation	.03	.12	.17**
Reputation	.08	.27***	.38***
Age	−.12	.00	−.05
Industry	−.32***	−.04	−.15*
Adj R^2	.12	.08	.19
ΔR^2	.05	.11	.20
F for ΔR^2	2.30*	5.13***	10.89***

***$p < .01$; **$p < .05$; *$p < .10$.

Table 5. Relationship of Stakeholder Responsiveness and Firm
Performance.

Variable	Tobin's Q	Altman's Z	ROA
Stakeholder responsiveness	−.06	.06	.16*
Age	−.12	.04	.01
Industry	−.34***	−.07	−.19**
Positive SR	−.19**	−.02	.17
Negative SR	−.16*	−.18*	−.09
Age	−.05	.08	.00
Industry	−.40***	−.11	−.18*
Customer responsiveness	.12	.20**	.19*
Employee responsiveness	.05	−.15	−.05
Shareholder responsiveness	.12	.27***	.19**
Supplier responsiveness	−.20**	−.27***	−.05
Regulatory responsiveness	−.02	−.12	−.15
Community responsiveness	−.22**	.11	.07
Age	−.05	.09	.02
Industry	−.30***	.00	−.10

***$p < .01$; **$p < .05$; *$p < .10$.

Eight combinations of responsiveness variables and mediators meet the
three conditions for mediation stipulated by Baron and Kenny (1986).
Table 6 shows the first set of tests for mediation of customer satisfaction
on firm performance. Model 1 examines the mediating role of customer
satisfaction on Tobin's Q, with positive stakeholder responsiveness as
the independent variable. Results show that positive stakeholder

Table 6. Mediating Analysis on Tobin's Q.

Variable	Model 1a	Model 1b	Model 2a	Model 2b
Positive SR	−.24***	−.24***		
Negative SR			−.22**	−.17*
Customer satisfaction		.20**		.16*
Age	−.08	−.06	−.08	−.07
Industry	−.37***	−.35***	−.40**	−.37***
Model F stat	8.64***	8.49***	7.95***	6.98***
R^2	.16	.20	.15	.17
Adj R^2	.14	.18	.13	.15
ΔR^2	.05	.10	.04	.02
F for ΔR^2	8.59***	7.93**	6.74**	3.60*

*** $p < .01$; ** $p < .05$; * $p < .10$.

responsiveness had a similar effect $(-.24 \ p < .01)$ when customer satisfaction was included, indicating that customer satisfaction is not supported as a mediator. Model 2 examines the mediating role of customer satisfaction on Tobin's Q, with negative stakeholder responsiveness as the independent variable. Results show that negative stakeholder responsiveness had a less negative effect when customer satisfaction was included, indicating that customer satisfaction is a partial mediator.

Table 7 shows the next set of tests for mediation of reputation on Altman's Z. Model 3 examines the mediation relationship with negative stakeholder responsiveness as the independent variable. Results show that the coefficient for negative responsiveness is slightly less negative when reputation is controlled, indicating a partial mediation effect of reputation on the relationship of negative stakeholder responsiveness to Altman's Z. Model 4 examines the mediation relationship with stakeholder responsiveness to shareholders as the independent variable. Results show that the coefficient for shareholder responsiveness $(.22 \ p < .05)$ is less when reputation is controlled $(.15 \ p < .10)$, indicating a partial mediation effect of reputation on the relationship of shareholder responsiveness to Altman's Z.

Table 8 shows the tests for mediation of innovation and reputation on the relationship between stakeholder responsiveness and ROA. In Models 5 and 6, the coefficients for the measures of stakeholder responsiveness are not significant in the models controlling for innovation, indicating full mediation of innovation in the relationship of overall stakeholder responsiveness and customer responsiveness to ROA. Similarly, in Models 7 and 8, the coefficients for the measures of stakeholder responsiveness are not significant in the models controlling for reputation, indicating full mediation

Table 7. Mediating Analysis on Altman's Z.

Variable	Model 3a	Model 3b	Model 4a	Model 4b
Negative SR	−.19**	−.17*		
Shareholder responsiveness			.22**	.15*
Reputation		.29***		.26***
Age	.08	.05	.06	.03
Industry	−.10	−.10	−.05	−.06
Model F stat	1.71	4.35***	2.47*	4.23***
R^2	.04	.12	.05	.11
Adj R^2	.02	.09	.03	.09
ΔR^2	.03	.08	.05	.06
F for ΔR^2	4.37**	11.87***	6.65**	9.06***

***$p < .01$; **$p < .05$; *$p < .10$.

Table 8. Mediating Analysis on Return on Assets.

Variable	Model 5a	Model 5b	Model 6a	Model 6b	Model 7a	Model 7b	Model 8a	Model 8b
SR Total	.16*	.10			.15*	.04		
Customer SR			.14*	.11				
Shareholder SR							.17**	.07
Innovation		.24***		.25***				
Reputation						.40***		.39***
Age	.01	−.02	.02	−.01	.00	−.04	.02	−.03
Industry	−.19*	−.15*	−.16*	−.13	−.17*	−.17**	−.15*	−.17**
Model F stat	2.65**	3.96***	2.43*	4.05***	2.09	7.95***	2.52*	8.11***
R^2	.06	.11	.05	.11	.05	.20	.05	.20
Adj R^2	.04	.08	.03	.08	.02	.17	.03	.17
ΔR^2	.03	.05	.02	.06	.02	.15	.03	.14
F for ΔR^2	3.52*	7.52***	2.90*	8.51***	2.09	7.95***	4.16**	23.76***

***$p < .01$; **$p < .05$; *$p < .10$.

of reputation in the relationship of overall stakeholder responsiveness and customer responsiveness to ROA.

DISCUSSION AND IMPLICATIONS

Our findings provide support for stakeholder marketing creating a strong relationship to organizational outcomes. A positive relationship between stakeholder responsiveness to customer satisfaction, innovation, and reputation is a significant contribution to knowledge. These mediators of firm performance are an important link in implementing stakeholder marketing for firm success. The relationship between stakeholder marketing and social responsibility is more complex and exists through enhancing relationships with key stakeholders and contributing to positive organizational outcomes.

Stakeholder Orientations and Stakeholder Responsiveness

In examining the results of the first hypothesis in our study (stakeholder orientation–stakeholder responsiveness), positive relationships emerge for customer and supplier orientations when measuring the prioritization that a firm places among the stakeholder groups. This finding is consistent with Greenley and Foxall (1996) where customer orientation emerged as the most important group in studies of stakeholder orientation. However, our results provide additional insights by treating positive stakeholder responsiveness as distinct from harmful activities (i.e., which have a greater effect). Prioritizing customers over other stakeholder groups reduces the negative responses overall. The results also suggest that greater prioritization of suppliers can improve positive stakeholder responses to all stakeholders. Focusing on suppliers has become increasingly important as firms rely on networks of suppliers (cf. Neill & Stovall, 2005). For example, Costco states in their annual report: "Our suppliers are our partners in business, and we believe in establishing alliances with them that enable both of us to prosper."

When measuring the extent that a firm values a stakeholder from the amount of attention given to a certain stakeholder in their annual report, stakeholder orientation had a negative relationship with responsiveness. Specifically, regulatory and shareholder orientations had the opposite effects on responsiveness than expected. These results suggest that orientation to specific stakeholder groups is a reflection of pressure to pay attention because of inadequate responses (Williams & Barrett, 2000). For example, Maurer and Sachs (2005) find that stakeholder orientation changes over time in reaction to triggering events, such as natural disasters, negative publicity over business practices, and legislative actions. This was also evident in one annual report in our study:

> Customers and regulators are increasingly measuring our performance against other leading utilities – and even service leaders in other industries – and they're expecting us to stay ahead of the curve. (PG&E Corporation, 2005, p. 4)

Managers should avoid adopting a "cookie cutter" approach to incorporating multiple stakeholders in their marketing strategy. The prioritization of stakeholders varies by industry as well as the level of scrutiny that a firm receives from the media, regulatory agencies, and activist groups. For instance, suppliers are a stakeholder group that is not receiving much attention, yet companies focusing on suppliers tend to have greater corporate social responsiveness scores. There is also a tendency to acknowledge and value a stakeholder defensively, in response to scrutiny. Companies adopting an orientation to a stakeholder group in response to negative publicity or legislative actions recognize that improving relationships with stakeholders takes time and resources.

Stakeholder Responsiveness and Marketing Outcomes

Our study corroborates some prior findings of the positive relationships between overall stakeholder responsiveness and marketing outcomes and extends those findings in a number of ways. For example, the standardized coefficient for stakeholder responsiveness to customer satisfaction of .24 is close to the significant coefficient for corporate social responsibility to customer satisfaction (.21) in a similar study in Luo and Bhattacharya (2006). However, by disaggregating responsiveness by positive and negative actions, we can provide insights in the relationship between responsiveness on customer satisfaction, innovation, and reputation beyond that of prior studies. For example, our results provide a better understanding of the relationship between "doing good" and customer satisfaction. While overall stakeholder responsiveness with aggregated strengths and concerns has a significantly positive relationship with customer satisfaction (.24 p <.01), the proactive actions reflected in positive stakeholder responsiveness is only slightly significant and much weaker (.17 p <.10). Negative responses have a stronger and negative relationship with customer satisfaction ($-.24$ p <.05), which is consistent with findings that unethical marketing that exploits or harms another party reduces the customer's satisfaction (Ingram, Skinner, & Taylor, 2005).

The positive relationship between stakeholder responsiveness and customer satisfaction may be more complex. For instance, Luo and Bhattacharya (2006) find that firms need to ensure that they are perceived as innovative and as makers of high-quality products before they undertake major corporate social responsibility initiatives since a low innovativeness capacity reduces customer satisfaction levels. The strong relationship between positive stakeholder responsiveness and innovation suggests that improvement in customer satisfaction from corporate social responsibility is through innovation. Aetna recognizes the link between innovation and customer satisfaction when stating that it "regained the confidence of customers through product and service innovation" (Aetna Inc., 2004, p. 6).

These findings highlight two views of how balancing multiple stakeholders influences innovation. Customer, community, and employee responsiveness have positive relationships with innovation, while regulatory responsiveness has a negative relationship (cf. Han et al., 1998). A customer orientation includes listening to customers and responding to their needs through innovative solutions. Best Buy embraces an employee orientation by creating a culture where "employees are energized because they have both the responsibility and the accountability to make decisions and drive innovation based on their knowledge of the customer" (Best Buy Co., Inc., 2004, p. 4). 3M acknowledges the role of customer orientation with innovation when stating: "A culture of customer-inspired innovation is at the core of this business model" (3M, 2005 p. 2).

Our results for community orientation support a social network perspective that innovations result in a particular need to consider a broad base of stakeholders (Bunn et al., 2002). An example of how a community orientation enhances innovation is an initiative by Bristol-Meyers Squibb. "Through support by 'Secure the Future' of a wide range of innovative community-based initiatives, we aim to help develop sustainable health care capacity that is greatly needed in the fight against AIDS" (Bristol-Meyers Squibb, 2004, p. 6). IBM seeks innovation through "the company's efforts to advance open technology standards and to engage with governments, academia, think tanks, and nongovernmental organizations on emerging trends in technology, society, and culture" (International Business Machines, Inc., 2004, p. 17).

The negative relationship of regulatory responsiveness provides support for scholars arguing that increasing regulation can hamper innovation. However, Gonzalez-Padron and Nason (2009) find that decreased innovation occurs when a firm focuses only on compliance with regulations, whereas innovation increases when firms embrace strategic-based approaches to regulatory issues. One recommendation is for firms to collaborate with industry-wide efforts or governmental/regulatory agencies. Rather than attract governmental intervention, Abbott participates in industry-wide efforts to help low-income, uninsured, or underinsured patients access free or discounted medications. Another recommendation is to seek regulatory changes or work with standards bodies.

Likewise, the relationship of positive and negative responsiveness to reputation is complex with a stronger negative relationship with harmful activities $(-.25\ p\ <.05)$ than the positive relationship with "doing good" $(.20\ p\ <.05)$. The recognition that corporate reputation may be slow to change through positive stakeholder responsiveness is due to the lingering effects of past corporate reputation. Pulling from attribution theory, studies find that a poor reputation for corporate social responsibility discredits charitable activities (Dean, 2003; Kuzma, Veltri, Kuzma, & Miller, 2003). A quotation from the 2004 annual report of Altria highlights this issue:

> We know that this is an evolving process and continually strive to improve our efforts to earn public trust and strengthen our reputation through a commitment to responsible marketing, quality assurance, ethical business practices and by giving back to our communities.

Effects on Firm Performance

Our results regarding the direct effects of customer satisfaction, innovation, and reputation on financial outcomes are somewhat consistent with a number of prior studies. We also extend these findings of these marketing outcomes in their roles as mediators between stakeholder responsiveness and performance. Providing a great deal of insight beyond prior studies is the analysis of the direct effects of overall, positive, and negative responsiveness to stakeholders on firm performance.

The measure for overall stakeholder responsiveness allows positive actions to counteract harmful actions. We find that overall stakeholder responsiveness positively affects ROA (cf. Orlitzky et al. (2003). Positive responsiveness has a negative relationship with market-based performance (Tobin's Q) that may reflect what Frederick (1987) refers to as a "trade-off problem" that exists when costs of compliance with social pressures and accepting positive duty to society conflict with corporate economic goals of profitability. However, harmful actions also have a negative relationship with market-based and financial-based performance, highlighting the stakeholder theoretical perspective that managers must satisfy various constituents that would withdraw support for the firm if important social responsibilities were unmet (Freeman, 1984).

Our study corroborates the stakeholder mismatching thesis of Wood and Jones (1995) by showing that effects of social responsive actions vary by stakeholder groups. Consistent with Berman et al. (1999), customer responsiveness has a positive relationship with Altman's Z and ROA. However, contrary to the earlier study, we find that employee responsiveness does not directly affect performance. Our results that employee responsiveness has a positive relationship with innovation and an insignificant effect on financial performance are comparable with those of Greenley and Foxall's (1998) findings that paying attention to employees affects new product success rather than financial performance. Although earlier tests show a supplier orientation as positively influencing the overall stakeholder responsiveness of the firm, we find that attention to suppliers lowers market and financial performance. A negative relationship of community responsiveness to Tobin's Q is consistent with findings of Seifert et al. (2004) that community philanthropy is not related to financial performance.

Regarding customer satisfaction, marketers strive to increase satisfaction with their products and services through cause marketing and philanthropic sponsorships. While studies show that social responsiveness can increase customer satisfaction, this has not necessarily translated into customer loyalty or purchasing. Our study shows that harmful activities have a greater effect on lowering customer satisfaction than social responsiveness has on increasing customer satisfaction by their effect on market-based performance.

We find that innovation fully mediates the relationship between stakeholder responsiveness and firm performance (cf. McWilliams & Siegel, 2000). We also found that positive social responsiveness increases firm performance through enhanced reputation, but negative reputational activities without positive actions reduce both reputation and financial performance. These findings suggest that overall stakeholder responsiveness and shareholder responsiveness influences ROA through the enhanced reputation of the firm. However, reputation only partially mediates the negative relationship of harmful responses and Altman's Z, providing further support that stakeholder responsiveness helps to mitigate negative actions. The partial mediation of reputation on shareholder responsiveness and financial performance reflects the focus on profits typically associated with a shareholder orientation.

These results would suggest that firms should increase programs focusing on multiple stakeholders to enhance their reputation. However, a poor reputation for corporate social responsibility discredits charitable activities and limits the effectiveness of community-oriented responses. A firm's reputation is slow to change, and attention to multiple stakeholders can help protect a positive reputation, but may not be able to repair a negative reputation. Harmful activities have a greater negative effect on reputation than stakeholder responsiveness activities. Therefore, paying attention to regulatory and governmental agencies to avoid legal sanctions is the best method of protecting reputation. As most reputation scores published are from an investor's view, paying attention to shareholders has the greatest effect on reputation.

CONCLUSIONS

Marketing strategy must align with strategic imperatives for companies to demonstrate responsible management, including goals of being a sustainable business. In the recent decade, increasing conceptual articles have called for marketers to adopt strategies that are socially and environmentally responsible (Baker & Sinkula, 2005; Bhattacharya & Korschun, 2008; Crittenden et al., 2011; Ferrell et al., 2010; Maignan et al., 2005). Marketers can build on expertise of managing customer relationship and generating customer value to develop a stakeholder marketing approach that addresses the economic, social, and environmental concerns of multiple stakeholders. We propose that stakeholder marketing includes a stakeholder orientation and stakeholder responsiveness that creates a competitive advantage in greater customer satisfaction, innovation, and reputation of a firm.

We further the discussion whether stakeholder marketing equates to greater corporate social responsibility. Our definition implies that stakeholder responsiveness is acting in the best interests of the stakeholder as a responsible business. We describe stakeholder responsiveness as the extent to which the organization implements policies and programs seeking to increase positive impacts and reduce negative impacts on stakeholder groups. This study shows that stakeholder marketing may not always represent socially responsible marketing. In our sample, attention to regulatory and community stakeholders related to greater irresponsible behavior. Further research could explore how and why firms may not respond ethically and responsibly to stakeholders.

It is heartening for managers to see another study supporting the financial benefits of adopting a sustainable and responsible business strategy. Including multiple stakeholders in the marketing function can increase the complexity of developing strategies that create value for the customer. However, the consequences of not integrating positive social, economic, and environmental impacts can harm the firm's reputation, reduce customer satisfaction, and stifle innovation. Stakeholder marketing that seeks to create value for multiple stakeholders can lead to a reputation of a sustainable business.

ACKNOWLEDGMENTS

We appreciate the financial support from the Center for International Business Education and Research at Michigan State University, and the input provided by Patrick L. Murphy, S. Tamer Cavusgil, and Robert Nason.

REFERENCES

3M. (2005). 3M 2004 Annual Report. St. Paul, MN.

Aetna Inc. (2004). The challenge of leadership: Aetna annual report 2004. Hartford, CT.

Altman, E. I. (1968). Financial ratios, discriminant analysis and the prediction of corporate bankruptcy. *Journal of Finance, 23*, 414–429.

Anderson, E. W., Fornell, C., & Mazvancheryl, S. K. (2004). Customer satisfaction and shareholder value. *Journal of Marketing, 68*(4), 172.

Aupperle, K. E., Carroll, A. B., & Hatfield, J. D. (1985). An empirical examination of the relationship between corporate social responsibility and profitability. *Academy of Management Journal, 28*(2), 446.

Baker, W. E., & Sinkula, J. M. (2005). Environmental marketing strategy and firm performance: Effects on new product performance and market share. *Journal of the Academy of Marketing Science, 33*(4), 461–475.

Banerjee, S. B., Iyer, E. S., & Kashyap, R. K. (2003). Corporate environmentalism: Antecedents and influence of industry type. *Journal of Marketing, 67*(2), 106.

Barney, J. B. (1991). Firm resources and sustained competitive advantage. *Journal of Management, 17*, 99–120.

Baron, R. M., & Kenny, D. A. (1986). The moderator mediator variable distinction in social psychological research: Conceptual, strategic, and statistical considerations. *Journal of Personality and Social Psychology, 51*, 1173–1182.

Berman, S. L., Wicks, A. C., Kotha, S., & Jones, T. M. (1999). Does stakeholder orientation matter? The relationship between stakeholder management models and firm financial performance. *Academy of Management Journal, 42*(5), 488–506.

Best Buy Co., Inc. (2004). Fiscal 2004 annual report. Richfield, MN.

Berry, G. R. (2003). Organizing against multinational corporate power in cancer alley: The activist community as primary stakeholder. *Organization & Environment, 16*(1), 3.

Bettman, J. R., & Weitz, B. A. (1983). Attributions in the board room: Causal reasoning in corporate annual reports. *Administrative Science Quarterly*, 165–183.

Bhattacharya, C. B., & Korschun, D. (2008). Stakeholder marketing: Beyond the four Ps and the customer. *Journal of Public Policy & Marketing, 27*(1), 113–116.

Bhattacharya, C. B., & Sen, S. (2003). Consumer-company identification: A framework for understanding consumers' relationships with companies. *Journal of Marketing, 67*(2), 76.

Bolton, R. N. (1998). A dynamic model of the duration of the customer's relationship with a continuous service provider: The role of satisfaction. *Journal of Marketing Research, 36*(2), 171–186.

Brammer, S., & Millington, A. (2003). The effect of stakeholder preferences, organizational structure and industry type on corporate community involvement. *Journal of Business Ethics, 45*(3), 213.

Brammer, S., & Millington, A. (2005). Corporate reputation and philanthropy: An empirical analysis. *Journal of Business Ethics, 61*(1), 29–44.

Branco, M. C., & Rodrigues, L. L. (2006). Communication of corporate social responsibility by Portuguese banks. *Corporate Communications, 11*(3), 232.

Bristol-Myers Squibb Company. (2005). Bristol-Myers Squibb Company 2004 annual report. New York, NY.

Bundy, J., Shropshire, C., & Buchholtz, A. K. (2013). Strategic cognition and issue salience: Toward an explanation of firm responsiveness to stakeholder concerns. *Academy of Management Review, 38*(3), 352–376.

Bunn, M. D., Savage, G. T., & Holloway, B. B. (2002). Stakeholder analysis for multi-sector innovations. *The Journal of Business & Industrial Marketing, 17*(2/3), 181.

Calantone, R. J., Cavusgil, S. T., & Zhao, Y. (2002). Learning orientation, firm innovation capability, and firm performance. *Industrial Marketing Management, 31*(6), 515.

Carroll, A. B. (1979). A three-dimensional conceptual model of corporate performance. *Academy of Management Review, 4*(4), 497–505.

Chabowski, B., Mena, J., & Gonzalez-Padron, T. (2011). The structure of sustainability research in marketing, 1958–2008: A basis for future research opportunities. *Journal of the Academy of Marketing Science, 39*(1), 55–70.

Choi, J., & Wang, H. (2009). Stakeholder relations and the persistence of corporate financial performance. *Strategic Management Journal, 30*(8), 895–907.

Clarkson, M. (1995). A stakeholder framework for analyzing and evaluating corporate social performance. *Academy of Management Review, 20*(1), 92–117.

Cohen, J. (1960). A coefficient of agreement of nominal scales. *Educational and Psychological Measurement, 20*(1), 37–46.

Cohen, J., Cohen, P., West, S. G., & Aiken, L. S. (2003). *Applied multiple regression/correlation analysis for the behavioral sciences.* Mahwah, NJ: Lawrence Erlbaum Associates.

Coulmont, M., & Berthelot, S. (2015). The financial benefits of a firm's affiliation with the UN Global Compact. *Business Ethics: A European Review, 24*(2), 144–157.

Crittenden, V., Crittenden, W., Ferrell, L., Ferrell, O., & Pinney, C. (2011). Market-oriented sustainability: A conceptual framework and propositions. *Journal of the Academy of Marketing Science, 39*(1), 71–85.

Cronin, J., Smith, J., Gleim, M., Ramirez, E., & Martinez, J. (2011). Green marketing strategies: An examination of stakeholders and the opportunities they present. *Journal of the Academy of Marketing Science, 39*(1), 158–174.

Damanpour, F. (1991). Organizational innovation: A meta-analysis of effects of determinants and moderators. *Academy of Management Journal, 34*(3), 555–590.

Davis, K. (1960). Can business afford to ignore social responsibilities? *California Management Review, 2*(Spring), 70–76.

Day, G. S. (1994). The capabilities of market-driven organizations. *Journal of Marketing, 58*(4), 37–52.

Dean, D. H. (2003). Consumer perception of corporate donations: Effects of company reputation for social responsibility and type of donation. *Journal of Advertising, 32*(4), 91.

Deniz-Deniz, M. d. l. C., & Saa-Perez, P. D. (2003). A resource-based view of corporate responsiveness toward employees. *Organization Studies, 24*(2), 299.

Deshpande, R., Farley, J. U., & Webster, F. E. (1993). Corporate culture, customer orientation, and innovativeness in Japanese firms: A quadrad analysis. *Journal of Marketing, 57*(1), 23–27.

Donaldson, T., & Preston, L. E. (1995). The stakeholder theory of the corporation: Concepts, evidence, and implications. *Academy of Management Review, 20*(1), 65.

Drumwright, M. E. (1994). Socially responsible organizational buying: Environmental concern as a noneconomic buying criterion. *Journal of Marketing, 58*(3), 1.

Eberl, M., & Schwaiger, M. (2005). Corporate reputation: Disentangling the effects on financial performance. *European Journal of Marketing, 39*(7–8), 838.

Elkington, J. (1998). *Cannibals with forks: The triple bottom line of 21st century business.* Stony Creek, CT: New Society Publishers.

Falkenberg, J., & Brunsæl, P. (2011). Corporate social responsibility: A strategic advantage or a strategic necessity? *Journal of Business Ethics, 99*, 9–16.

Ferrell, O. C. (2004). Business ethics and customer stakeholders. *The Academy of Management Executive, 18*(2), 126.

Ferrell, O. C., Gonzalez-Padron, T. L., Hult, G. T. M., & Maignan, I. (2010). From market orientation to stakeholder orientation. *Journal of Public Policy & Marketing, 29*(1), 93–96.

Fombrun, C. (1996). *Reputation: Realizing value from the corporate image.* Harvard, MA: Harvard Business School Press.

Fombrun, C., & Shanley, M. (1990). "What's in a name? Reputation building and corporate strategy." *Academy of Management Journal, 33*(2), 233–258.

Fornell, C. (1992). A national customer satisfaction barometer: The Swedish experience. *Journal of Marketing, 6*(January), 1–21.

Fornell, C., Johnson, M. D., Anderson, E. W., Cha, J., & Everitt Bryant, B. (1996). The American customer satisfaction index: Nature, purpose, and findings. *Journal of Marketing, 60*(4), 7.

Frederick, W. C. (1987). Theories of corporate social performance. In S. P. Sethi & C. Falbe (Eds.), *Business and society: Dimensions of conflict and cooperation.* New York, NY: Lexington Books.

Freeman, R. E. (1984). *Strategic management: A stakeholder approach.* Englewood Cliffs, NJ: Prentice-Hall.

Friedman, A., & Miles, S. (2006). *Stakeholders: Theory and practice.* New York, NY: Oxford University Press.

Fussler, C. (2004). Responsible excellence pays! *Journal of Corporate Citizenship, 16*, 33–44.

Glavas, A., & Mish, J. (2015). Resources and capabilities of triple bottom line firms: Going over old or breaking new ground? *Journal of Business Ethics, 127*(3), 623–642.

Gonzalez-Padron, T. L., & Nason, R. W. (2009). Market responsiveness to societal interests. *Journal of Macromarketing, 29*(4), 392–405.

Greenley, G. E., & Foxall, G. R. (1996). Consumer and nonconsumer stakeholder orientation in UK companies. *Journal of Business Research, 35*(2), 105.

Greenley, G. E., & Foxall, G. R. (1997). Multiple stakeholder orientation in UK companies and the implications for company performance. *The Journal of Management Studies*, *34*(2), 259.

Greenley, G. E., & Foxall, G. R. (1998). External moderation of associations among stakeholder orientations and company performance. *International Journal of Research in Marketing*, *15*(1), 51–69.

Greenley, G. E., Hooley, G. J., Broderick, A. J., & Rudd, J. M. (2004). Strategic planning differences among different multiple stakeholder orientation profiles. *Journal of Strategic Marketing*, *12*(September), 163–182.

Greenwood, M. (2007). Stakeholder engagement: Beyond the myth of corporate responsibility. *Journal of Business Ethics*, *74*(4), 315–327.

Han, J. K., Kim, N., & Srivastava, R. K. (1998). Market orientation and organizational performance: Is innovation a missing link? *Journal of Marketing*, *62*(4), 30.

Harris, H. (2001). Content analysis of secondary data: A study of courage in managerial decision making. *Journal of Business Ethics*, *34*, 191–208.

Harrison, J. S., & St John, C. H. (1996). Managing and partnering with external stakeholders. *The Academy of Management Executive*, *10*(2), 46.

Harwood, T. G., & Garry, T. (2003). An overview of content analysis. *Marketing Review*, *3*, 479–498.

Hillman, A. J., & Keim, G. D. (2001). Shareholder value, stakeholder management, and social issues: What's the bottom line? *Strategic Management Journal*, *22*(2), 125.

Hult, G. T. M., & Ketchen, D. J. (2001). Does market orientation matter?: A test of the relationship between positional advantage and performance. *Strategic Management Journal*, *22*(9), 899–906.

Hult, G. T. M., Mena, J. A., Ferrell, O. C., & Ferrell, L. (2011). Stakeholder marketing: A definition and conceptual framework. *AMS Review*, *1*(1), 44–65.

Hunt, S. D., & Morgan, R. M. (1995). The comparative advantage theory of competition. *Journal of Marketing*, *59*(2), 1–15.

Hurley, R. F., & Hult, T. M. (1998). Innovation, market orientation, and organizational learning: An integration and empirical examination. *Journal of Marketing*, *62*(3), 42–54.

Ingram, R., Skinner, S. J., & Taylor, V. A. (2005). 'Consumers' evaluation of unethical marketing behaviors: The role of customer commitment. *Journal of Business Ethics*, *62*(3), 237.

International Business Machines Corporation. (2004). IBM annual report 2004. New York, USA.

Jackson, J. (2001). Prioritising customers and other stakeholders using the AHP. *European Journal of Marketing*, *35*(7–8), 858.

Judd, V. C., & Tims, B. J. (1991). How annual reports communicate a customer orientation. *Industrial Marketing Management*, *20*, 353–360.

Ketchen, D. J., Hult, G. T. M., & Slater, S. F. (2007). Toward greater understanding of market orientation and the resource-based view. *Strategic Management Journal*, *28*(9), 961–964.

Kohli, A. K., & Jaworski, B. J. (1990). Market orientation: The construct, research propositions, and managerial implications. *Journal of Marketing*, *54*(2), 1–18.

Kuzma, J. R., Veltri, F. R., Kuzma, A. T., & Miller, J. J. (2003). Negative corporate sponsor information: The impact on consumer attitudes and purchase intentions. *International Sports Journal*, *7*(2), 140.

Laasch, O., & Conaway, R. N. (2015). *Principles of responsible management: Glocal sustainability, responsibility, and ethics*. Stamford, CT: Cengage Learning.

Laczniak, G. R., & Murphy, P. M. (2006). Normative perspectives for ethical and socially responsible marketing. *Journal of Macromarketing, 26*(2), 154–177.

Laszlo, C., Sherman, D., Whalen, J., & Ellison, J. (2005). Expanding the value horizon: How stakeholder value contributes to competitive advantage. *The Journal of Corporate Citizenship, 20*, 65.

Lee, R. P., & Grewal, R. (2004). Strategic responses to new technologies and their impact of firm performance. *Journal of Marketing, 68*(4), 157.

Li, T., & Calantone, R. J. (1998). The impact of market knowledge competence on new product advantage: Conceptualization and empirical examination. *Journal of Marketing, 62*(4), 13.

Lindsay, V. J. (2004). Computer-assisted qualitative data analysis: Application in an export study. In R. Marschan-Piekkari & C. Welch (Eds.), *Handbook of qualitative research methods for international business*. Northampton, MA: Edward Edgar Publishing Ltd.

Luo, X., & Bhattacharya, C. B. (2006). Corporate social responsibility, customer satisfaction, and market value. *Journal of Marketing, 70*(4), 1–18.

Maignan, I., & Ferrell, O. C. (2004). Corporate social responsibility and marketing: An integrative framework. *Journal of Academy of Marketing Science, 32*(1), 3–19.

Maignan, I., Ferrell, O. C., & Ferrell, L. (2005). A stakeholder model for implementing social responsibility in marketing. *European Journal of Marketing, 39*(9–10), 956.

Maignan, I., Ferrell, O. C., & Hult, G. T. M. (1999). Corporate citizenship: Cultural antecedents and business benefits. *Journal of Academy of Marketing Science, 27*(4), 455–469.

Maignan, I., Gonzalez-Padron, T. L., Hult, G. T. M., & Ferrell, O. C. (2011). Stakeholder orientation: Development and testing of a framework for socially responsible marketing. *Journal of Strategic Marketing, 19*(4), 313–338.

Margolis, J. D., & Walsh, J. P. (2003). Misery loves companies: Rethinking social initiatives by business. *Administrative Science Quarterly, 48*(2), 268.

Martinez, R. J., & Norman, P. M. (2004). Whither reputation? The effects of different stakeholders. *Business Horizons, 47*(5), 25.

Mattingly, J. E., & Berman, S. L. (2006). Measurement of corporate social action: Discovering taxonomy in the Kinder Lydenburg Domini ratings data. *Business and Society, 45*(1), 20.

Maurer, M., & Sachs, S. (2005). Implementing the stakeholder view: Learning processes for a changed stakeholder orientation. *The Journal of Corporate Citizenship, 17*, 93.

McWilliams, A., & Siegel, D. S. (2000). Corporate social responsibility and financial performance: Correlation or misspecification? *Strategic Management Journal, 21*(5), 603.

McWilliams, A., & Siegel, D. S. (2001). Corporate social responsibility: A theory of the firm perspective. *Academy of Management Review, 26*(1), 117.

McWilliams, A., Siegel, D. S., & Wright, P. M. (2006). Corporate social responsibility: Strategic implications. *Journal of Management Studies, 43*(1), 1–18.

Mena, J., & Chabowski, B. (2015). The role of organizational learning in stakeholder marketing. *Journal of the Academy of Marketing Science, 43*(4), 429–452.

Menon, A., & Menon, A. (1997). Enviropreneurial marketing strategy: The emergence of corporate environmentalism as market strategy. *Journal of Marketing, 61*(1), 51.

Montiel, I. (2008). Corporate social responsibility and corporate sustainability – Separate pasts, common futures. *Organization & Environment, 21*(3), 245–269.

Montoya-Weiss, M. M., & Calantone, R. (1994). Determinants of new product performance: A review and meta-analysis. *Journal of Product Innovation Management, 11*, 377−417.

Muhr, T., & Friese, S. (2004). *User's manual for Atlas.Ti 5.0* (2nd ed.). Berlin: Scientific Software Development.

Murphy, B., Maguiness, P., Pescott, C., Wislang, S., Ma, J., & Wang, R. (2005). Stakeholder perceptions presage holistic stakeholder relationship marketing performance. *European Journal of Marketing, 39*(9−10), 1049.

Narver, J. C., & Slater, S. F. (1990). The effect of a market orientation on business profitability. *Journal of Marketing, 54*(4), 20−35.

Neill, J. D., & Stovall, O. S. (2005). Stakeholder salience and corporate social responsibility: Evidence from three companies. *Journal of Applied Business Research, 21*(3), 71−78.

Noble, C. H., Sinha, R. K., & Kumar, A. (2002). Market orientation and alternative strategic orientations: A longitudinal assessment of performance implications. *Journal of Marketing, 66*(4), 25−39.

Ogden, S., & Watson, R. (1999). Corporate performance and stakeholder management: Balancing shareholder and customer interests in the U.K. privatized water industry. *Academy of Management Journal, 42*(5), 526.

Orlitzky, M., & Benjamin, J. D. (2001). Corporate social performance and firm risk: A meta-analytic review. *Business and Society, 40*(4), 369.

Orlitzky, M., Schmidt, F. L., & Rynes, S. L. (2003). Corporate social and financial performance: A meta-analysis. *Organization Studies, 24*(3), 403.

Parmar, B. L., Freeman, R. E., Harrison, J. S., Wicks, A. C., Purnell, L., & de Colle, S. (2010). Stakeholder theory: The state of the art. *The Academy of Management Annals, 4*(1), 403−445.

Peloza, J., & Shang, J. (2011). How can corporate social responsibility activities create value for stakeholders? A systematic review. *Journal of the Academy of Marketing Science, 39*(1), 117−135.

PG&E Corporation. (2005). PG&E Corporation Annual Report 2004. San Francisco, CA.

Phillips, R., & Caldwell, C. (2005). Value chain responsibility: A farewell to arm's length. *Business and Society Review, 110*(4), 345−370.

PG&E Corporation. (2005). PG&E Corporation annual report 2004. San Francisco, CA.

Preston, L. E., & Sapienza, H. J. (1990). Stakeholder management and corporate performance. *Journal of Behavioral Economics, 19*(4), 361.

Rietveld, T., & van Hout, R. (1993). *Statistical techniques for the behavioral sciences*. Berlin: Mouton de Gruyter.

Roberts, P. W., & Dowling, G. R. (2002). Corporate reputation and sustained superior financial performance. *Strategic Management Journal, 23*(12), 1141.

Roca-Puig, V., Beltrin-Martin, I., Escrig-Tena, A. B., & Bou-Llusar, J. C. (2005). Strategic flexibility as a moderator of the relationship between commitment to employees and performance in service firms. *International Journal of Human Resource Management, 16*(11), 2075−2093.

Ruf, B. M., Muralidhar, K., Brown, R. M., Janney, J. J., & Paul, K. (2001). An empirical investigation of the relationship between change in corporate social performance and financial performance: A stakeholder theory perspective. *Journal of Business Ethics, 32*(2), 143.

Seifert, B., Morris, S. A., & Bartkus, B. R. (2004). Having, giving, and getting: Slack resources, corporate philanthropy and firm financial performance. *Business & Society, 43*(2), 135−161.

Sharfman, M. (1996). The construct validity of the Kinder, Lydenberg & Domini social performance ratings data. *Journal of Business Ethics, 15*(3), 287.

Sharma, S., & Vredenburg, H. (1998). Proactive corporate environmental strategy and the development of competitively valuable organizational capabilities. *Strategic Management Journal, 19*(8), 729.

Sheth, J. N. (2012). The reincarnation of relationship marketing. *Marketing News, 46*(16), 11.

Sheth, J. N., & Uslay, C. (2007). Implications of the revised definition of marketing: From exchange to value creation. *Journal of Public Policy & Marketing, 26*(2), 302–307.

Siltaoja, M. E. (2006). Value priorities as combining core factors between CSR and reputation – A qualitative study. *Journal of Business Ethics, 68*(1), 91.

Spurgin, E. W. (2001). Do shareholder have obligations to stakeholders? *Journal of Business Ethics, 33*(4), 287.

Steurer, R., Langer, M. E., Konrad, A., & Martinuzzi, A. (2005). Corporations, stakeholders and sustainable development I: A theoretical exploration of business-society relations. *Journal of Business Ethics, 61*(3), 263–281.

Swenson-Lepper, T. (2005). Ethical sensitivity for organizational communication issues: Examining individual and organizational differences. *Journal of Business Ethics, 59*(3), 205.

Symanski, D. M., & Henard, D. H. (2001). Customer satisfaction: A meta-analysis of the empirical evidence. *Journal of Academy of Marketing Science, 20*(Winter), 19–35.

Szwajkowski, E., & Figlewicz, R. E. (1999). Evaluating corporate performance: A comparison of the fortune reputation survey and the Socrates social rating database. *Journal of Managerial Issues, 11*(2), 137.

van Marrewijk, M. (2003). Concepts and definitions of CSR and corporate sustainability: Between agency and communion. *Journal of Business Ethics, 44*(2), 95–105.

Voorhes, M. (2006). *Support grows for social proposals*. Institutional Shareholder Services Inc. Retrieved from http://www.issproxy.com/governance/publications/2006archived/195.jsp. Accessed on December 20, 2006.

Waddock, S., & Graves, S. B. (1997). Quality of management and quality of stakeholder relations. *Business and Society, 36*(3), 250.

Wartick, S. L., & Cochran, P. L. (1985). The evolution of the corporate social performance model. *Academy of Management Review, 10*(4), 758–769.

Weiss, A. M., Anderson, E., & MacInnis, D. J. (1999). Reputation management as a motivation for sales structure decisions. *Journal of Marketing, 63*(4), 74.

Wernerfelt, B. (1984). A resource-based view of the firm. *Strategic Management Journal, 5*(2), 171–180.

Williams, R. J., & Barrett, J. D. (2000). Corporate philanthropy, criminal activity, and firm reputation: Is there a link? *Journal of Business Ethics, 26*(4), 341–350.

Wolf, J. (2014). The relationship between sustainable supply chain management, stakeholder pressure and corporate sustainability performance. *Journal of Business Ethics, 119*(3), 317–328.

Wood, D. J., & Jones, R. E. (1995). Stakeholder mismatching: A theoretical problem in empirical research on corporate social performance. *International Journal of Organizational Analysis, 3*, 229–267.

World Commission on Environment and Development. (1987). *Our common future*. Oxford: Oxford University Press.

Yoon, E., Guffey, H. J., & Kijewski, V. (1993). The effects of information and company reputation on intentions to buy a business service. *Journal of Business Research, 27*(3), 215–228.

TURNING TO SUSTAINABLE BUSINESS PRACTICES: A MACROMARKETING PERSPECTIVE

Mark Peterson and Matthew B. Lunde

ABSTRACT

Purpose — *This paper reviews recent developments in marketing-related sustainable business practices (SBP) that macromarketing scholars have researched and debated for four decades. Such SBPs should be regarded as positive steps toward a future where business does more good than harm in society.*

Methodology/approach — *Using the approach of a literature review, this paper highlights the actions of entrepreneurs and firms to implement SBPs resulting from analysis of the interplay between markets, marketing and society. Such analysis is in the tradition of macromarketing scholarship.*

Findings — *The study identifies important developments about an important shift toward adopting SBPs among many firms, as well as among consumers — especially, in developed countries of the world.*

Marketing In and For a Sustainable Society
Review of Marketing Research, Volume 13, 103–137
Copyright © 2016 by Emerald Group Publishing Limited
All rights of reproduction in any form reserved
ISSN: 1548-6435/doi:10.1108/S1548-643520160000013013

Research implications — *The study suggests that taking a macromarketing view offers scholars a broad lens on current complex marketplace phenomena that will prove effective in better understanding sustainability issues.*

Practical implications — *The results of the study underline the value of macromarketing scholarship through the last four decades. By being daring enough to consider other stakeholders other than marketers and owners of firms, macromarketers have provided scholars a more holistic understanding of business' role in society.*

Originality/value — *Today, enlightened practitioners who utilize knowledge from macromarketing scholarship can gain a competitive advantage as they navigate markets increasingly influenced by a wider set of stakeholders. Such influential stakeholders include partner firms, employees, society and local communities, NGOs, media, government, as well as the environment and future generations. Scholars can gain perspective on the phenomena they investigate with such a macromarketing lens.*

Keywords: Sustainability; sustainable business practices; macromarketing; consumer attitudes; green products; sustainable development goals

According to veteran marketing scholar Kotler (2011a), business-related degradation of the environment must now be dramatically reduced because of the perilous outcomes of such degradation. Kotler sees danger for society from (1) climate change, (2) shortages of fresh water, and (3) depletion of natural resources. To become sustainable, firms now need to make significant changes in their approach to business. According to Kotler, this is the "environmental imperative." Others have termed this the "sustainability imperative" (Lubin & Esty, 2010). Kotler's assertion that business must be the cure for the environmental degradation that business has caused reframes a question debated for years by macromarketers, as well as social critics — can business do more societal good, than harm? (Chouinard, Ellison, & Ridgeway, 2011; Fisk, 2006; Friedman, 2008; Mittelstaedt, Shultz, Kilbourne, & Peterson, 2014).

The purpose of this paper is to review recent developments in marketing-related sustainable business practices (SBP) that would be regarded as positive steps toward a future where business does more good than harm in society. When a mainstream marketing scholar such as Kotler rebukes business for degrading the natural environment, it is time to look at the net effect of business on society. Many of these developments favorable to SBP can be seen to be coping responses by firms and by consumers to changes in the markets where these firms and consumers interact. Such changes could be due to new technologies, new competitors, new norms, and new rules in these markets – just to name a few causes of market dynamism. The aim of this paper is to examine SBP from a macromarketing viewpoint.

Macromarketing examines marketing ideas through a large-scale lens where "markets are systems...markets are heterogeneous, and the actions of market participants have consequences far beyond the boundaries of firms" (Mittelstaedt, Kilbourne, & Mittelstaedt, 2006, p. 131). The *Journal of Macromarketing* (*JMK*), since 1981, has provided an outlet for research on these larger, societal issues (Fisk, 1981; Layton & Grossbart, 2006). Over the years, six sub-domains of macromarketing emerged. These are (1) quality of life, (2) ethics, (3) environment, (4) systems, (5) history, and (6) poor countries. The first letters of these six areas comprise the acrostic "QuEEnSHiP" (Peterson, 2013). Importantly, more than 30 articles have focused on sustainability issues in over 30 articles (McDonagh & Prothero, 2014).

The journal has had three special issues on sustainability issues in 2010, 2014, and 2015. The 2010 special issue, "The Challenge of Sustainability in a Changing World" featured five articles that focused on sustainability and SBP issues "beyond the traditional marketing approach centering on recycling, green products, and energy consumption" (Kilbourne, 2010, p. 109). According authors in this special issue, sustainability is driven by sustainable consumption (Thogersen, 2010), through transformative change (Varey, 2010) with a holistic and global lens (Prothero, McDonagh, & Dobscha, 2010), that can form a sustainable market orientation (Mitchell, Wooliscroft, & Higham, 2010). Such a sustainable market orientation can be catalytic for the development of more sustainable business practices (Prothero & Fitchett, 2000).

In 2014, the second sustainability special issue focused on "Sustainability as Megatrend I." Researchers were asked to act on what should be done about sustainability (McDonagh & Prothero, 2014). Nine articles contemplated whether sustainability is a "megatrend," in which Mittelstaedt et al. (2014) concluded that indeed it is. The authors in the special issue examined a variety of SBP issues, including (1) how the idea of sustainability is framed for businesses and consumers (Humphreys, 2014), (2) how it is communicated and advertised (Cummins, Reilly, Carlson, Grove, & Dorsch, 2014; Ourahmoune, Binninger, & Robert, 2014), and (3) how it is intertwined in local and global public markets (Visconti, Minowa, & Maclaran, 2014).

In 2015, the most recent *JMK* sustainability issue, "Sustainability as Megatrend II" examined pertinent macro issues facing sustainability (Prothero, & McDonagh, 2015). A few major themes included (1) consumption sufficiency (Gorge, Herbert, Ozcaglar-Toulouse, & Robert, 2015), (2) sustainability of water resources (Patsiaouras, Saren, & Fitchett, 2015), (3) citizen-consumer influence of food channels (Chaudhury & Albinsson, 2015), and (4) slow fashion (as opposed to fad-oriented garment marketing featuring garments destined for disposal after wearing them two or three times) (Ertekin & Atik, 2015).

Uniquely, macromarketing scholarship can put sustainability efforts into context. For example, instead of focusing on how a business can be responsible to the environment and to society, Humphreys (2014) asks the question of how sustainability has evolved over the years. She finds that over time, sustainability has shifted from just protecting the environment by government actors to improving the environment by company and consumer stakeholders. Arriving at the triple-bottom-line (Savitz & Weber, 2006), Humphreys emphasizes that sustainability is more than just not letting the environment get worse. Humphreys goes on to assert that improving the environment for all stakeholders is the proactive approach to SBP.

Most of the macromarketing literature in sustainability falls into two broad categories: (1) the developmental school and (2) the critical school (Mittelstaedt et al., 2014). The developmental school of thought states, "marketing systems play a positive role in economic development and societal well-being" (p. 258). That is, markets can develop sustainable systems to create sustainable businesses and societies. In this view emphasizing the supply side of market exchanges, sustainability is a problem to be solved. However, the critical school of thought states that marketing systems are not stable or sustainable, and that "most problems facing humanity have a consumption solution" (p. 259). This idea criticizes the idea that sustainability can be "fixed" by individuals and society. In this view emphasizing the demand side of market exchanges, sustainability starts with how consumers and businesses "make collective decision, as in the decisions, themselves" (p. 259). The critical school extends the traditional role of macromarketing as being the "kvetch" (continual complainer) in marketing scholarship (Carman, 1999) and takes it to a new level of skepticism about markets and marketing.

Lest one mistake critical marketing as the troll underneath marketing's bridge to other disciplines, Verganti (2016) asserts that new product development efforts are typically overwhelmed by new ideas and that institutionalized criticism is needed for any hope of regular occurring success − or the occasional breakthrough. By analogy, one can discern that marketing scholarship just might need a corrective lens on what might be an overly optimistic view of marketing's place in society. For example, Varey (2012) criticized responsible marketing behavior as not aligning with sustainable marketing. Varey asserted that to be truly sustainable, responsible marketing needs to focus on not more products and services, but on better products and services.

EARLY ACCOMPLISHMENTS FOR SUSTAINABLE BUSINESS PRACTICES

As a response to environmental degradation and to business' proximity to social problems, many firms have adopted the "triple bottom line" (people, planet, profit). By doing this, these firms signal that they are beginning to account for their net social and environmental impact in addition to the traditional metric of economic profit (Eccles & Krzus, 2015; Savitz & Weber, 2006). Positive environmental outcomes include (1) improving air and water quality, (2) conserving energy, and (3) reducing waste and air pollution. Positive social outcomes include improvements in (1) labor practices, (2) community health, (3) better-educated consumers, and (4) social justice resulting from businesses insisting on better outcomes for members of local communities where these businesses operate around the world now (Savitz &Weber, 2013). Adopting such a triple-bottom-line approach that emphasizes regard for multiple stakeholders and nonfinancial goals can prove financially rewarding for firms (Peterson, 2013).

The building industry is a sector of the U.S. economy that has noticeably embraced the stakeholder concept and SBP. Through organizations such as (1) the United States Green Building Council (USGBC) that sponsors the LEED (Leadership in Energy and Environmental Design) certification program, (2) PassivHaus, (3) Green Globes, (4) Living Building Challenge, and (5) Net-Zero Energy Building, sustainability has become a strong force influencing architects, engineers, business owners, and consumers (Yudelson, 2008). As of January 2015, the USGBC has certified over 77,000 buildings in the United States and an additional 69,000 worldwide have been certified as LEED sustainable (USGBC.org, 2015).

According to Yudelson (2008), a sustainable building, also known as a "green building," "high performance building," or "smart building" is "one that considers and reduces its negative impact on the environment and human health...[it] is designed to use less energy and water and considers the life cycle of the materials used..." (p. 3). In 2015, the USGBC estimated that 40–48 percent of non-residential buildings in the United States would be classified as sustainable. This represents a significant investment in infrastructure of with sustainability features worth more than $140 billion.

As the recent history of the building sector illustrates, the wider adoption of macro sustainability principles is creating marked economic, societal, and environmental benefits. Not only can a business save money by incorporating SBP concepts, but also it can lead to more efficient operations, to more engaged and more productive employees, as well as to a safer and cleaner environment. Today, for example, Whole Foods Market Co-CEO John Mackey is leading a movement of firms called "Conscious Capitalism." These firms, such as Whole Foods Market and South-Korean steelmakers POSCO, have successfully integrated a stakeholder approach and an ever-increasing number of sustainable business practices (Mackey, & Sisodia, 2013).

CHALLENGES FOR BUSINESSES ADOPTING SUSTAINABLE BUSINESS PRACTICES

Consumer Product Adoption Challenges

Macromarketers of the critical school have asserted that consumers routinely make decisions in the marketplace without questioning much of marketing that furthers an ethos of "more is better" (Kilbourne, McDonagh, & Prothero, 1997). Such macromarketers would assert that many consumers do not realize their consumption decisions are culturally influenced by a dominant social paradigm leading to excessive consumption, rather than sustainable consumption. As sustainability is such a macro-scale issue, consumers may not grasp why sustainability is important. While consumers' reluctance to adopt green product innovations has macromarketing implications, much of this research is "micro," rather than "macro" because of its focus on individual consumer behavior, rather than on marketing systems or society.

Nath, Kumar, Agrawal, Gautman, and Sharma (2014) examined consumer impediments to green product adoption. After doing a review of the literature from the marketing, operations, production, and supply-chain realms from 1970 to 2012, they developed a list of ten factors to explain why consumers resist adopting green products. In general, these factors are similar to those facing all products – especially innovative products that are new to the world which require some learning on the part of consumers to fully understand their relative advantages (Nidumolu, Prahalad, & Rangaswami, 2009; Rogers, 2010).

First, consumers are not always willing to pay a premium for sustainable products. Even if the products are not actually more expensive, many consumers still assume the sustainable product is more than the other product promotion (Dangelico & Pujari, 2010; Drozdenko, Jensen, & Coelho, 2011).

Second, consumers may not trust the sustainable advertisement or promotion. Coddington (1993) stated that "corporate communications are neither relied nor generally trusted as a source of environmental information" (p. 201). Consumers become skeptical of the product and even sustainability in general. Some products will fall victim to greenwashing, which is "intentionally misleading or deceiving consumers with false claims about a firm's environmental practices and impact" (Nyilasy, Gangadharbatla, & Paladino, 2014). TerraChoice (2010) identified that more than 95 percent of the 5,296 products they analyzed committed one or more of seven sins of greenwashing that firms need to avoid. The seven sins include the sins of (1) hidden tradeoff, (2) no proof, (3) vagueness, (4) irrelevance, (5) lesser of two evils, (6) fibbing, and (7) worshiping false labels. Notably, the U.S. Federal Trade Commission issued revised Green Guides to help marketers avoid making misleading claims in 2012 (Federal Trade Commission, 2012).

Third, many consumers may not be aware of environmental issues, why sustainability is important, and how the sustainable product will help the Earth. There has been an abundance of research over the years related to the effectiveness eco-labeling. Rahbar and Wahid (2011) concluded that when customers were not aware of environmental issues, it made eco-labels ineffective.

Fourth, the more consumers become educated about environmental issues, the faster these consumers will adopt sustainable products (Diamantopoulos, Schlegelmilch, Sinkovics, & Bohlen, 2003; Widegren, 1998). In other words, environmentally conscious behaviors tend to increase as education levels rise.

Fifth, in some geographic locations, consumers may have difficulty locating sustainable products. For most consumers, if a sustainable product is not readily available at the time they want to purchase the product, they will not wait and will purchase the unsustainable alternative (Coddington, 1993; Nath, Kumar, Agrawal, Gautam, & Sharma, 2012).

Sixth, there may be many sustainable product alternatives; however, there may not be the support services needed (Nath et al., 2012). For example, if a business in a small community purchases a wind turbine, there might not be the support services there to service the wind turbine when needed. Regarding alternative-fuel vehicles, researchers have found that consumers are hesitant to purchase electric cars because the infrastructure of electricity stations is still scarce in many parts of the United States (Lane & Potter, 2007; Thakur, & Murgai, 2012). While companies like IBM are developing solutions through big data analytics to remedy support service infrastructure problems for electric cars, many consumers remain wary of becoming a pioneer user of electric vehicles (Mayer-Schonberger & Cukier, 2013).

The National Academies of Science has made efforts to bring in the view of marketing academics in advancing the development of electric vehicles by appointing marketing scholar Jakki Mohr of the University of Montana to its Committee on Overcoming Barriers to Electric Vehicle Deployment in 2012 (UM News, 2012). In this way, Mohr and her committee members have helped identify market barriers slowing the purchase of electric vehicles and plug-in hybrids in the United States.

Seventh, consumers might be hesitant to purchase and/or adopt a sustainable product if there is a lack of incentives, such as coupons, tax waivers, grants, and other sources of funding (Drozdenko et al., 2011; Gallagher & Muehlegger, 2011; Nathan, 2011). To combat the lack of incentives, many companies (and governments) have provided tax credits and promotions for those buying sustainable products, such as Hunter Douglas window treatments (some made from recycled materials) that help improve the energy efficiency of buildings (Hunter Douglas, 2013), solar panels for residential buildings (Macintosh, 2011), and fuel-efficient vehicles (Gallagher & Muehlegger, 2011).

Eighth, consumers might feel that sustainable products are not as functional, will not perform as well, and are not as reliable as their unsustainable alternatives (Coddington, 1993). For example, Salmela and Varho (2006) found that consumers perceived green electricity (i.e., solar, wind, etc.) to be not as functional as fossil fuel electricity (i.e., gas, coal, oil, among others.). Researchers have also found evidence that consumers regard products such as detergents and cleansers to be weaker, if the products carry a sustainability labeling (Luchs, Naylor, Irwin, & Raghunathan, 2010).

Ninth, some consumers simply just do not trust sustainable products as well as their unsustainable alternatives (Salmela & Varho, 2006).

Consumers might not trust the product's performance, durability, or long-evity. Additionally, some will not trust the company or the company's mes-saging about the sustainable product or service. Arkesteijn and Oerlemans (2005) found that when consumers were asked why they were hesitant to adopt green electricity, these consumers reported that they did not trust the electric company's claims that the product they were buying (and for which they likely would be paying a premium) was actually sustainable.

Tenth, consumers cautious of sustainable products are not educated on how to integrate them into their daily lives. If consumers are not sure how the green product will change their normal routine, they will stick with the unsustainable alternative (Arkesteijn & Oerlemans, 2005; Salmela & Varho, 2006).

In sum, such challenges to adoption face many new products. Accordingly, marketers of sustainability-oriented products and services should take confidence that similar challenges have been confronted and overcome by successful marketing programs using elements of the market-ing mix (product, place, price, and promotion). Encouragingly, macromar-keting scholars have noted that green marketers have had noticeable success in the marketplace in recent years (Prothero et al., 2010).

Sustainable Communication Challenges

Sustainable Message Framing

The way a sustainable message is framed (e.g., public announcement, gov-ernment order, advertisement, marketing message, etc.) has the ability to influence attitudes and intentions, both positively and negatively, which ultimately influence decision-making behaviors. Chandran and Menon (2004) illustrated through three different studies that positive message framing (showing a "gain") versus negative framing influenced attitudes toward consumer products.

Morton, Rabinobich, Marshall, and Bretschneider (2011) found that a high degree of uncertainty about negative environmental impact using negative framing decreased the intentions for sustainable behavior. By comparison, positive framing about sustainable behaviors increased consu-mers' intentions to pursue sustainable behaviors. Additionally, gain fram-ing led to increased engagement intentions for sustainable behaviors (Gifford & Comeau, 2011). Such gain framing also led to more abstract thinking (vs. concrete) (Cheng, Woon, & Lynes, 2011), and a broader way of thinking about how sustainable reactions might have global implications

(White, MacDonnell, & Dahl, 2011). However, Cheng et al. (2011) concluded that the type of message frame used for sustainability ultimately lies in the type of message communicated (i.e., gain, loss, or threat). In sum, the way a sustainable message is framed and communicated has profound effects on whether consumers will act sustainably.

Sustainable Intentions and Behaviors

Sustainable intentions do not always lead to sustainable behaviors (Barr, Gilg, & Shaw, 2006). To promote sustainable consumption and behaviors, barriers often need to be reduced. Kollmuss and Agyeman (2010) proposed different barriers to pro-environmental behavior: (1) demographic factors, (2) external factors, and (3) internal factors. Demographic factors, such as gender and years of education were not found to influence pro-environmental behavior. However, these researchers did find evidence for the influence of external and internal factors on adopting pro-environmental behaviors. External factors included institutional barriers (no recycling programs in a community) economic barriers (including sustainability payback and lack of money to purchase more expensive sustainable products), as well as social and cultural barriers. Finally, internal factors included cognitive dimensions, such as lack of knowledge about sustainability and perceived locus of control. Internal factors included motivational dimensions, such as attitudes toward environmentally oriented behaviors.

To remove those barriers of sustainable intentions leading to sustainable behaviors, Barr et al. (2006) recommended strategies, such as (1) removing the barriers of change (through education, training, and importance), (2) using policy to promote sustainability, and (3) making sure there is a collective movement toward sustainability. Meng (2015) and Dolan (2002) have echoed the importance of group behavior by proposing that the more widespread sustainable behaviors are in the population, the more likely sustainable intentions will lead to sustainable behaviors.

One part of developing a sustainability movement can be seen in the emergence of online games for learning about sustainability practices. Learningforsustainability.net is one online source for accessing such games (Learning about Sustainability, 2015). Another important part of this collective effect for adopting sustainable practices, such as recycling, comes from the infrastructural support that develops over time. Acquiring recycling bins and implementing a schedule of pick-ups from those bins are examples of hard and soft infrastructure that often can lead to the realization of the goals of sustainability programs.

Researchers have also investigated how consumers' political ideology can influence their receptivity to sustainability messages. In studying how sustainable intentions might lead to sustainable recycling behaviors, researchers found evidence that appealing to the moral foundations of liberals and conservatives can significantly boost recycling behavior (Kidwell, Farmer, & Hardesty, 2013). In sum, if firms want to communicate sustainable business practices effectively, marketers at these firms will have to gauge astutely how politically tinged messages might affect targeted consumers in specific contexts. This might mean creating messages to appeal to political liberals by highlighting how a group will not experience harm by the use of a product or service. For communicating to political conservatives, the same firm might highlight how using the product or service will respect tradition. Alternatively, the same firm might decide to keep politically tinged messages out of their communication campaigns.

Greenburg, KS, a very sustainable U.S. city, had to learn how to communicate sustainable strategies to its residents without overt connections to political affiliation. After a devastating EF-5 tornado flattened the community in 2007, Greensburg had to decide how to pick up the pieces and rebuild (GreensburgGreenTown.org, 2015). They decided to rebuild sustainably. As a result, the community has become a very sustainable small community as evidenced by sustainable buildings and residents who go beyond intending to live sustainably and actually live this way.

When educating the residents, Greensburg leaders decided to keep politically charged phrases out of its sustainable marketing communication. During field research in this Kansas town during the spring of 2015, the second author interviewed town officials about steps taken in the rebuilding of the once devastated town. These officials reported that they deliberately chose to avoid using phrases such as "global warming," "climate change," and "tree hugger." Instead, they used phrases such as "smart living," "sustainable living," and "smart business practices" and avoided the misunderstanding that might have occurred by using terms with political overtones.

THE CHANGING CONSUMER

Consumers' Attitudes Change toward Sustainability

Some macromarketing scholars do assert that increasing numbers of consumers are changing their attitudes and lifestyles to reflect more concern for the environment and society today (Prothero et al., 2010). Three factors that likely account for some of the change in attitudes and lifestyles of consumers include (1) the Great Recession, (2) the emergence of environmentally oriented media and social media, and (3) recommended approaches to business offered by NGOs.

First, the global economic meltdown of 2008 and years-long Great Recession made many consumers re-think the promises of unsustainable economic growth. Although appealing during the boom years of 2004–2007, the economic growth of these years led to the bust that occurred in 2008. Later, leaders of important institutions in societies (such as major depository banks, investment banks, and central banks) appeared misguided and even naïve regarding their own perceptions of risk for their operations.

Although new regulations followed the Economic Crisis of 2008, such as the 2,319-page Dodd-Frank Wall Street Reform and Consumer Protection Act of 2010, it will take years to prove how effective this legislation will be in reducing risk for the financial system (Acharya, Cooley, Richardson, Sylla, & Walter, 2011). Ominously, many former senior executives at the Federal Reserve Bank admit that crises remain hard to prevent and that the Dodd-Frank Act restricts the Fed from taking the drastic actions in future crises that it took in 2008 to save the economy (Appelbaum, 2015).

With the Great Recession still in recent memory, individuals are reconsidering the latitude society had previously accorded to the conduct of business by large corporations and financial institutions. Consumers are turning to other means to save money, gain employment, and give back to society.

Many consumers are moving into smaller houses (Gram-Hanssen, 2015), buying fuel-efficient automobiles, and/or using public transportation (Garling & Friman, 2015). In recent years, many sustainability jobs in architecture, engineering, technology, and business have created new employment opportunities. Consumers are demanding sustainable buildings not only because they are environmentally friendly but also because they save them money. Through the installation of solar panels, wind turbines, low-flow plumbing fixtures, and proper insulation, sustainable buildings can markedly reduce the building owner's recurring expenditures for energy and water usage (Yudelson, 2008). Building smaller buildings and working from home are two other ways to reduce energy consumption.

Chastened by the skepticism of firms many consumers adopted toward business during the Great Recession, many firms implemented corporate social responsibility (CSR) initiatives to become more sustainable. The

European Commission has defined CSR as "a concept whereby companies integrate social and environmental concerns in their business operations and in their interaction with their stakeholders (clients) on a voluntary basis" (Commission of the European Communities, 2001, p. 6). Researchers have found that many firms are using CSR to gain competitive advantage because of a perceived moral obligation ("to do the right thing"), and a desire to boost the reputation of the firm (Piercy & Lane, 2009). Firms are finding that increasing numbers of customers do value CSR initiatives.

Encouragingly, entire communities are turning to sustainable practices. Such initiatives include adding public transportation upgrades (for people who face mobility, hearing, vision, or other impairments), recycling programs, energy conservation measures, and waste management initiatives. Such cities include Greensburg, KS, Chicago, IL, San Francisco, CA, Georgetown, TX, and others. For example, Greensburg, KS has more LEED-certified sustainable buildings per capita than any other city in the United States (GreensburgKS.org, 2015). Chicago Mayor Rahm Emanuel is committed to making Chicago one of the greenest cities in the world (Environment Programs & Initiatives, 2015). San Francisco has banned the sale of water bottles (Timm, 2014), and recently, Georgetown, TX, announced that the city will "get 100 percent of the electricity it provides from renewables" (relying on solar energy during the day, and then using battery-stored energy and wind energy at night) (Gross, 2015).

Second, the emergence of environmentally oriented media and social media has reinforced nurturing attitudes toward care of the earth (Phipps et al., 2013; Prothero et al., 2010). Magazines that promote simple living, such as *Mother Earth News*, and others that focus on environmental issues, such *E − the Environmental Magazine*, are now abundant. Additionally, many books continue to be published about sustainability. These books help raise awareness for environmental issues and what can be done about them.

Video series/movies have been created documenting sustainability. Al Gore's 2006 documentary, *An Inconvenient Truth,* proved to be very influential in raising awareness of global climate change and the role of humans in this change. In the United States, the Public Broadcasting System's e^2 video series is a collection of videos envisioning sustainability through social, cultural, economic, and ecological stances (PBS: e^2, 2010). Case studies and stories are documented from design, energy, transport, water, food, and urban development. For a final example, Discovery Channel did a documentary program called "Build it Bigger: Rebuilding Greensburg" on the devastating tornado and subsequent sustainable rebuilding of Greensburg, KS (DiscoveryEducation.com, 2015).

The Home and Garden TV channel now distributes a show called "Flea Market Flip" where the goal is to buy used items for a home, add value to them, and then sell it for a profit at a flea market. In this way, conservation is reinforced as these used items are up-cycled, instead of being sent to the landfill for disposal.

Social media marketing is also a media platform that has been transforming consumers' attitudes and behaviors toward sustainability. Through social media outlets, such as Facebook, Twitter, Instagram, Pinterest, and others, consumers can follow sustainable businesses, interact with businesses, create grassroots groups to advocate sustainability, pin pictures, and initiate conversation related to sustainability and environmental concerns. Sustainable videos turn viral, grassroots groups can communicate instantaneously with others, and pictures can help depict the reasons for being sustainable (Williams, Page, & Petrosky, 2014).

Third, NGOs have developed and offered recommended approaches to business for accomplishing sustainable business practices (Epstein & Buhovac, 2014). These include initiatives of the United Nations, such as the Millennium Development Goals (Millennium Development Goals, 2015) and the Global Compact for businesses (established in 2001). (The UN Global Compact asked firms to support a set of core values in the areas of human rights, labor standards, the environment, and anti-corruption.) The Millennium Development Goals focused on poverty, health, and the environment issues and proposed a target for completion by 2015. However, while significant gains were made by 2015, the UN adopted a new set of goals called the Sustainability Development Goals (SDG) in September 2015 with a proposed completion date of 2030 (Sustainability Development Goals, 2015). Table 1 presents the 17 goals of the SDG. As can be seen, these correspond to the people, planet and profit dimensions of the triple-bottom-line (Savitz & Weber, 2006), so the important role for businesses in attaining these goals is clear.

The UN Environmental Program (UNEP) created the program "D4S" (Design for Sustainability) for "companies to improve profit margins, product quality, market opportunities, environmental performance, and social benefits" (Design for Sustainability, 2015). The D4S program focuses on a life-cycle model for sustainable products and provides worksheets for firms that guide these firms through the steps required to design sustainable products. Organizations, such as USGBC's LEED-certification program

Table 1. The UN's Sustainable Development Goals for 2030.

Goal 1	End poverty in all its forms everywhere
Goal 2	End hunger, achieve food security and improved nutrition, and promote sustainable agriculture
Goal 3	Ensure healthy lives and promote well-being for all at all ages
Goal 4	Ensure inclusive and equitable quality education and promote lifelong learning opportunities for all
Goal 5	Achieve gender equality and empower all women and girls
Goal 6	Ensure availability and sustainable management of water and sanitation for all
Goal 7	Ensure access to affordable, reliable, sustainable, and modern energy for all
Goal 8	Promote sustained, inclusive and sustainable economic growth, full and productive employment, and decent work for all
Goal 9	Build resilient infrastructure, promote inclusive and sustainable industrialization, and foster innovation
Goal 10	Reduce inequality within and among countries
Goal 11	Make cities and human settlements inclusive, safe, resilient, and sustainable
Goal 12	Ensure sustainable consumption and production patterns
Goal 13	Take urgent action to combat climate change and its impacts*
Goal 14	Conserve and sustainably use the oceans, seas, and marine resources for sustainable development
Goal 15	Protect, restore, and promote sustainable use of terrestrial ecosystems, sustainably manage forests, combat desertification, and halt and reverse land degradation and halt biodiversity loss
Goal 16	Promote peaceful and inclusive societies for sustainable development, provide access to justice for all and build effective, accountable, and inclusive institutions at all levels
Goal 17	Strengthen the means of implementation and revitalize the global partnership for sustainable development

and CarbonTrust, and other NGOs have contributed to raising awareness of issues related to developing sustainable products.

Other organizations, such as the Clinton Climate Initiative, CERES, and Natural Step have helped customers see the value in sustainability and environmentally friendly behaviors. The Clinton Climate Initiative, created by former U.S. President Bill Clinton, helps "energy-hungry cities become more efficient, ramping up green power generation, and keeping the world's carbon-storing forests standing" (Climate Change, 2015). CERES works with firms to incorporate sustainability into their business goals and practices (Ceres.org, 2015). In addition, the organization mandates that results of reports on the environmental impact of the firm be made public. Natural Step Framework, developed by Swedish oncologist Dr. Karl-Henrik Robèrt was adopted and made popular by Interface, Inc.'s founder and CEO Ray

Anderson (Anderson, & White, 2009). The principles of the Natural Step to become a sustainable society include (1) reducing the progressive buildup of substances extracted from the earth's crust (such as heavy metals and fossil fuels), (2) the chemicals and compounds produced by industrial processes (dioxins, DDT, PVC), (3) the progressive physical degradation of nature and natural processes (over-harvesting of forests), and (4) conditions that undermine individuals' capacities to their basic human needs (such as unsafe working conditions and meager wages) (Mager & Sibilia, 2010).

Consumers Notice Changes in Business Operations

Macromarketers have applauded firms becoming more sustainability-oriented in recent years. Wal-Mart's transition typifies some of the most earnest efforts to adopt sustainable business practices. In choosing to emphasize energy conservation, Wal-Mart put compact fluorescent light bulbs (CFLs) at eye level for consumers on the top three shelves (Bonini & Oppenheim, 2008). To increase comfort for the spiral shapes of the CFLs, Wal-Mart installed them in displays of ceiling fans in the stores (Humes, 2011). Wal-Mart pressed its case for CFLs suggesting that it could create its own private label brand of CFLs if light bulb manufacturers did not meet its orders for the CFLs. The results were astounding: Wal-Mart exceeded its sales goals and Wal-Mart customers saved an estimated $40 on electricity over the life of each CFL. For all of the 137 million bulbs sold, $10 billion in electric bills would be saved over the life of the bulbs.

Many consumers are seeing environmentally friendly changes in the company's physical infrastructure: the store. For example, many Wal-Mart stores have installed a grid of skylights on the roofs of their stores. During the day, when it is bright outside, the stores' lighting will automatically turn off when it senses enough daylight. Additionally, many stores are using natural concrete flooring as the finished floor rather than installing a tile or other type of flooring on top of the concrete (Wal-Mart Environmental Sustainability, 2015).

A business that has been implementing sustainability for years is the Japanese-based car manufacturer, Toyota. With their signature Prius hybrid car, Toyota implements sustainability initiatives that focus on society, the environment, and social contribution. With the hybrid Prius getting upwards of 45–50 mpg and the Plug-in Hybrid Prius getting over 95 miles per gallon (mpg), customers have recognized Toyota to be a leader in developing sustainable cars (Toyota.com, 2015). Environmentally, Toyota has positioned the company to be environmental stewards, reducing carbon emissions and greenhouse gasses, managing chemical substances, and contributing to a recycling-based society. Finally, relating to social contributions, Toyota is committed to increasing its research in traffic safety, giving money and its volunteers' time to society, and supporting Toyota employees' volunteer activities and ideas.

Marketers at other auto manufacturers have taken note of Toyota's initial success with more sustainable autos. There is even a luxury hybrid market now where manufacturers, such as Tesla, Mercedez-Benz, BMW, Cadillac, Lexus, and Infiniti are ranked (US News and World Report, 2015).

Businesses and environmentalists have increasingly been working together. For example, McDonald's and Greenpeace have combined efforts to avoid further destruction of the Amazon rainforest (Prothero et al., 2010). After initially criticizing McDonald's in 2006 for buying chickens raised on soybeans grown on illegal farms carved out of the Amazon rainforest in Brazil, the following year Greenpeace joined forces with McDonald's to pressure the major soy traders in Brazil into placing an unprecedented two-year moratorium on the purchase of any soy from newly deforested areas (Butler, 2009).

Consumers Turn toward Green

Segmentation studies of U.S. consumers in recent years have identified the Lifestyles of Health and Sustainability (LOHAS) segment that is the most interested in green products and services (Ottman, 2011). Approximately 13−19 percent of U.S. consumers (nearly 41 million people) would be assigned to the LOHAS segment in 2014 (LOHAS, 2015). These consumers are the most environmentally conscious and physically active of the consumer segments. Demographically, these consumers tend to be married, educated, middle-aged, and female. LOHAS consumers have the second highest income level, so they have the means needed to buy a variety of products and services − and perhaps paying a premium for some of these. This demographic segment represents "an estimated \$290 billion U.S. marketplace for goods and services focused on health, the environment, social justice, personal development, and sustainable living" (LOHAS, 2015).

LOHAS consumers are active in their communities and support environmental, as well as social causes. They are conscious stewards of the environment as evidenced by their energy and water conservation, their use of cloth shopping bags, and their advocacy for environmental causes. They will use the Internet to investigate new green brands, and 71 percent of them report a willingness to boycott brands that offend their values (this is twice as high as any other segment).

Importantly, they are early adopters of green technologies, and are vocal in recommending green products and services to friends. This means that they have an impact (positive or negative) in the diffusion of innovations for any green product of which they form an opinion. In other words, they would play the role of a valued expert on green products and services in their social network. In research conducted by the Natural Marketing Institute, other segments express varying degrees of interest in sustainable living (Ottman, 2011). However, no segment is as committed to green purchasing as the LOHAS segment.

Research aimed at understanding consumers' perceptions of products and services promoted as green or sustainable is rapidly emerging. As previously noted, one set of studies found evidence that consumers may not always view sustainability as an asset for companies or products. Consumers' desire for sustainability dimensions in products depends on the type of benefit they most value for the product category. As previously noted, Luchs et al. (2010) found that consumers associated higher product-ethicality with gentleness-related attributes and lower product-ethicality with strength-related attributes. In categories such as shampoo, tires, and liquid hand-sanitizer, sustainability is a liability for product choice when strength is especially valued. Here, a lack of ethicality is associated with being especially concerned with "getting the job done," even if it comes at a price to others. By comparison, ethicality carries an association of being "gentle" and perhaps even "weak."

An analysis of these results is in order. For example, the study did not perform sub-group analysis on consumers with pro-sustainability attitudes. By focusing on this sub-group the researchers could have understood how consumers, who are the most likely to purchase green products, made associations between the ethicality of companies or products with terms such as "gentle" or "strong."

Another set of studies found evidence that altruism − in the form of buying green products that cost more − signals one's willingness and ability to incur costs for others' benefit (Griskevicius, Tybur, & Van den Bergh, 2010). These results suggest that such altruism is a "costly signal" associated with status. In other words, in addition to signaling that a person is prosocial (doing things for others), altruism can demonstrate both one has the resources (time, energy, money, relationships, or other) and the ability to incur the costs of self-sacrifice for public welfare. Interestingly, eliciting status motives for respondents increased the desire for green products when shopping in public (but not private) and when green products cost more (but not less) than non-green products.

A final set of studies suggested that consumers are becoming more and more aware of green products by the use of green labeling (Whitson, Ozkaya, & Roxas, 2014). In their study, they used Green Seal and Environmental Protection Agency (EPA) green labels and logos on laundry detergent to determine whether respondents would regard the detergent as environmentally friendly or not. The researchers found that over the past 15 years (from 1999 to 2014), environmental awareness because of green labeling has increased. Numerous other studies have demonstrated similar findings that green labels do promote buying environmentally friendly products, however, only to a certain price point. After a certain price point, cost superseded the sustainability attributes of the product (D'Souza, Taghian, & Lamb, 2006; D'Souza, Taghian, Lamb, & Peretiatko, 2007; Sedjo & Swallow, 1999).

It appears that the key question about green consumption is "how rapidly is it being adopted by consumers around the world?" Studies have now identified LOHAS consumer segments of substantial size in 23 countries (LOHAS, 2015). With Wal-Mart's decision to promote green products, such as CFLs, it is likely that green consumption will become part of mainstream consumption in the future. With the accountability mechanisms of the Web and social media in the 21st century, no firm wants to be known for providing products and services that are more harmful to the natural environment and communities.

THE CHANGING FIRM

Factors Influencing Businesses to Adopt Sustainable Business Practices

The study of individual firm behavior would be "micro" in focus, while the study of firms in the aggregate would be "macro" in focus. While explanations of why firms tend to adopt sustainable business practices have been studied for many years, several likely contributing macro factors can be identified (Hollender & Breen, 2010; Millar, Hind, & Magala, 2012; Peterson, 2013). These macro factors can influence firms adopting

Table 2.   Factors Influencing Firms to Adopt
Sustainable Business Practices.

1.	Technological improvements
2.	Rising prosperity and environmental values
3.	Awareness of Earth's limits
4.	Firms can "Do the right thing"
5.	Increasing importance of intangible assets
6.	Rise of non-governmental organizations
7.	Branding as a social phenomenon

sustainable business practices. Even though these seven macro factors do not constitute a complete list, Table 2 presents seven prominent macro reasons more firms are moving to adopt sustainable business practices now. Two of these macro factors deserve special note because of their likely influence on firms adopting sustainable business practices in the future.

First, improvements in technology — especially telecommunications technology — increasingly gives power to individual consumers and citizens. In the networked world of the 21st century, accountability is more timely and powerful than ever. Savitz and Weber (2006) called this the "Age of Accountability." Accordingly, externalities generated by firms, such as the variety and breath of pollutants generated, the amount of waste produced, or the amount of energy wasted, are no longer disregarded. On the other hand, firms that embrace stewardship of the planet and concern for people in their pursuit of profits are more likely to be recognized and rewarded for such an approach to business. Many CSR and sustainability lists and awards recognize sustainability achievements. UPS, for example, uses predictive analytics and sensor data to monitor over 60,000 of its vehicles. In the past to prevent breakdowns, UPS would replace parts on its vehicles every 2–3 years. However, UPS now only replaces parts when needed based on the sensor data (Mayer-Schonberger & Cukier, 2013).

Second, firms now know better how to "do the right thing." Integrated reporting and biomimicry in new product development efforts are two examples of such improved knowledge about how firms can adopt SBP. In integrated reporting, some firms are going beyond creating separate reports for financial and nonfinancial results (e.g., corporate social responsibility or sustainability reports) and combining these into a single integrated report (Eccles & Krzus, 2010, 2015). The Internet, with social media, instantaneous reporting, and word-of-mouth advertising, is reporting more detailed and transparent results to all of their stakeholders, improving their level of dialogue and engagement with a wider set of stakeholders. Wall Street financial analysts have begun to take note in recent years because such integrated reporting contributes noticeable value to the company. Contributions to sound business practices and a more sustainable society make enlightened firms more appealing to many stakeholders – including shareholders (Peterson, 2013).

Using Nature's Principles

In biomimicry, firms can use nature's principles in new product development. Through the imitation of nature (i.e., biomimicry), firms, such as Wal-Mart and Dell are creating more sustainable products and are implementing more effective sustainable business practices. The concept of biomimicry (using nature's principles and imitating its processes) has become a widely used term in sustainability (Nature's Inspiration, 2008). Benyus (2002) defined biomimicry as "a new science that studies nature's models and then imitates or takes inspiration from these designs and processes to solve human problems ... a new way of viewing and valuing nature ... on what we can learn from it" (front pages). Because of the usefulness of sustainability as a strategic business practices framework for improving the efficiency and effectiveness of businesses and society, further consideration of how nature can inform approaches to human activities is warranted.

The "cradle-to-grave" approach in product design features products that eventually wear out and go to a landfill after their useful life. Some of these discarded products are made of plastics termed "monstrous hybrids," such as polyvinylchloride (PVC) that take thousands of years to decompose. Alternatively, architect William McDonough and his chemist business-partner, Michael Braungart, have become leading advocates for a "cradle-to-cradle" approach in product design. Using the McDonough Braungart Design Chemistry (MBDC) cradle-to-cradle (C2C) design protocol, the concept of waste goes away. Using C2C, firms design products, packaging, and systems from the very beginning to be fully recyclable (McDonough & Braungart, 2002a). The C2C concept also designs monstrous hybrids out of products. McDonough & Braungart compared the C2C approach to traditional practice in the following way:

> The characteristic design approach of the last century was "cradle to grave." It involved digging up, cutting down, or burning natural resources – releasing toxic material into the environment in the process – to make products that became useless waste at the end of their useful lives. By contrast, [the] cradle-to-cradle approach mirrors nature's

regenerative cycles so that at the end of its useful life, a product and its component materials are used to make equally valuable products. C2C thinking does not just focus on minimizing toxic pollution and reducing natural resources waste. It goes one-step further, demanding that companies redesign industrial processes so that they don't generate pollution and waste in the first place. (Lee & Bony, 2008, p. 5)

Using as few raw materials as possible in the design of products mimics nature's ways (i.e., "biomimicry"). This makes recycling easier than using many (often synthetic) materials in the manufacture of modern products. For example, MBDC examined the composition of the Aeron desk chair made by furniture manufacturer Herman Miller based in Zeeland, Michigan, and operating in more than 40 countries (Miller, 2011). MBDC found that more than 200 components made from more than 800 chemical compounds were used in the manufacture of the Aeron. Herman Miller used the analysis conducted by MBDC to design its award-winning Mirra desk chair whose dramatically simplified set of materials allows the Mirra to be 96 percent recyclable (Unruh, 2008). Reinforcing the design concept of recycling, instructions for disassembling the Mirra at the end of its life were included with each chair.

Diffusion of Sustainable Business Practices

As previously discussed, the building sector of the U.S. economy offers a rich example of sustainable business practice adoption (Lunde, 2013). Architects and building developers striving to obtain LEED certification for the environmental sustainability of their buildings can use inputs such as ecoScorecard information (from ecoScorecard.org) in choosing the materials and office equipment for their buildings (USGBC.org, 2015). Points toward LEED certification are gained by using environmentally certified products in a building being considered for LEED certification. Products with high ratings not only contribute to the sustainability of the building but also make such buildings less costly to maintain.

Importantly, such green buildings are places that are more productive for employees because such green buildings have better indoor air-quality, superior lighting, and toxin-free furniture. Such products can qualify for the U.S. EPA Environmentally Preferable Purchase Program (www.epa.gov/epp), and for sale on eBay's site for socially and environmentally just products (www.worldofgood.ebay.com). In these ways, environmental certification can give access to buyers and marketplaces where green has benefit.

Firms such as Herman Miller have gained numerous advantages from adopting closed-loop recycling principles of nature's ways in pursuing sustainability for their products. For example, Herman Miller has become a more flexible market player because their procurement process seeks materials that will not be regulated or restricted in the future (MBDC.com, 2011). Herman Miller stopped producing the paneled exterior of its iconic Eames chairs out of rosewood because it recognized rosewood was an endangered species (Michler & Fehrenbacher, 2011). By switching to walnut for the Eames chair, Herman Miller avoided a more expensive material (and one likely to be regulated or restricted in the future).

In the manufacturing process, Herman Miller gained financial benefits by avoiding employee exposure to harmful chemicals and reducing regulatory costs. In the design process, Herman Miller created a source of more readily accessible raw materials by designing products for end-of-life material recovery. The ability to forecast the return of materials to the industry for future use will be the most significant economic gain from intelligent product design imparted by a C2C approach (McDonough & Braungart, 2002b). Finally, Herman Miller won a more defensible position in the marketplace with its products characterized by strong environmental performance. That is, Herman Miller products are higher quality because they were better designed by using the healthiest materials for users that can later be recycled into products of equal or greater value in the next cycle (up-cycling).

Using recycled materials drastically reduces costs. For example, Patagonia's Common Threads Recycling program turns last season's Patagonia's Capilene brand performance underwear into this season's second-generation polyester fibers used in the manufacture of Patagonia clothing. It has also extended this recycling to fleece. Energy costs for making such second-generation polyester are 76 percent below those for virgin sourcing (Unruh, 2008).

Taking a cradle-to-cradle perspective for Patagonia means that the Patagonia website prominently profiles how to (1) buy and sell used Patagonia gear on eBay, (2) send in Patagonia gear for repair at a modest cost, and (3) send in gear for donation to the recycling program (Patagonia.com, 2015). In this way, Patagonia reinforces the idea of the durability of its products in the mind of consumers – an important reason to choose Patagonia (Tueth, 2010). It also positions itself as not only a manufacturer, but also a collaborator with customers interested in reducing consumption. By taking back used products for recycling, Patagonia also assumes a role in reverse logistics — getting the product back from the user for re-processing. This is accomplished through the mail for underwear (that it hopes is clean) and through drop-off bins at retail outlets (Unruh, 2008). In this way, Patagonia nurtures relationships with customers important to its future.

Dell, the computer company founded by Michael Dell, introduced a new policy for all of its employees a few years ago. After hearing reports that firms where computers and monitors are left running overnight were wasting up to $4 billion of electricity annually, Dell decided to require its employees turn off their computers every night before leaving (Dell.com, 2015). After the first year, Dell Computers saved $1.8 million for its 50,000 computers. In Dell's case, the simple process of having employees turn off their computers nightly, it cut costs, reduced energy usage, and increased profits (Harris, 2012).

Along with businesses adopting sustainable business practices, communities have also been focusing on quality of life issues, sustainable community programs, sustainable buildings and subdivisions, and social change policies (McMichael, 2012). Communities such as Greensburg, KS, Chicago, IL, New York, NY, Georgetown, TX, Joplin, MO, and many others have embraced sustainability as a way of life. Some cities develop sustainability policies, such as San Francisco banning plastic water bottles (Timm, 2014), whereas other communities, such as Greensburg, KS, have adopted non-mandated sustainability plans (GreensburgKS.org, 2015). Many of the buildings use wind turbines and solar panels to produce energy. Many of the community's residents grow their own food in gardens. The schoolchildren learn about sustainability every day from their LEED-Platinum school. In sum, many residents look at sustainability as a smart living — a way of life, rather than some policy or thing they are mandated to do.

Sustainable Business Practices Merely a Fad?

Is the embrace of sustainable business practices by more firms merely a fad? Kumar, Rahman, Kazmi, and Goyal (2012) questioned whether the emergence of sustainability as a marketing strategy is the beginning of a new era. However, other researchers affirm that sustainable business practices are here to stay (Windolph, Harms, & Schaltegger, 2013).

Previously, marketers assumed that unlimited consumption was good, the planet's resources and its carrying capacity for waste and pollution were infinite, and that quality of life increased as consumption did, too. In short, resource limitations and externality costs were abstract notions reserved for academic debates. However, these constraints are more evident today as Kotler (2011a) has emphatically asserted.

Despite decades of disseminating marketing principles and techniques focused on finding out what customers want and giving it to them, Kotler (2011b) now emphasizes a new turn for marketing in which marketers need to replace a narrow view of meeting one need for the customer with a more complete view of the customer. People today have many concerns about the future. They hear about water shortages, air pollution, fat in their diet, and rising healthcare costs, among other things. Kotler has called marketers to replace their vertical perspective of a customer with a horizontal perspective where they see the customer's full humanity. "Firms need to show that they share the same concerns that customers do and that they are acting on these concerns" (Kotler, 2011b, p. 34).

Importantly, the adoption of SBP can open the door cost savings (through CSR initiatives, and energy conservation), and innovation (e.g., creating a new sustainable strategy can innovate the marketplace for consumers leading to higher profits and a stronger competitive advantage).

Mish and Scammon (2010) found in their study on triple-bottom-line firms that "these firms develop and offer value propositions based on the inherent interconnectedness of all stakeholders in the marketplace" (p. 12). These researchers asserted that firms wanting to stay interconnected with all stakeholders of the macro-marketplace must change not only their organization, but also engage in channel-wide intelligence gathering, dissemination, and responsiveness. In this regard, firms that want to practice sustainable marketing and the triple-bottom-line cannot only focus on themselves and their own customers, but they have to focus on the macro-market, societal influences, and public policy implications.

Laczniak and Murphy (2012) examined the stakeholder approach to marketing and found that sustainable marketing has to include all stakeholders, and firms have to move from a firm centric to a social perspective. They concluded that if firms want to be successful, they "must realize that serving stakeholders sometimes requires sacrificing maximum profits to mitigate outcomes that would inflict damage on other stakeholders, especially society" (p. 284).

Astute firms these days are working with select NGOs rather than resisting them. For example, as mentioned earlier in the paper, USGBC's LEED-certification program is certifying billions of square feet for sustainable buildings. Existing buildings and/or new buildings can be certified as

LEED-Certified, LEED-Silver, LEED-Gold, or LEED-Platinum through a sustainability checklist (USGBC.org, 2015).

Research has shown that when green behaviors become normal behaviors, as they would when living and/or working in a sustainable building, customers and employees are more apt to behave sustainably (Rettie, Burchell, & Riley, 2012). One example of a NGO that is effective in its work with for-profit businesses is CarbonTrust based in the United Kingdom. CarbonTrust helps businesses reduce their carbon usage and emissions and be overall better stewards to society (CarbonTrust.com, 2015).

Another example of an effective NGO helping to diffuse SBP emerged in the aftermath of the devastating 2007 tornado in Greensburg, Kansas, as a NGO came into existence to help local businesses, as well as the entire community become more sustainable. Greensburg GreenTown, which calls itself a "grassroots community-based organization," worked with city and county officials, as well as with business owners and with the town's residents to integrate sustainable principles into their rebuilding process (GreensburgGreenTown.org, 2015).

THE CHANGING SOCIETY

The influential potential of NGOs in furthering SBP can be seen in NGOs helping firms become more aware of societal changes and their implications for firms (Baker & Lesch, 2013). Much institutional change comes from innovations (Maixé-Altés & Balaguer, 2015; Markin & Duncan, 1981). Examples of innovations can be seen in the realm of NGOs, and in the realm of social media.

First, Kiva is a NGO that most know through its online crowdfunding website (http://www.kiva.org/) Kiva's mission is to connect people through lending in order to alleviate poverty. Kiva networks across the world with microfinance institutions in order to enable individuals online to lend as little as $25 to help create opportunities in developing countries.

Since Kiva was founded in 2005, it has enabled more than 1.3 million to lend more than $792 million in loans. The repayment rate has been an astounding 98.44 percent.

Second, social media has helped sustainability and SBP gain wider acceptance. Before sites such as Facebook, Twitter, and others, it was much harder for businesses and grassroots groups to communicate their sustainability messages (Hutter & Hoffmann, 2013). However, with the rise in social media, SBP initiatives can touch consumers on a daily basis.

Businesses now can easily communicate their role in large-scale sustainability movements, such as reducing carbon emissions to minimize global warming.

New arrangements in society can emerge through the action of governments and regulating bodies (Maixé-Altés & Balaguer, 2015). Businesses can self-regulate themselves, but they may be forced or advised to adopt SBP by governments. For example, in December 2015, the United Nations Climate Change Summit concluded in Paris, France. Representatives of 195 countries negotiated an agreement to reduce greenhouse emissions to mitigate climate change (Davenport, 2015). In the United States, the Environmental Protection Agency finalized the Clean Power Plan Rule to cut carbon pollution from existing power plants. In the electricity-generation sector of the economy, electrical energy service companies will be required to limit their carbon emissions in order to mitigate global warming. However, in other U.S. industries, businesses are not forced but are advised to adopt sustainable business to help lower greenhouse emissions (Pylas, 2015). Other regulations include sustainability policies, recycling initiatives, sustainable building codes, energy, and water reduction bills, among others (Koppenjan & Enserink, 2009).

Market structures change over time. The rise of the Internet over the past few decades made firms fundamentally change how they conduct business. Most businesses today cannot survive without an online presence. Through online presence, businesses have the ability to share their CSR initiatives and other sustainable business practices with stakeholders and society (Quinn & Thorne, 2014).

All businesses are interconnected to create the institution of markets (Bjerrisgaard & Kjeldgaard, 2013). Almost all markets are interconnected today to create the global market. When businesses decide to adopt or not adopt SBP, they are not only affecting their immediate shareholders, but they are affecting society, as well as societies of the world. The interconnectivity of those on the planet has never been more pronounced than today.

CONCLUSION

Naturalists define sustainability as the capacity of healthy ecosystems to continue functioning indefinitely (Unruh, 2008). One can perceive the idea of ecosystem sustainability in the United Nations' Brundtland Commission report as the Commission defined sustainable development as meeting "the needs of the present without compromising the ability of future generations to meet their own needs" (World Commission on Environment and Development, 1987). Today, more firms are pursuing sustainable marketing initiatives, CSR practices, employee training, research and development, product design and promotion, and building design in increasing number (Tueth, 2010).

In this era of the environmental imperative, when sustainability is becoming a force changing the orientation of society, firms will not want to appear indifferent to larger economic, social, and environmental concerns (Kotler, 2011a). As a result, accountability has increased markedly for firms in society (Meyer & Kirby, 2010). With the Internet and social media, entrepreneurs with green innovations are able to keep these in front of possible consumers and investors much longer because of new communication technologies. Sustainability initiatives and marketing strategies are appearing in smartphone apps, websites, restaurant menus, college campuses, corporate strategic mission and vision statements, building codes to name a few.

In sum, calls from macromarketing scholars from Fisk (1981) to Prothero and McDonagh (2015) for business to adopt SBP are now being answered by firms in impressive ways. While sustainable business practices will likely be an increasingly important part of marketing and operations for global firms in the developed world, much remains to be done in moving sustainability forward in firms from developing countries, such as China and India (Kahn & Yardley, 2007). What happens in developing countries in the coming years regarding sustainability will determine how truly sustainability can be said to be a widespread trend in business. Now, more sustainable-oriented firms must commit to global standards of operations (Weybrecht, 2014). Consumers must increasingly choose brands managed by leaders who "do the right thing" for the natural environment and other stakeholders. Marketers would do well not to only adopt sustainability concepts, but to contribute to the development of sustainable business practices, as well. In this way, both consumers and marketers can strengthen the turn to sustainable business practices in societies around the world.

REFERENCES

Acharya, V. V., Cooley, T., Richardson, M., Sylla, R., & Walter, I. (2011). Prologue: A bird's-eye view, The Dodd-Frank Wall Street reform and consumer protection act. In V. Acharya, T. Cooley, M. Richardson, R. Sylla, & I. Walter (Eds.), *Regulating wall street: The Dodd-Frank Act and the new architecture of global finance* (pp. 1–32). New York, NY: Wiley.

Anderson, R. C., & White, R. (2009). *Confessions of a radical industrialist.* Toronto: McClelland & Stewart.

Appelbaum, B. (2015). Skepticism prevails on preventing crisis. *The New York Times*, October 5, p. B1.

Arkesteijn, K., & Oerlemans, L. (2005). The early adoption of green power by Dutch households an empirical exploration of factors influencing the early adoption of green electricity for domestic purposes. *Energy Policy, 33*, 183–196.

Baker, B. L., & Lesch, W. C. (2013). Equity and ethical environmental influences on regulated business-to-consumer exchange. *Journal of Macromarketing, 33*(4), 322–341.

Barr, S., Gilg, A., & Shaw, G. (2006). *Promoting sustainable lifestyles: A social marketing approach.* Exeter: University of Exeter.

Benyus, J. (2002). *Biomimicry: Innovation inspired by nature.* New York, NY: Harper Perennial.

Bjerrisgaard, S. M., & Kjeldgaard, D. (2013). How market research shapes market spatiality a global governmentality perspective. *Journal of Macromarketing, 33*(1), 29–40.

Bonini, S. M. J., & Oppenheim, J. M. (2008, October). Helping 'green' products grow. *The McKinsey Quarterly.* Retrieved from http://www.mckinseyquarterly.com

Butler, K. (2009). Greenpeace: Lovin' McDonald's. *Mother Jones*, August 18. Retrieved from http://motherjones.com

CarbonTrust.com. (2015). *Carbon trust.* Retrieved from http://www.carbontrust.com

Carman, J. (1999). Is macromarketing the kvetch of marketing academia? 24th Macromarketing Conference, Nebraska City, NE.

Ceres.org. (2015). *CERES: Mobilizing business leadership for a sustainable world.* Retrieved from http://www.ceres.org

Chandran, S., & Menon, G. (2004). When a day means more than a year: Effects of temporal framing on judgments of health risk. *Journal of Consumer Research, 31*(2), 375–389.

Chaudhury, S. R., & Albinsson, P. A. (2015). Citizen-consumer oriented practices in naturalistic foodways: The case of slow food movement. *Journal of Macromarketing, 35*(1), 36–52.

Cheng, T., Woon, D. K., & Lynes, J. K. (2011). The use of message framing in the promotion of environmentally sustainable behaviors. *Social Marketing Quarterly, 17*(48), 48–62.

Chouinard, Y., Ellison, J., & Ridgeway, R. (2011). The sustainable economy. *Harvard Business Review*, (October), 52–62.

Climate Change. (2015). *Clinton climate imperative.* Retrieved from http://www.clintonfoundation.org/our-work/by-topic/climate-change

Coddington, W. (1993). *Environmental marketing: Positive strategies for reaching the green consumer.* New York, NY: McGraw-Hill Inc.

Commission of the European Communities. (2001). Green paper: Promoting a European framework for corporate social responsibility. *COM, 366*, 6. Retrieved from http://ec.europa.eu/

Cummins, S., Reilly, T. M., Carlson, L., Grove, S. J., & Dorsch, M. J. (2014). Investigating the portrayal and influence of sustainability claims in an environmental advertising context. *Journal of Macromarketing, 34*(3), 332–348.

Dangelico, R. M., & Pujari, D. (2010). Mainstream green product innovation: Why and how companies integrate environmental sustainability. *Journal of Business Ethics, 95*, 471–486.

Davenport, C. (2015). A climate deal, 6 fateful years in the making. *The New York Times*, December 14, p. A1.

Dell.com. (2015). *Dell environment webpage*. Retrieved from http://www.dell.com

Design for Sustainability. (2015). *Environment for development*. UNEP: United nations environment programme. Retrieved from http://www.unep.org

Diamantopoulos, A., Schlegelmilch, B. B., Sinkovics, R. R., & Bohlen, G. M. (2003). Can socio-demographics still play a role in profiling green consumers? A review of the evidence and an empirical investigation. *Journal of Business Research, 56*, 465–480.

DiscoveryEducation.com. (2015). *Build it better: Rebuilding Greensburg: Green goes home DVD*. Retrieved from http://www.discoveryeducation.com

Dolan, P. (2002). The sustainability of "sustainable consumption". *Journal of Macromarketing, 22*(2), 170–181.

Drozdenko, R., Jensen, M., & Coelho, D. (2011). Pricing of green products: Premiums paid, consumer characteristics and incentives. *International Journal of Business, Marketing and Decision Sciences, 4*, 106–116.

D'Souza, C., Taghian, M., & Lamb, P. (2006). An empirical study on the influence of environmental labels on consumers. *Corporate Communication: An International Journal, 11*, 162–173.

D'Souza, C., Taghian, M., Lamb, P., & Peretiatko, R. (2007). Green decisions: Demographics and consumer understanding of environmental labels. *International Journal of Consumer Studies, 31*, 371–376.

Eccles, R. G., & Krzus, M. P. (2010). *One report: Integrated reporting for a sustainable strategy*. Hoboken, NJ: Wiley.

Eccles, R. G., & Krzus, M. P. (2015). *The integrated reporting movement: Meaning, momentum, motives, and materiality*. Hoboken, NJ: Wiley.

Environment Programs & Initiatives. (2015). *City of Chicago website*. Retrieved from http://www.cityofchicago.org

Epstein, M. J., & Buhovac, A. R. (2014). *Making sustainability work: Best practices in managing and measuring corporate social, environmental, and economic impacts*. San Francisco, CA: Berrett-Koehler Publishers, Inc.

Ertekin, Z. O., & Atik, D. (2015). Sustainable markets: Motivating factors, barriers, and remedies for mobilization of slow fashion. *Journal of Macromarketing, 35*(1), 53–69.

Federal Trade Commission. (2012, October 1). FTC issues revised "Green Guides." Retrieved from https://www.ftc.gov/news-events/press-releases/2012/10/ftc-issues-revised-green-guides. Accessed on October 14, 2015.

Fisk, G. (1981). An invitation to participate in affairs of the Journal of Macromarketing. *Journal of Macromarketing, 1*(Spring), 3–6.

Fisk, G. (2006). Envisioning a future for macromarketing. *Journal of Macromarketing, 26*(2), 214–218.

Friedman, T. (2008). *Hot, flat, and crowded: Why we need a green revolution*. New York, NY: Farrar, Straus, and Giroux.

Gallagher, K., & Muehlegger, E. (2011). Giving green to get green: Incentives and consumer adoption of hybrid vehicle technology. *Journal of Environmental Economics and Management, 61*(1), 1–15.

Garling, T., & Friman, M. (2015). Unsustainable travel becoming (more) sustainable. In L. A. Reisch & J. Thogersen (Eds.), *Handbook of research on sustainable consumption*. Northampton, MA: Edward Elgar Publishing, Inc.

Gifford, R., & Comeau, L. A. (2011). Message framing influences perceived climate change competence, engagement, and behavioral intentions. *Global Environmental Change, 21*(4), 1301–1307.

Gorge, H., Herbert, M., Ozcaglar-Toulouse, N., & Robert, I. (2015). What do we really need? Questioning consumption through sufficiency. *Journal of Macromarketing, 35*(1), 1–12.

Gram-Hanssen. (2015). Housing in a sustainable consumption perspective. In L. A. Reisch & J. Thogersen (Eds.), *Handbook of research on sustainable consumption*. Northampton, MA: Edward Elgar Publishing, Inc.

GreensburgGreenTown.org. (2015). *Greensburg GreenTown website*. Retrieved from http://www.greensburggreentown.org/history

GreensburgKS.org. (2015). *Greensburg community website*. Retrieved from http://www.greensburgKS.org

Griskevicius, V., Tybur, J. M., & Van den Bergh, B. (2010). Going green to be seen: Status, reputation, and conspicuous conservation. *Journal of Personality and Social Psychology, 98*(3), 392–404.

Gross, D. (2015). The Texas town that just quit fossil fuels. *Slate.com*. Retrieved from http://www.slate.com

Harris, J. (2012). Six surprising sustainability facts. *Environmental & Energy Management News*. Retrieved from http://www.environmentalleader.com

Hollender, J., & Breen, B. (2010). *The responsibility revolution: How the next generation of businesses will win*. San Francisco, CA: Jossey-Bass.

Humes, E. (2011). *Force of nature: The unlikely story of Wal-Mart's green revolution*. New York, NY: Harper Business.

Humphreys, A. (2014). How is sustainability structured? The discursive life of environmentalism. *Journal of Macromarketing, 34*(3), 265–281.

Hunter Douglas. (2013, March 15). Federal energy tax credits reinstated for 2012–2013. *Energy Business Journal, 5*(3), 228.

Hutter, K., & Hoffmann, S. (2013). Carrotmob and anticonsumption: Same motives but different willingness to make sacrifices? *Journal of Macromarketing, 33*(3), 217–231.

Kahn, J., & Yardley, J. (2007). As China roars, pollution reaches deadly extremes. *The New York Times*, August 26. Retrieved from http://www.nytimes.com

Kidwell, B., Farmer, A., & Hardesty, D. M. (2013). Getting liberals and conservatives to go green: Political ideology and congruent appeals. *Journal of Consumer Research, 40*(2013), 350–367.

Kilbourne, W., McDonagh, P., & Prothero, A. (1997). Sustainable consumption and the quality of life: A macromarketing challenge to the dominant social paradigm. *Journal of Macromarketing, 17*(1), 4–24.

Kilbourne, W. E. (2010). Facing the challenge of sustainability in a changing world: An introduction to the special issue. *Journal of Macromarketing, 30*(2), 109–111.

Kollmuss, A., & Agyeman, J. (2010). Mind the gap: Why do people act environmentally and what are the barriers to pro-environmental behavior? *Environmental Education Research, 8*(3), 239–260.

Koppenjan, J. F. M., & Enserink, B. (2009). Public-private partnerships in urban infrastructures: Reconciling private sector participation and sustainability. *Public Administration Review, 69*(2), 284–296.

Kotler, P. (2011a). Reinventing marketing to manage the environmental imperative. *Journal of Marketing, 75*, 132–135.

Kotler, P. (2011b). How I do it. *Marketing News*, April 30, p. 34.

Kumar, V., Rahman, Z., Kazmi, A. A., & Goyal, P. (2012). Evolution of sustainability as marketing strategy: Beginning of new era. *Procedia: Social and Behavioral Sciences, 37*(2012), 482–489.

Laczniak, G. R., & Murphy, P. E. (2012). Stakeholder theory and marketing: Moving from a firm-centric to a societal perspective. *Journal of Public Policy & Marketing, 31*(2), 284–292.

Lane, B., & Potter, S. (2007). The adoption of cleaner vehicles in the UK: Exploring the consumer attitude action gap. *Journal of Cleaner Production, 15*, 1085–1092.

Layton, R. A., & Grossbart, S. (2006). Macromarketing: Past, present, and possible future. *Journal of Macromarketing, 26*(2), 193–213.

Learning about Sustainability. (2015). *On-line games for learning about sustainability.* Retrieved from http://learningforsustainability.net/internet/online_games.php. Accessed on October 14, 2015.

Lee, D., & Bony, L. (2008). *Cradle-to-cradle design at Herman Miller: Moving toward environmental sustainability.* Case number 9-607-003. Boston, MA: Harvard Business School Press.

LOHAS. (2015). *LOHAS online.* Retrieved from www.lohas.com

Lubin, D. A., & Esty, D. C. (2010). The sustainability imperative. *Harvard Business Review, 88*(May), 42–50.

Luchs, M. G., Naylor, R. W., Irwin, J. R., & Raghunathan, R. (2010). The sustainability liability: Potential negative effects of ethicality on product preference. *Journal of Marketing, 74*(5), 18–31.

Lunde, M. (2013). Socially responsible green marketing in architecture. *International Journal of Sustainability Policy and Practice, 8*(1), 259–278.

Macintosh, A. (2011). Searching for public benefits in solar subsidies: A case study on the Australian government's residential photovoltaic rebate program. *Energy Policy, 396*, 3199.

Mackey, J., & Sisodia, R. (2013). *Conscious capitalism: Liberating the Heroic spirit of business.* Boston, MA: Arvard Business Review Publishers.

Mager, D., & Sibilia, J. (2010). *Street smart sustainability: The entrepreneur's guide to profitably greening your organization's DNA.* San Francisco, CA: Berrett-Koehler Publishers, Inc.

Maixé-Altés, J. C., & Balaguer, R. C. (2015). Structural change in peripheral European markets Spanish grocery retailing, 1950–2007. *Journal of Macromarketing, 35*(4), 448–465.

Markin, R. J., & Duncan, C. P. (1981). The transformation of retailing institutions: Beyond the wheel of retailing and life cycle theories. *Journal of Macromarketing, 1*(1), 58–61.

Mayer-Schonberger, V., & Cukier, K. (2013). *Big data.* Boston, MA: First Mariner Books.

MBDC.com. (2011). *Value of certification.* Retrieved from www.mbdc.com

McDonagh, P., & Prothero, A. (2014). Introduction to the special issue: Sustainability as megatrend I. *Journal of Macromarketing, 34*(3), 248–252.

McDonough, W., & Braungart, M. (2002a). *Cradle to cradle.* New York, NY: North Point Press.

McDonough, W., & Braungart, M. (2002b). *The anatomy of transformation: Herman Miller's journey to sustainability.* Retrieved from http://www.mcdonough.com

McMichael, P. (2012). *Development and social change: A global perspective.* Thousand Oaks, CA: Sage.

Meng, J. (2015). Sustainability: A framework of typology based on efficiency and effectiveness. *Journal of Macromarketing, 35*(1), 84–98.

Meyer, C., & Kirby, J. (2010). Leadership in the age of transparency. *Harvard Business Review, 88* (April), 38–46.

Michler, A., & Fehrenbacher, J. (2011, April 24). Inhabit interview: Green architect & cradle to cradle founder William McDonough. *Inhabit*. Retrieved from http://inhabitat.com/inhabitat-interview-green-architect-cradle-to-cradle-founder-william-mcdonough/

Millar, C., Hind, P., & Magala, S. (2012). Sustainability and the need for change: Organisational change and transformational vision. *Journal of Organizational Change Management, 25*(4), 489–500.

Millennium Development Goals. (2015). *Millennium development goals and beyond 2015*. UN website. Retrieved from http://www.un.org/milleniumgoals/bkgrd.shtml

Miller, H. (2011). *Where we are*. Retrieved from http://www.hermanmiller.com

Mish, J., & Scammon, D. L. (2010). Principle-based stakeholder marketing: Insights from private triple-bottom-line firms. *Journal of Public Policy & Marketing, 29*(1), 12–26.

Mitchell, R. W., Wooliscroft, B., & Higham, J. (2010). Sustainable market orientation: A new approach to managing marketing strategy. *Journal of Macromarketing, 30*(2), 160–170.

Mittelstaedt, J. D., Kilbourne, W. E., & Mittelstaedt, R. A. (2006). Macromarketing as agrology: Macromarketing theory and the study of the agora. *Journal of Macromarketing, 26*(2), 131–142.

Mittelstaedt, J. D., Shultz II, C. J., Kilbourne, W. E., & Peterson, M. (2014). Sustainability as megatrend: Two schools of macromarketing thought. *Journal of Macromarketing, 34*(3), 253–264.

Morton, T. A., Rabinobich, A., Marshall, D., & Bretschneider, P. (2011). The future that may (or may not) come: How framing changes responses to uncertainty in climate change communications. *Global Environmental Change, 21*(2011), 103–109.

Nath, V., Kumar, R., Agrawal, R., Gautam, A., & Sharma, V. (2012). Green behaviors of Indian consumers. *International Journal of Research in Management, Economics and Commerce, 2*(11), 488–498.

Nath, V., Kumar, R., Agrawal, R., Gautman, A., & Sharma, V. (2014). Impediments to adoption of green products: An ISM analysis. *Journal of Promotion Management, 20*(5), 501–520.

Nathan, C. S. (2011). Marketing strategies for modifying consumer behavior towards green products. *Marketing Mastermind, 5*, 47–52.

Nature's Inspiration. (2008). Nature's inspiration: Solving sustainability challenges. *Strategic Direction, 24*(9), 33–35.

Nidumolu, R., Prahalad, C. K., & Rangaswami, M. R. (2009). Why sustainability is now the key driver of innovation. *Harvard Business Review, 87*(9), 56–64.

Nyilasy, G., Gangadharbatla, H., & Paladino, A. (2014). Perceived greenwashing: The interactive effects of green advertising and corporate environmental performance on consumer reactions. *Journal of Business Ethics, 125*, 693–707.

Ottman, J. A. (2011). *The new rules of green marketing: Strategies, tools, and inspiration for sustainable branding*. London: Berrett Koehler.

Ourahmoune, N., Binninger, A. S., & Robert, I. (2014). Brand narratives, sustainability, and gender: A socio-semiotic approach. *Journal of Macromarketing, 34*(3), 313–331.

Patagonia.com. (2015). *Patagonia's mission statement*. Retrieved from http://www.patagonia.com

Patsiaouras, G., Saren, M., & Fitchett, J. A. (2015). The marketplace of life? An exploratory study of the commercialization of water resources through the lens of macromarketing. *Journal of Macromarketing*, 35(1), 23–35.

PBS. (2010). *e²: The economies of being environmentally conscious*. PBS website. Retrieved from http://www.pbs.org/e2/

Peterson, M. (2013). *Sustainable enterprise: A macromarketing approach*. Thousand Hills, CA: Sage.

Phipps, M., Ozanne, L. K., Luchs, M. G., Subrahmanjan, S., Kapitan, S., Catlin, J. R., ... Weaver, T. (2013). Understanding the inherent complexity of sustainable consumption: A social cognitive framework. *Journal of Business Research*, 66, 1227–1234.

Piercy, N. F., & Lane, N. (2009). Corporate social responsibility: Impacts on strategic marketing and customer value. *Marketing Review*, 9(4), 335–360.

Prothero, A., & Fitchett, J. A. (2000). Greening capitalism: Opportunities for a green commodity. *Journal of Macromarketing*, 20(1), 46–55.

Prothero, A., & McDonagh. (2015). Introduction to the special issue: Sustainability as megatrend II. *Journal of Macromarketing*, 35(1), 7–10.

Prothero, A., McDonagh, P., & Dobscha, S. (2010). Is green the new black? Reflections on a green commodity discourse. *Journal of Macromarketing*, 30(2), 147–159.

Pylas, P. (2015, December 15). Businesses get climate certainty they wanted; now for action. *WRAL.com*. Retrieved from http://www.waral.com

Quinn, F. F., & Thorne, D. M. (2014). Effective communication with stakeholders. In R. P. Hill & R. Langan (Eds.), *Handbook of research on marketing and corporate social responsibility* (pp. 108–134). Northampton, MA: Edward Elgar Publishing Limited.

Rahbar, E., & Wahid, N. A. (2011). Investigation of green marketing tools' effect on consumers' purchase behavior. *Business Strategy Series*, 12(2), 73–83.

Rettie, R., Burchell, K., & Riley, D. (2012). Normalising green behaviours: A new approach to sustainability marketing. *Journal of Marketing Management*, 28(3–4), 420–444.

Rogers, E. M. (2010). *Diffusion of innovations*. New York, NY: Simon and Schuster.

Salmela, S., & Varho, V. (2006). Consumers in the green electricity market in Finland. *Energy Policy*, 24, 3669–3683.

Savitz, A. W., & Weber, K. (2006). *The triple bottom line: How today's best-run companies are achieving economic, social, and environmental success – and how you can too*. San Francisco, CA: Jossey-Bass.

Savitz, A. W., & Weber, K. (2013). *Talent, transformation, and the triple bottom line: How companies can leverage human resources to achieve sustainable growth*. San Francisco, CA: Jossey-Bass.

Sedjo, R., & Swallow, S. (1999). *Eco-labeling and the price premium*. Department of Environmental and Natural Resource Economics, University of Rhode Island. Retrieved from http://www.rff.org

Sustainability Development Goals. (2015). *UN's sustainability development goals*. Retrieved from http://www.un.org/sustainabledevelopment/sustainable-development-goals/

TerraChoice. (2010). *The sins of greenwashing: Home and family edition 2010*. A report on environmental claims made in the North American consumer market. Retrieved from http://sinsofgreenwashing.org

Thakur, A., & Murgai, S. (2012). Is India ready for a green drive? *Indian Management*, 51(6), 22–24.

Thogersen, J. (2010). Country differences in sustainable consumption: The case of organic food. *Journal of Macromarketing*, 30(2), 171–185.

Timm, J. C. (2014). San Francisco bans sale of plastic water bottles on city property. *MSNBC website*. Retrieved from http://www.msnbc.com

Toyota.com. (2015). *Toyota global sustainability*. Retrieved from http://www.toyota-global.com/sustainability/

Tueth, M. (2010). *Fundamentals of sustainable business*. Hackensack, NJ: World Scientific Publishing Co.

UM News. (2012). Press release, October 19, 2012. Retrieved from http://news.umt.edu/2012/10/101912mohr.aspx. Accessed on October 14, 2015.

Unruh, G. C. (2008). The biosphere rules. *Harvard Business Review*. Retrieved from http://hbr.org/2008/02/the-biosphere-rules/ar/1

USGBC.org. (2015). *United States Green Building Council website*. Retrieved from http://www.usgbc.org

US News and World Report. (2015). *Car rankings: Hybrid luxury*. Retrieved from http://usnews.rankingsandreviews.com/cars-trucks/rankings/Hybrid-Luxury/. Accessed on October 14, 2015.

Varey, R. J. (2010). Marketing means and ends for a sustainable society: A welfare agenda for transformative change. *Journal of Macromarketing, 30*(2), 112–126.

Varey, R. J. (2012). The marketing future beyond the limits of growth. *Journal of Macromarketing, 32*(4), 424–433.

Verganti, R. (2016). The innovative power of criticism. *Harvard Business Review*, 88–95.

Visconti, L. M., Minowa, Y., & Maclaran, P. (2014). Public markets: An ecological perspective on sustainability as a megatrend. *Journal of Macromarketing, 34*(3), 349–368.

Wal-Mart Environmental Sustainability. (2015). *Wal-Mart website*. Retrieved from http://corporate.walmart.com/global-responsibility/environmental-sustainability

Weybrecht, G. (2014). *The sustainable MBA: A guide to sustainability* (2nd ed.). San Francisco, CA: Wiley.

White, K., MacDonnell, R., & Dahl, D. W. (2011). It's the mind-set that matters: The role of construal level and message framing in influencing consumer efficacy and conservation behaviors. *Journal of Marketing Research, 48*, 472–485.

Whitson, D., Ozkaya, E., & Roxas, J. (2014). Changes in consumer segments and preferences to green labelling. *International Journal of Consumer Studies, 38*(5), 458–466.

Widegren, O. (1998). The new environmental paradigm and personal norms. *Environment and Behavior, 30*(1), 75–100.

Williams, K. C., Page, R. A., & Petrosky, A. R. (2014). Green sustainability and new social media. *Journal of Strategic Innovation and Sustainability, 9*(1/2), 11–33.

Windolph, S. E., Harms, D., & Schaltegger, S. (2013). Motivations for corporate sustainability management: Contrasting survey results and implementation. *Corporate Social Responsibility and Environmental Management, 21*(5), 272–285.

World Commission on Environment and Development. (1987). *Our common future*. New York, NY: Oxford University Press USA.

Yudelson, J. (2008). *Marketing green building services: Strategies for success*. Burlington, MA: Elsevier, Ltd.

NO THROUGH ROAD: A CRITICAL EXAMINATION OF RESEARCHER ASSUMPTIONS AND APPROACHES TO RESEARCHING SUSTAINABILITY

Seonaidh McDonald, Caroline J. Oates and Panayiota J. Alevizou

ABSTRACT

Purpose — *The purpose of this paper is to examine the ways in which academic researchers frame and conduct sustainability research and to ask to what extent we are limited by these frames.*

Methodology/approach — *Our approach is based on an epistemological critique. We begin with a discussion of the ways in which sustainable consumption has been conceptualised within marketing; we question the influence of positivist social science research traditions and examine how research on sustainability is impacted by the structure of academia.*

Findings — *Our critical reflection leads us to suggest three ways in which sustainability research might be re-framed: a reconsideration of language, a shift in the locus of responsibility and the adoption of a holistic approach.*

Marketing In and For a Sustainable Society
Review of Marketing Research, Volume 13, 139–168
ISSN: 1548-6435/doi:10.1108/S1548-643520160000013014

Research implications — *We propose that in order to make progress in sustainability research, alternative frames, terms, units of analysis, method(ologies) and research ambitions are needed.*

Originality/value — *By making visible our collective, unexamined assumptions, we can now move forward with new questions and agendas for sustainability research.*

Keywords: sustainable consumption; sustainable practices; qualitative research; households; sustainability definitions; attitude behaviour gap

Forty years after marketing academics began to research issues related to sustainability we can look back on much industry within the academy, but not much progress (Baker, 2015; Peattie, 2010). Although many commentators suggest that the problems lie with green consumers who express their wish for, but do not buy green products, we offer here an alternative view: that the approaches favoured by marketing researchers and the assumptions implicit within the these approaches are problematic for studying sustainability. We aim to turn the mirror upon ourselves and thus provide insights based on an epistemological critique.

In this paper we will look critically at the academic literatures that are engaged in addressing aspects of sustainability. By drawing attention to the assumptions implicit within some of these literatures we are able to consider the effect that these assumptions are having on the shape and progress of the marketing field with regards to understanding and facilitating sustainable consumption. We will focus on three inter-related issues: the way that green consumers have been conceptualised; the problems inherent in positivist approaches to researching green consumers and finally the effects of privileging the researcher perspective. Each of these will be considered in turn with reference to work done by ourselves and by others that is situated in the marketing and related social science literatures.

CONCEPTUALISATION OF SUSTAINABLE CONSUMPTION

In this section we will argue that some of the assumptions that marketing researchers have made about green consumers, although understandable, are problematic for advancing our understanding of sustainable consumption. This includes the fact that we have traditionally taken the unit of analysis to be the individual, that we have looked at consumption in isolation and that we have conceptualised individual consumption as either green or not green. We will examine the effect on the discipline of each of these implicit assumptions in turn. First however we will consider the terms used to describe people who participate in sustainable consumption.

The Framing of the Green Consumer

What 'sustainable' means often provokes a lot of technical debate. For example, people question whether it is more sustainable to collect recyclables door-to-door if that means two large vehicles driving around collecting our rubbish instead of one and/or transporting materials over long distances in order to process them, suggesting that the extra fuel consumed wipes out any potential environmental benefit to be had from not simply burying them in the ground. Examples of these narratives abound in both the academic literature and the general media. There are also expert debates on whether sustainability is, for example, best served by buying organic vegetables from a supermarket or buying whatever is in your local independent greengrocer, regardless of organic status. It can be argued either way. And that is because what 'sustainable' is means many different things to many different people, both personally and as part of societal stakeholder groups. Different people will privilege different elements of sustainability according to their own values or preferences in that moment. In our view, these debates are both inevitable, because 'sustainable' is a contested term and pointless because what is 'sustainable' is socially constructed. We prefer to resist attempts to either define or defend sustainability as a term, deferring instead to the multiple meanings we see in our qualitative data. Our concern here is rather to discuss how the terms we use to label sustainable consumption and those who practise elements of it suggest different framings of the same issue(s) and reveal something of the assumptions that different communities of researchers have made about how it can and should be studied.

In the marketing literature, the term 'green consumer' is one which is often employed. This term can be viewed as paradoxical. If we understand 'green' to imply environmental concern, used in this context it suggests someone who deliberately changes or reduces their consumption. The term 'consumer' used in isolation would however tend to suggest someone whose role it is to consume, someone driven by consumption. This point has been made many times before (Peattie, 2001; Pettit & Sheppard, 1992; Redclift, 2005). However there are other problems with this term. If 'green' as a term suggests 'environmental' then some argue that this ignores a wide range of issues related to the social justice (such as fair trade) or the non-anthropocentric (such as animal welfare) elements that they see as an important parts of sustainability. Academics considering these issues often use the term 'ethical consumer' in preference to 'green consumer' in order to signal the kinds of issues they privilege within the notion of sustainability (Bray, Johns, & Kilburn, 2011; Carrigan & Attalla, 2001; Newholm & Shaw, 2007). The term ethical consumer can also incorporate notions of 'doing without' as in reducing consumption, for example voluntary simplifiers (McDonald, Oates, Young, & Hwang, 2006), as well as indicating engagement in alternative consumption patterns, such as moving to fair trade brands. However some use the terms 'green consumer' (McDonald, Aitken, & Oates, 2012) or 'ethical consumer' (Shaw & Shiu, 2002) to encompass all these ideas and more, some use both together (Bartels & Onwezen, 2014) to signal a wider conception than either term alone, some commentators have developed green/ethical as a joint term (Chatzidakis, Maclaran, & Bradshaw, 2012) and some use them interchangeably as if they were synonyms (Young, Hwang, McDonald, & Oates, 2010). Despite the focus on debating (sometimes explicitly, more often implicitly) whether we should be labelling people 'green' or 'ethical' consumers, we will argue later in this paper that two of the assumptions underpinning the notion 'consumer' are potentially far more problematic for researching sustainable consumption than either 'green' or 'ethical'. First the term 'consumer' suggests that the individual is (and perhaps even, should be) the unit of analysis when researching sustainable consumption; secondly 'consumer' suggests a primary focus on the act of obtaining goods and services, as distinct from producing them, using them or disposing of them.

Problems with Adopting the Individual as the Unit of Analysis

Within the Marketing literature as a whole, two units of analysis have traditionally been privileged: the individual and the firm. A great deal of the work done in the field is interested in determining the characteristics and behaviour of the individual and how that translates into markets for products and services offered by firms. Drawing on the norms of base disciplines such as Economics, where the individual is conceptualised as essentially rational and Social Psychology where they are considered as cognitive actors, a picture of the consumer is formed which depicts the individual as independent of context and motivated to maximise economic benefit and/or personal utility. When Marketing turned its attention to matters of sustainable consumption, these same norms have naturally become adopted as part of the lens through which we consider the green consumer.

Consumption is Located at the Household Level
However by listening to research participants engaged in various research projects over a number of years it has become clear to us that these assumptions are not necessarily appropriate for understanding the green consumer. Firstly, we have found that many activities are negotiated at a household level. The most straightforward example of this is the weekly shop. It is easy to see that what is actually bought in a weekly trip to the supermarket represents the needs and preferences of a household rather than the person(s) who is(are) doing the shopping (Miller, 1998). Someone in a household might prefer fair trade coffee; another member might be brand loyal to a specific mainstream brand. This might mean that alternate brands are bought depending on who is actually doing the shopping on a particular week, on the basis of 'turns' or one brand might be privileged based on the negotiation skills or power structures between household members (Scott, Oates, & Young, 2015). We have found the same to be true of other decisions about, for example holiday travel (Oates & McDonald, 2014).

However this is also manifested in less obvious ways. In a project about the process of purchasing sustainable household technologies respondents in rented accommodation reported not being able to buy low energy light bulbs or switch to green energy tariffs (McDonald, Aitken et al., 2012) without their landlord's permission. Consider also the issue of recycling, which is also undertaken at the household level, raising questions about how recycling activities sit within the context of other domestic tasks. Reflecting on these issues led to a study which asked households to tell us who initiated and who practiced the recycling within their households (Oates & McDonald, 2006). The findings of this study show that that different people may initiate and maintain recycling schemes within households and that there may be a gendered element to these roles. There is also a literature about the presence and role of children in inculcating pro-sustainability behaviours within households. Within the education literature, for example, researchers have studied what they term 'reverse socialisation' processes whereby environmental education received by children at school (Evans, Gill, & Marchant, 1996), or through the media (Oates, McDonald, Blades, & Laing, 2013), is brought home and influences the behaviours of adults within the household (Gentina & Muratore, 2012; Gentina & Singh, 2015).

For all of these reasons, the 'consumer', the individual, is too small a unit of analysis for the examination of sustainable practices. Instead we should be looking at the household, or, as Moisander (2007) points out, even the community as a unit of analysis for sustainability.

Rational Actors versus Evidence of Inconsistency
The second concern that we have with using the individual as the unit of analysis is that, as Peattie pointed out in 1999, consumers are not consistent. Having borrowed the notion of the rational, optimisation seeking consumer from Economics, we have made a range of assumptions about the extent to which (non)green behaviours can be explained by individuals, attributed to market segments and predicted by researchers. However researchers point out that many purchases are context specific and that purchase criteria can vary between purchases (McDonald, Oates, Thyne, Alevizou, & McMorland, 2009).

Inconsistency between Attitudes and Behaviours. One of the few things that all researchers engaged in studying sustainability agree about is that there is a discrepancy between what people say they currently do, or will do in the future, and what they actually do (Belz & Peattie, 2012). This phenomenon is known as the Attitude-Behaviour Gap and it takes several forms. In a very few studies the claims (e.g. about amounts recycled) of a specific group are compared to the concrete outcomes of a specific initiative (Barker, Fong, Grossman, Quin, & Reid, 1994; Hamad, Bettinger, Cooper, & Semb,1980). More often however, general reporting of high levels of green attitudes, values or intentions are compared with a lack of sea changes in demand for green products generally (for a discussion of this, see Peattie, 2010) or a low uptake of specific sustainability activities, such as recycling (Perrin & Barton, 2001). The most common approach to studying the Attitude-Behaviour Gap is to firstly conceive of it as a negative effect that is treated as a black box in otherwise logical models of consumer behaviour (such as Theory of Reasoned Action (TRA) or Theory or Planned Behaviour (TPB)) that must be predicted and eradicated. For a recent review of work in this area, see Caruana, Carrington, and Chatzidakis (2015). We have argued elsewhere that this phenomenon is exacerbated by the convention of using self-reports in quantitative research designs (McDonald, Oates, Alevizou, Young, & Hwang, 2012). As qualitative researchers we see levels of self-reported behaviour as revealing the social norms individuals feel compelled to comply with, rather than understanding them as a deliberate attempt to mislead researchers. We will return to this issue in the section on positivist approaches. In fact we believe that these norms mean that self-reported environmental values, attitudes and intentions are all over-reported as well as environmental behaviours. This is a point on which the Attitude-Behaviour Gap literature is completely silent.

Researchers do tend to assume that the gap between attitudes and behaviours that they routinely uncover is the responsibility of the researched and not the researcher. This is an interesting assumption which bears some examination. It is worth bearing in mind that the self-reported behaviour that turns out to be exaggerated is not offered by respondents spontaneously. Rather it is deliberately sought out by researchers who elicit estimates of amounts, frequencies and numbers of sustainable activities from their research subjects, whilst simultaneously invoking the powerful social norms they know skew the very results they are asking for, in the moment in which they are given. In other words, the research design is not a neutral, apolitical vehicle for collecting 'truths', but a socially constructed, loaded instrument that invokes meaning and situated reaction from both the researcher and the researched. Added to this is the oft used convention of using hypothetical questions. It is common, for example, within green marketing to ask members of the public not just how often they buy organic vegetables (thus seeking self-reported behaviour) but also whether they would pay a premium for organic vegetables. Sometimes consumers are asked to estimate how much of a premium they would pay (see Davis, 2013). These research designs are going beyond self-reporting into the realms of asking the individual to imagine how they might respond in a hypothetical, future situation. Obviously, the problems that we have already discussed for self-reporting, would also hold for these hypothetical questions, but we would argue that hypothetical questions have a further set of problems. In our experience, when you ask individuals to talk about recent, actual purchases or behaviours, they tend to describe their behaviours. However when you invite them to talk about what they 'would' do they tend to give answers which describe, not actual purchases or behaviours, but idealised ones (Oates & McDonald, 2014). In other words, what the researcher using hypothetical questions is eliciting is not behaviours, but attitudes or values. The trouble is that researchers, particularly, but not exclusively, within the quantitative domain often do not distinguish between these behaviour and attitude data, conflating them and reporting them all as behaviour without reflection.

Inconsistency between Product Categories. As well as the documented inconsistencies between the attitudes and behaviours of individuals, we have uncovered other inconsistencies through our own research, which we think could be key to understanding how sustainable consumption actually takes place in practice. By asking individuals in a lot of detail about how they approached the recent purchase of technology-based products for their households, we found huge differences between the processes and purchase criteria adopted by the same people for researching and purchasing different products. Our initial reason for asking people to describe the purchase of more than one technology-based product was to build up as large a dataset as possible of detailed purchase narratives that were based on the (non) purchase of each product type. We had assumed, like others before us, that the narratives sourced from the individuals that we interviewed would surface a variety of consumer strategies that would vary *by consumer* but be roughly similar across all a single person's purchases. As marketers would predict that some purchase processes would entail higher levels of consumer involvement than others (DePelsmacker, Geuens, & Van Den Berg, 2013), we felt that we would find differences in the way an individual approached the purchase of a refrigerator and their weekly food shopping. However, because we implicitly fell in with the notion that an individual's knowledge, attitudes and values with respect to sustainability underpin their consumer behaviour we felt it would be reasonable to expect that if someone was the sort of consumer who did a lot of research before they bought a fridge, and then based their choices on the energy performance of the appliance, that they might apply the same process and criteria to their purchase, later the same year, of a washing machine. However, by collecting multiple examples of purchases of white goods and other technology-based household products (from cars and solar panels, to music systems and green energy tariffs) what we found was that there was more similarity between the purchases made by different people in the same product category than there was between the different purchases made by the same person (McDonald et al., 2009). In other words, the same individual will approach purchases in different product categories completely differently in terms of information seeking, purchase criteria and priorities.

There could be a number of reasons for the patterns we uncovered. One might be that some of the sustainability issues are competing and need to be traded off against each other in terms of personal sustainability priorities. For example when shopping for fruit and vegetables, an individual engaged in trying to green their lifestyle might choose to privilege fair trade vegetables over organic ones, or fruit produced locally over fair trade alternatives that have travelled more 'food miles', depending on the aspect of sustainability that they personally felt was most important. Another reason that different criteria might prevail in different product categories is that different sustainability issues are regarded as salient for different products. For example, recyclability might be an important criteria for a product packaged in a plastic bottle (such as ketchup (see Holusha, 1990 for an overview of this 1990s controversy)), but less important for the purchase of a motor car. Although cars are often recyclable, most consumers would tend to view the fuel efficiency of a vehicle as a more significant environmental criterion (Moons & De Pelsmacker, 2015). The criteria that are selected for scrutiny (or not) by consumers is also heavily influenced by advertisers and retailers who privilege some information and information sources over others, as illustrated by the fact that energy ratings are heavily promoted (and thus used by consumers) to judge refrigerators, but the same is not true for televisions. This suggests that individuals acting differently in different product sectors may be a sign of a very sophisticated understanding of both sustainability and the framing of sustainability by the media, rather than the lack of it.

Inconsistency between Contexts. Evidence is also gathering of inconsistency across contexts. Researchers within the travel and tourism domain have been discussing this for some time. They have long established the fact that green views do not translate into green tourism (Budeanu, 2007; Higham, Cohen, & Cavaliere, 2014; Prillwitz & Barr, 2011), in line with parallel discussions of the Attitude-Behaviour Gap in marketing more generally. However a less emphasised variation on this theme is that the same consumer who recycles or buys fair trade or eschews car travel for their commute to work in their everyday lives can act very differently whilst on holiday (Barr, Shaw, Coles, & Prillwitz, 2010). This moves away from the much established refrain that 'attitudes do not predict behaviour' which has attracted a great deal of academic interest from across the social sciences to a different insight: behaviours do not predict behaviours. This is not a new idea. We already know that green purchasing behaviour in one market segment (such as household cleaning products) will not predict purchasing behaviour for a different product group (such as a washing machine) (McDonald et al., 2009). However this new thread underlines a slightly more perplexing variant on this theme: the *same* people don't necessarily demonstrate the *same* behaviours if the context is different. These findings are echoed in waste management research, where we have demonstrated that the same individuals, who have well established recycling routines at home, do not translate that into recycling in their workplaces (McDonald, 2011). In her research looking at household decision-making around a wide range of sustainability issues, Scott (2009) showed that students who held strong pro-environmental attitudes and would always recycle whilst at home, failed to do so whilst living in their term-time accommodation. The reason that some of these differences have not come to light is that research tends to focus on a single context and also focus on behaviour within the domestic context (Oke, 2015).

This evidence suggests that the 'consumer' is in fact too large a unit of analysis. If people are not consistent over time, between product categories, or across contexts then we should instead, as Peattie (2001) suggests be looking at individual (non)purchases as a more appropriate unit of analysis for examining sustainable behaviours. It also suggests that studying non-purchases would be as potentially revealing and valuable for marketers as studying purchases.

Individuals Are Conceptualised as Either Green or Not
Across the social sciences the language used to describe people involved in sustainability tends to suggest that individuals are either green, or not green. Thus in the social psychology literature we find discussion of voluntary simplifiers (Etzioni, 1998) and non-voluntary simplifiers (Shaw & Newholm, 2002). Within the waste management literature, it is usual to refer to recyclers (Vining & Ebreo, 1990) and non-recyclers (McDonald & Oates, 2003). Although marketers implicitly differentiate between consumers who are green (or in some strands of the literature, ethical) and others who are not, there is a tendency not to define what the consumers who cannot be described as 'green consumers' or 'ethical consumers' ought to be called. This is perhaps because, in focusing on one aspect of a consumer's shopping, such as whether they buy fair trade foodstuffs, it might be considered a stretch to refer to consumers who buy fair trade as 'green' (or ethical) even if the researchers only have evidence for one element of that person's green or ethical consumption, but this is a much smaller and less offensive leap of logic that it would be to term someone who does not show any evidence of supporting fair trade a non-green or unethical consumer. This highlights the fact that calling someone a green consumer because one aspect of their consumption is green is problematic. It also

suggests that marketers regard 'green consumer' as a socially acceptable label which will not offend people, and by contrast underlines the unease that marketers feel in labelling a consumer non-green or unethical (the logical opposites of these terms). Wagner (1997) uses 'grey consumer' to describe the group of consumers who are not green consumers and this is a term we have also adopted. This term can be seen as problematic because 'grey consumer' is also used in the marketing literature to signal a focus on older consumers (Carrigan, 1998). Perhaps Ottman's (2011) use of 'browns' to describe those who are not green would be a better alternative. What is important is that we do not simply leave the consumers who are not green undescribed because if we do not offer an explicit opposite for 'green consumer' or 'ethical consumer' (and therefore, if you follow the tenets of sociology, the meaning of the terms themselves) then the unspoken assumption is perhaps that the opposite is the mainstream or (in terms often used by our students) normal consumer. As green marketers, we definitely need to think through the implications of this assumption. Not least because, by extension, this is an assumption that pervades most of marketing, turning green or social marketing into a specialist concern for those colleagues keen to label themselves in this way, rather than a problem that concerns marketing as a whole discipline. In other words, green marketing is conceived of as working to serve specialist interests rather than towards a paradigm shift.

Whether the opposites of terms like 'green consumer' and 'ethical consumer' are made explicit or not, the fact remains that within these social science literatures it has become the norm to conceptualise these as two, mutually exclusive groups. There are two ways in which researchers have tried to complexify this picture. The first is by conceptualising more than two (still mutually exclusive) groups, usually placed along a continuum. For example, Prothero (1990) uses the terms 'light green' and 'dark green' and Barry (1994) examines the notions 'shallow green' and 'deep green'. What is implied here is that people might start off in the less green groups and move gradually towards the more green groups. We have taken this approach in the past, arguing that rather than just voluntary simplifiers and non-voluntary simplifiers, it was useful also to consider a middle, transitionary group, that we termed beginner voluntary simplifiers (McDonald et al., 2006). The second approach is to produce typologies of green consumers which emphasise different ways of being green as opposed to different degrees of greenness. The most famous of these is probably the typology produced by Ottman (1993), based on work by The Roper Organisation (1992) which segregates individuals into two non-green groups (basic browns who have no interest in green issues and grousers who feel that it is someone else's problem), two green groups (greenback greens who spend money to be green but otherwise don't change their lifestyles, and true blue greens who are very active in a range of areas) and a 'swing' group (sprouts) who are uncertain on whether to back the environment or the economy in their decision-making. Even where attempts have been made to offer multiple groups, or different positions on a continuum (such as do Paço & Raposo, 2010) there is still an implicit assumption that these groups are homogeneous: that one green consumer is like another.

In our research we have also surfaced a typology of green consumers who we distinguish from each other in terms of the ways that they are greening their lifestyles (McDonald, Oates et al., 2012). Our qualitative work uncovered people who concentrated on one (or several) specific area(s) of consumption, such as waste, or organic food (selectors), people who passively waited to be told how to respond to sustainability, but then more or less responded as directed (translators) and people with a sophisticated and active orientation to comprehensively greening their lifestyles who nevertheless allowed themselves one or more non-green exceptions (exceptors). These sorts of typologies are more meaningful because they help us to understand that different people can be equally (or perhaps better to say equivalently) green in very different ways. By emphasising the similarities of greening processes and examining *how* people are greening, rather than *what* they are greening, it is possible to draw out similarities within groups of people that are meaningful for marketers but still allow for an appreciation of the heterogeneity of individual experiences. This rather goes against the quantitative research conventions embedded within segmentation approaches and we will come back to this issue when we discuss the limitations of quantitative approaches in the section 'Positivist Approaches'.

To characterise individuals (or households, or purchases) as green or not green is an increasingly unrealistic shortcut in thinking. Over the course of our research it is becoming harder and harder to find people who have no sustainable behaviours at all. It is still possible to find people who have wholly anti-sustainability attitudes, of course, but since social norms across Europe around recycling have changed beyond recognition and some decisions are being taken out of consumers' hands (such as Cadbury making all of its product offerings with fair trade chocolate and the EU law changes making it impossible to buy incandescent light bulbs) it is less and less likely that we will find European consumers who have no green elements in their lifestyles, whether they like it or not. Equally, no matter how hard a household tries to reduce its environmental impact or control its carbon emissions, it is very hard indeed wholly to embrace sustainability in the context of Western capitalism without seeking the kinds of self-sufficiency and off-grid living that would permit households to live without earning income and interacting with society. The research that underpins our typology (McDonald, Oates et al., 2012) helped us to re-examine this assumption that people are 'green' or 'grey' (or any other set of poles on a continuum) and understand that every one of us is caught in a tension between green and grey, or perhaps between social pressures to be green and social pressures to ignore green. Equally, it underlined the need to conceptualise everyone, even very committed green consumers, or the most cynical 'browns' as being in the process of greening whether this process is conscious and willing or not.

A Shift in How We Conceptualise Individuals Approaching Sustainability
In the section 'Consumption Is Located at the Household Level' we reflected that since consumption, use and disposal are located at the household, rather than individual, level that the consumer is too small a unit of analysis. In the section 'Rational Actors versus Evidence of Inconsistency' we argued that because consumers do not necessarily act on their espoused values and are not consistent over time, between product categories or across contexts that the consumer is too large a unit of analysis. In the section 'Individuals Are Conceptualised as Either Green or Not' we pointed out that because no one is wholly 'green' or 'not green' but rather caught between the two, it doesn't make sense to think of any person or purchase in these terms. Taken together, what we are proposing is that the individual is both too small and too large a unit of analysis for researching sustainability. We suggest that what is needed instead is analysis at the level of the stream of (probably inconsistent) individual purchases and activities but examined in the context of whole households, or even communities. We further suggest that this requires a dynamic rather than static understanding of 'green' which will need to be supported by research that looks at these households over time.

   This view of greening raises a number of quite profound critiques of the extant marketing literature. For example, research which centres on the notion of the Attitude-Behaviour Gap is assuming that there is, or could be, a relationship between an individual's attitudes (or in some work, values/beliefs) and their behaviour. However our discussion of inconsistencies demonstrates that this is unlikely to be the case as we have demonstrated in previous work that the same people act differently over time, between product types and across different contexts. If there was a straightforward relationship between attitudes and behaviours then you would expect to find that people tended to make the same, or similar decisions each time, approach the purchase of different product types in roughly equivalent ways and transfer their behaviour in one part of their lives (home) to other parts (such as work). So this reconceptualisation represents a rejection of the assumptions that much of the work that discussions of the Attitude-Behaviour Gap is based upon. This will include popular models such as the Theory of Planned Behaviour and the Theory of Reasoned Action which have been widely used in green consumer behaviour research (Armitage & Conner, 2001 for a review) and these insights suggest that a careful review of the usefulness of this kind of work for understanding greening would be appropriate.

This reconceptualisation offers an important insight into the problems associated with another major area of marketing endeavour: the quest to identify (and then segment) the green consumer. There is a vast academic literature and a great deal of practitioner market research aimed at trying to pin down the green consumer using demographics, psychographics and socio-demographics. The intent is clear: If you can identify them, you can segment and then target them with green products or services. This is seen as an important endeavour both for those designing green products and services and for those trying to promote their uptake. There is some agreement amongst commentators that this endeavour has been somewhat less than successful (Diamantopoulos, Schlegelmilch, Sinkovics, & Bohlen, 2003; Peattie, 2010; Straughan & Roberts, 1999). The challenges presented to the notion of a 'green consumer' outlined here help to explain this failure to identify such a creature. In other words, the inability of all the studies of demographics and psychographics and socio-demographics to identify the green consumer is not really a failure: it is a resounding endorsement of the points made here.

Problems of conceptualising the individual as the unit of analysis are not however confined to quantitative approaches. With the emphasis on the individual interview as the research approach of choice within the qualitative research community, this assumption has also been allowed to go largely unquestioned within many qualitative studies. This technique also allows an implicit privileging of the individual viewpoint, an acceptance that the espoused narratives will represent actual rather than idealised accounts (Potter & Hepburn, 2005) of pro-sustainability behaviours and provides the researcher the opportunity to use the account of one person as a proxy for understanding the behaviours of a household in the same way as a quantitative study would.

Returning to the earlier discussion of how to label people engaged in sustainable consumption having considered the problems of using individuals as a unit of analysis we question the framing of terms such as 'green consumer' or 'ethical consumer' which both assume and perpetuate the norm of making individuals the focus of our inquiry. In order to move away from this mindset, terms like 'sustainable consumption', 'greening' or even 'green behaviour' are more appropriate, although they still have problems of association ('consumption' precludes production and disposal; 'green' suggests only environmental aspects) for a conceptualisation of sustainability research which is concerned with (inconsistent) streams of activities set within shared household contexts. Despite its limitations, 'greening' has the advantage of signalling the dynamic and incomplete nature of change and also highlights the notion of process rather than implicitly emphasising the role of values as 'green consumer' does. New terms like 'sustainable behaviours' or 'sustainable practices' (Black & Cherrier, 2010) are even more neutral, and we suggest therefore useful, in this respect.

The Emphasis Is on Consumption

The second problem with the term 'consumer' is that it implies an emphasis on consumption (or even just purchase) (McDonald & Oates, 2006) rather than seeing it as part of a much larger, integrated, inter-dependent system of production, consumption (including both purchase and use) and disposal (Alevizou, 2011). The preoccupation with the point of purchase is a natural one for marketing as an academic domain. It is also broadly in keeping with the norms of free-market capitalism where the consumer is the key figure at the meeting point between the forces of supply and demand. Even in the broader focused domains of social marketing and public policy, the consumer is often depicted as a key instrument of change, shouldering the responsibility for changing the world though their personal agency and their purchasing power. It could be argued that although many marketing literatures are silent on the issues of production, and disposal, this falls outside the scope of their domain. There are of course whole other literatures dedicated to production. There are green debates within the design, production, quality, energy and supply chain management literatures, to name a few. The same is true of disposal, with separate, well-developed environmental literatures in the field of waste management. These do tend to focus on technical aspects and are predominantly quantitative in nature. Perhaps because social sciences such as marketing are seen as taking care of the problem of the consumer, and perhaps because they are heavily grounded in the norms of natural science, production (and to some extent disposal) is seen as neutral and unproblematic and as something that is ultimately caused by the (bad) consumer.

It is important to focus research on specific parts of this whole, but it is equally important not to lose sight of the fact that they are just that: parts of a whole. We will argue in the next section that researchers have been keen to implement positivist conventions of simplifying reality in order to research it, and reducing systems to their constituent parts in order to study them, but we have forgotten that they are positivist conventions and that they do not represent our social reality: we have forgotten to put them back together and see individual studies, and even individual disciplines as pieces of a much bigger jigsaw.

POSITIVIST APPROACHES

Positivist understandings of economic behaviour have been translated for greening. So for example, consumers' decisions are imagined to be consistent and rational. As we have discussed already, both of these assumptions are unhelpful in the study of sustainability. They are also assumed to be apolitical.

Positivist approaches are evident throughout marketing thinking about sustainability at the micro, practical level of individual research designs. For example, our earlier discussion about surveying individuals, asking them what they recycle and then mapping their demographic, psychographic or socio-demographic characteristics against self-reports of behaviour demonstrates a number of positivist assumptions that are problematic for understanding sustainability. The assumption that self-reported behaviour (or in the willingness to pay literature, intention to act in a hypothetical situation) will approximate actual behaviour is one made out of a wish to (a) simplify the situation and (b) make it researchable using a survey. We contend that the question should not be: how can we frame a research question that can be answered using a survey; but rather, what do we need to know about recycling habits and what research instrument would best approach these issues. What is problematic here is that it is a convention that has become largely unquestioned in the marketing, and wider management literature. However even a cursory reflection on whether self-reported behaviour or hypothetical questions will be an accurate representation of actual behaviour would lead most of us to see this as an unconvincing conflation of intention with behaviour. The other positivist convention at work here is to conflate behaviour with intention. In other words, if someone recycles, we 'count' them as a recycler without any knowledge of their intentions. In a study of plastics recycling in the 1990s (McDonald & Ball, 1998), a questionnaire was developed to ask people about their recycling habits. Five hundred people were stopped in the street and asked about their perceptions of different materials, their recycling of these same materials and some classification data were gathered relating to their age, gender, employment and income level. Imagine that one of the authors of this paper had answered these questions. A picture might be painted from their data of an informed and committed recycler. And this would be more or less an accurate and appropriate description. However imagine now that one of our long suffering partners was stopped in the street and asked the same questions. Their reported recycling behaviour is excellent, as befits a person living with an informed and committed recycler. However the question of whether they would have developed these recycling activities independently is something that a survey recording their behaviour and collecting their classification data cannot inform. The effect that their classification data will have on the aggregate picture of 'who recycles' will be to contribute to a misleading view of the recycler. Equally, if someone refuses to be part of a kerbside paper recycling scheme we might decide that they are a 'non-recycler' without realising that they have decided to share a paper bin with their neighbour in order to minimise the environmental impact of the council collecting two half full bins (McDonald & Oates, 2003). This is best explained with reference to a different study. We found that two people can buy the same very energy efficient fridge in the same city, with a similar amount of background research within a few months of each other for an identical price, but do so with very different intentions, criteria and, ultimately meanings attached to these purchases. One might select the fridge for its A + + energy rating, whilst the other might buy it because it matches his kitchen. Annoyingly these fridge shoppers could even belong to the same household and be relating the (completely different) stories of how they came to buy the same fridge. This is not a problem for a qualitative study like ours, trying to understand how people buy fridges (Young et al., 2010) because we accept that the fridge has simultaneous, contested meanings and that there is no single 'true' story of how it came to be purchased. However it is easy to see how a researcher looking at the results of a quantitative survey could record the A + + fridge as an environmental purchase, associating this with the demographic characteristics of only the survey participant and conflating behaviours with intentions. People carry out sustainable actions for a whole host of reasons. They cycle to work to keep fit rather than reduce carbon, they eat organic food for taste reasons, not caring whether they reduce the use of pesticides. We have even found that many people who start 'green' businesses do so because they see it as an entrepreneurial opportunity rather than because they have environmental values (Gan, 2010). The simplification of concepts required to operationalise research questions through a questionnaire and the habit of conflating intentions and behaviours conspire to make data collection less meaningful in these situations. Further, a reliance on quantitative instruments has long masked problems with individuals as a unit of analysis, as discussed above.

There is also evidence of positivist assumptions running through the field of marketing at a macro level. It is our view that a positivistic drive to dissect and simplify complex problems has reinforced the fragmentation in the ways in which we study sustainability issues. Once split up at the level of individual approaches to specific activities (e.g. by studying only purchasing of fair trade coffee, or only the recycling of plastics in the United Kingdom) this is compounded by the need to undertake a degree of simplification of the problem so that individual components can be reliably measured, and their relationships modelled. Within this reductionist approach there is an implicit assumption that the pieces can be put back together, but often this is never attempted. There is a conspicuous dearth of sense-making work which seeks to stand back and look at how all the incremental measuring and modelling activity actually looks as a body of explanation within each fragment of the literature, let alone how each of the fragments fits together. Worse, we suspect that if this was attempted that we would find that the sum was in fact much less than the sum of its parts. This is at least in part due to the faulty positivistic assumptions that activity in one realm might be thought of as 'equivalent' to activity in another. Quantitative researchers hope that at worst this will mean that what we learn about recycling will transfer to the purchase of ethical bank accounts, and at best the presence of activity in one domain will allow the prediction of activity in another. However qualitative approaches demonstrate that this is simply not the case (McDonald, Oates et al., 2012).

Throughout a number of the marketing discourses surrounding the green consumer, the failure to identify the green consumer and/or predict their behaviour has been implicitly understood as a failing on the part of the green (or not-so-green) consumer. In the work on Attitude-Behaviour Gap, for example, when these models such as TPB and TRA fail to explain or predict consumer behaviour it is often implied that consumers are over-reporting their intentions. Sometimes this is portrayed in a relatively neutral way, depicting consumers as subject to social pressures to be 'seen to be green' or as exaggerating in order to please the (presumably green) researcher as part of a natural social process of emphasising what you have in common with those with whom you interact. Sometimes, though the implication is framed (but never stated) more negatively: consumers do not answer surveys honestly; consumers say they are green but they are too lazy/uncaring/selfish/short-termist/miserly to actually do what they have said they will.

Related to this is the reaction of the research community to research like ours which surfaces the inconsistencies in individual behaviour. Reporting of inconsistencies is often met with the assumption from our peers that we regard this as a negative finding: that inconsistency is bad. There is of course no reason to assume that inconsistency is negative, but it is a positivist convention to assume that consistency (predictability) is positive and inconsistency is therefore not. Flowing from this assumption, as a field we tend to read these as inconsistencies as due to some lack in the consumer, such as a lack of complete knowledge, a lack of capacity to take a large number of complex factors into account, or simply (and more neutrally) a lack of agency associated with financial or other constraints. In fact we suggest (from a qualitative perspective) that these are not evidence that the inconsistent consumer is bad, but that instead it may speak to the importance that context plays on sustainability decisions. Equally it suggests that methods of inquiry based on assumptions of rational actors that concern themselves with developing models with causality at their heart that have the ability to predict behaviour might not be best suited to the work of examining sustainability.

These negative framings of the consumer are interesting to us because they suggest that researchers (and policy makers) lay the blame for the lack of green consumption at the door of the consumers. In fact we suggest that there is another type of 'failure' which is not being considered. If research is not identifying and explaining green behaviour, might that not in part be a failure of the research design? We suggest that this disconnect between the theory and reality of green consumption can at least be partly explained by the problems of relying on positivist assumptions about behaviour and using positivist research instruments for the task of researching green behaviour. This lack of critical reflection about the limitations of our own assumptions and approaches is linked to the problem, set out in the next section, of privileging the researcher perspective.

PRIVILEGING THE RESEARCHER PERSPECTIVE

Within the social science discourses surrounding sustainable consumption there is an explicit privileging of the view of sustainability that is framed by the assumptions and needs of the academy. This is of course inevitable because the discourses are produced by and intended for fellow academics. However some of the assumptions implicit in this framing are worth highlighting because of the effects that they have on the research that is and can be done on sustainable consumption. We will consider two main issues here: the academic lens and the structures of the academy.

The Academic Lens

When academics enter the field they bring social science terms for the things they see. This can help by tying the phenomena they observe back to wider debates, however it can also hinder the progress of the field. Following an immersion in the plastics recycling literature, a waste management academic would be forgiven for developing a tendency for naming bottles according to the names of the polymers used to manufacture them. Those commonly present in UK domestic waste are PET, PVC, LDPE and HDPE. On entering the field however she might learn that consumers, who do not purchase plastic bottles in order to own them, but rather to consume their contents know them by what they contain (coke bottles, water bottles, milk bottles and washing up liquid bottles), or by where they are stored within the household (bathroom bottles, kitchen bottles). The assumption that the naming of things belongs to academics is a positivist one (see section on Positivist Approaches) and can hamper dialogue within the field, weakening research results and dissemination of research findings to the field, reducing its impact on practice.

In fact inductive research with householders in Sheffield led us to the revelation that although as academics we conceive of recycling as a green activity, an everyday act of green consumerism (or even green activism) our respondents understood it quite differently: as housework (Oates & McDonald, 2002). Similarly, although production, consumption and disposal might all seem like separate issues to an academic and thus be reported in different and separate literatures we find that these are not understood or treated as separate issues by consumers (McDonald & Oates, 2006) who see traces of the whole system embedded in the products and services they select. So in a real life decision-making process the energy efficiency of production, the ethics of the retailer, the organic status of the product and the recyclability of the packaging might all be considered simultaneously, or traded off against each other for a single purchase.

The Structure of the Academy

We have already alluded to the fact that there is a high degree of fragmentation of research into various aspects of sustainability across the social sciences. Some of the divisions of labour that have grown up within disciplines and between literatures seem quite straightforward and understandable. It is easy to see the logic of writing about purchasing behaviours in the marketing literature, but discuss recycling activity in the waste management literature. However others seem more arbitrary to the casual observer. For example, discussions about holiday travel are situated in the travel and tourism literature but journeys related to commuting are considered in the transport literature. This leaves us wondering what happens to studies of academics travelling to far flung destinations in order to attend sustainability conferences as this would be work-related travel which could not be considered commuting. Similarly, studies of recycling at home can be found in the waste management literature but studies of recycling at work are part of the Organisational Citizenship Behaviour literature, which is part of Organisational Behaviour, a strand of the Management literature. And if your purchasing behaviour is related to a green energy tariff you should expect to find this discussed, not in the marketing literature alongside a myriad of other purchasing behaviours, but in the energy literature. As previously mentioned, there is also a disconnect between literature which considers the environmental aspects of the production, purchase, use and disposal of the same object. So the chances of anyone putting together any kind of big picture from this wealth of knowledge is quite small and it is beginning to look like the work in these areas is parallel and not cumulative.

Just to complicate the issue further, these issue-specific debates are underpinned by a variety of base disciplines including social psychology, geography, management, marketing and social marketing. Each of these disciplines favours slightly different research conventions. This can be illustrated by the somewhat trivial example of the range of labels that are used to describe people engaged in sustainability activities. Some of these labels are discipline specific; for example, they are referred to as green consumers in the mainstream marketing literature and ethical consumers in the ethics literature and the sustainable development literature, as discussed above. In other parts of the literature they are variously termed voluntary simplifiers (McDonald et al., 2006), downshifters (Nelson, Rademacher, & Paek, 2007), ecologically conscious consumers (ECC) (Roberts & Bacon, 1997) or citizen consumers (Scammell, 2003). Terms used to describe their behaviours include: Environmentally Responsible Behaviours (ERBs) (De Young, 2000); pro-environmental behaviours (Steg & Vlek, 2009); Organisational Citizenship Behaviours (Daily, Bishop, & Govindarajulu, 2009) and ecological consumer behaviour (Fraj & Martinez, 2007). This plethora of terms is unhelpful, as previously discussed, at a conceptual level, but also, importantly, at a practical level. It is simply very difficult to find work from disciplines other than your own because searching won't necessarily pick them up if you don't already know what terms they use.

These are all ways of dividing the debates and although they are helpful to academics in that they reduce the scope of the field making the vast and unruly literature which is relevant to sustainable consumption more manageable in terms of the individual paper, ultimately this false partitioning of the field (through discipline boundaries and language) is unhelpful because it stops the insights garnered in one academic's work flowing through the whole community of scholars engaged in sustainability research. This means that we are channelled into tackling the problem of greening as a series of separate activities. It also means that we are reinventing the wheel. The alternative is cross disciplinary scholarship which means either teams of social scientists or large (career slowing) investments by individuals in many literatures.

The problem of compartmentalising discipline-based fragments of the sustainability debate is reinforced by the institutional structures in the academy. In many disciplines (Business & Management and Marketing among them) the emphasis is on the peer-reviewed journal article as the most privileged form of output (Wells, 2010). This means that all of our insights need to be delivered in circa 8,000 word fragments. Other, less constrained vehicles for the dissemination of research ideas such as books are much less valued within some academic disciplines and will not win an individual who writes them the peer esteem or publication record required to access any of the career rewards available from appointments panels, promotions boards and funding bodies. For some disciplines (again, we speak from a position of familiarity with the Marketing and Business & Management literatures) it is not sufficient to constrain researchers in terms of the type of output that is acceptable, but there is also a privileging of journals that are considered to be within discipline. This discourages individuals from publishing in (and therefore reading and engaging with) research written by researchers outside their immediate field. With increasing competition for publications in the top journals, journals have become gatekeepers for academic success. They privilege work which is squarely within their discipline norms and it becomes very difficult to publish multi-disciplinary work, or work which steps outside or challenges those norms. This makes the very kind of work that is needed to address problems of sustainability the very kind of work that you would not recommend to your colleagues in career progression terms.

The game becomes to publish papers on sustainable consumption rather than to solve the problems of sustainable consumption.

IN SUMMARY

In summary then, what we are saying is that *pro-sustainability attitudes (or intentions) will not predict pro-sustainability behaviour*. Although we have argued that research designs conflate attitudes and behaviours and that the approaches to recording and 'measuring' these are both flawed, we are suggesting that even if we resolved these methodological and empirical issues, researchers would still not find a strong correlation between attitudes and behaviours. This is not a novel statement. It has been borne out by the cumulative efforts of 40 years of social psychology and green consumer behaviour research and is conceptualised within these literatures as the Attitude-Behaviour Gap. However we further suggest that evidence of *pro-sustainability behaviour will not predict pro-sustainability attitudes*. It is misleading to interpret statistics about the use of public transport or the purchase of organic food as evidence of a greening population, as we have demonstrated here with illustrative anecdotes from our own research. Crucially though, we would also maintain that emerging evidence from the research of others, as well as ourselves shows that *pro-sustainability behaviour will not predict pro-sustainability behaviour* over time, between product categories or across contexts. Thus whilst we are saying that segmentation approaches have been deeply flawed methodologically we suggest that the deeper understanding of greening strategies and the meanings and minutiae of sustainable practices that our work represents present a more profound, epistemological and ontological challenge to extant approaches to green marketing. It is not that segmentation approaches and assumptions about the ability of marketers to interest a consumer engaged in one 'green' activity to take up another are just badly designed: it is that they are wholly irrelevant. And that this is partly made inevitable by the very structures and practices of the academic institutions of which we are all a part.

NO THROUGH ROAD: MOVING FORWARD

Based on the cumulative insights from work done by ourselves and others whose approaches have kinship with our own, this critical reflection on the norms and assumptions of marketing as a discipline and as an academy suggests a number of ways forward for researching sustainability. As will be evident from the discussion that follows, these should be viewed as inter-dependent.

We suggest that debates about what to call what we do are not trivial: These terms underpin our conceptualisations going forward and profoundly affect the research we design and the questions we can ask and cannot ask. In terms of how to label our research endeavours in the field of sustainability, in light of our discussions about the connotations of specific terms, the plethora of naming conventions, the problems inherent in framing sustainability at the level of the individual, the need to capture decisions not to buy as well as to buy, and to understand (non)purchases as part of a wider system of production, consumption and disposal, we suggest using 'sustainable practices' as a more inclusive term which is also appropriate with respect to both unit and level of analysis. This is in line with our belief that there is a need for sustainability research to make a conceptual and practical shift towards *households (or even communities) as a stream of (inconsistent) practices*. 'Practices' infers a link with a sociological framing of the problems raised by sustainability and this we think is a helpful conceptualisation as it underlines the need for understanding the wider context (social norms) as well as the immediate contexts (households, organisations, communities) within which practices are set. Thinking of practices as the unit of analysis will also help researchers engage with sustainability as part of the private, every day, habitual, unquestioned domestic sphere of a household's existence, rather than conceiving of it as a series of miniature acts of public activism. Further it suggests a need to study actions and meanings in a lot of detail (Fuentes, 2014). This work is best suited to qualitative approaches, at least until such times as strong theoretical frameworks can be offered by the grounded, crafting of theories from data relating to actual behaviours, or decisions not to act. Qualitative approaches are not perfect, of course, and as discussed above, have also tended to focus on the individual as a unit of analysis, but they offer the opportunity to move us away from blind attempts at measurement, at least until we understand what we are measuring. An important part of moving away from quantitative approaches will be finally letting go of the implicit positivist assumptions that individuals are rational, consistent and predictable.

The next big challenge for researchers is to begin to take a much wider range of research into account. Although there will always be a place for focused, single activity research in order for us to understand the challenges of sustainability at a detailed level, there is also a need to join up the results of these individual studies in order to see a bigger picture and be able to move the whole field(s) forward. This means looking at sustainability holistically, as it is viewed by households: as an infuriating set of contradictory, overlapping and inter-dependent, socially constrained and globally expressed set of issues, rather than isolating specific activities, or privileging production, consumption or disposal phases. In order to do this *it will be necessary to look across literatures* and therefore activities and at the same time across activities and therefore literatures. It will mean reading, and even publishing outside our own narrow disciplines. This is a tall order for researchers practically, because of the sheer volume of research and the myriad of terms and approaches used, but also politically and personally, because it will surely slow down the rate of their personal output and complexify the process of publication significantly. This will have an inevitable impact on progression and promotion for the individuals who attempt it. These are sacrifices that many individuals may not be able or prepared to make on a personal level. One possible way to ameliorate these effects is through genuinely multi-disciplinary approaches designed by teams of academics representing wide ranges of disciplines and approaches. This will allow individual researchers to harness insights from different issues and cut down the investments required by individuals to reach a big picture view that incorporates multiple literatures and streams of research practices.

As a research community we would do well to deal with the question of the locus of responsibility for change in a more explicit manner. We need to begin by chasing out the notions implicit in our language that individuals are bad. Of course the cumulative effect of individual behaviour is to blame for the predicament we find ourselves in at the beginning of the 21st century. But *individuals are not bad* they are just not rational or consistent and are acting in accord with powerful social norms (see for example, work on the Dominant Social Paradigm Kilbourne, McDonagh, & Prothero,

1997). It is economics that is wrong here, not people: rationality is a simplification too far. (Un)sustainable practices are very complex and cannot be
understood without understanding the contexts they operate through and
within. Consumers are not to 'blame' for the problem of non/partial compliance. Neither are they the only locus for solutions and change, despite
the assumptions of a free-market society. Individuals, households and communities do need to change. However institutional structures and *social
norms also need to change* as these constrain practices both conceptually
and practically. This is not an easy thing to do, but there are a few examples of success that we can look to for inspiration. Norms have recently
been tackled by placing *real* constraints upon the consumer through simply
taking less sustainable options out of the marketplace. This has been
accomplished both by large organisations (such as Cadbury changing all its
chocolate to fair trade) and by Governments (such as the European Union
ban on light bulbs that are not energy efficient or the Scottish Government
ban on retailers supplying free carrier bags). However they can also be
tackled by placing *cultural* constraints on the consumer. Looking at the
fact that smoking in the United Kingdom has gone from a ubiquitous,
socially accepted behaviour to a socially derided act of the few shows us
that it can be done, and that there is a very real role for marketers in
achieving this. Once researchers start to look at actual practices rather than
(or as well as) espoused values/attitudes/behaviours they can move beyond
asking 'what is the difference between attitudes and behaviours' to asking
'why are attitudes and behaviours different'. This will need an examination
of current behaviour as a stream of (non)actions set within a social context
that is bound by pervasive, unquestioned and invisible norms. We need to
treat gaps between attitudes and behaviours as signs of these norms at play
rather than misinterpreting them as laziness or stupidity on behalf of
the consumer.

The path that our collective, unexamined assumptions have ushered us
down has turned out to be a dead end street. We have done our best to
examine it in minute detail. We have learned a lot but essentially we are
looking in the wrong place. It is time to admit that we have navigated into
a cul-de-sac and look together for new paths.

REFERENCES

Alevizou, P. J. (2011). *Sustainability claims on FMCGs: Consumers' perceptions and company
practice in the UK and in Greece.* Unpublished PhD thesis, University of Sheffield.

Armitage, C. J., & Conner, M. (2001). Efficacy of the theory of planned behaviour: A meta-analytic review. *British Journal of Social Psychology, 40*(4), 471–499.

Baker, M. (2015). Social business, business as if people mattered: Variations on a theme by Schumacher (1973). *Sustainability, 7*(6), 6478–6496.

Barker, K., Fong, L., Grossman, S., Quin, C., & Reid, R. (1994). Comparison of self-reported recycling attitudes and behaviors with actual behavior. *Psychological Reports, 75*(1), 571–577.

Barr, S. W., Shaw, G., Coles, T., & Prillwitz, J. (2010). 'A holiday is a holiday': Practicing sustainability, home and away. *Journal of Transport Geography, 18*, 474–481. doi:10.1016/j.jtrangeo.2009.08.007

Barry, J. (1994). The limits of the shallow and the deep: Green politics, philosophy, and praxis. *Environmental Politics, 3*(3), 369–394.

Bartels, J., & Onwezen, M. C. (2014). Consumers' willingness to buy products with environmental and ethical claims: The roles of social representations and social identity. *International Journal of Consumer Studies, 38*, 82–89.

Belz, F. M., & Peattie, K. (2012). *Sustainability marketing A global perspective.* Chichester: Wiley.

Black, I. R., & Cherrier, H. (2010). Anti-consumption as part of living a sustainable lifestyle: Daily practices, contextual motivations and subjective values. *Journal of Consumer Behaviour, 9*(6), 437–453.

Bray, J., Johns, N., & Kilburn, D. (2011). An exploratory study into the factors impeding ethical consumption. *Journal of Business Ethics, 98*(4), 597–608.

Budeanu, A. (2007). Sustainable tourist behaviour – A discussion of opportunities for change. *International Journal of Consumer Studies, 31*, 499–508.

Carrigan, M. (1998). Segmenting the grey market: The case for fifty-plus "lifegroups". *Journal of Marketing Practice: Applied Marketing Science, 4*(2), 43–56.

Carrigan, M., & Attalla, A. (2001). The myth of the ethical consumer – Do ethics matter in purchase behaviour? *Journal of Consumer Marketing, 18*(7), 560–578.

Caruana, R., Carrington, M. J., & Chatzidakis, A. (2015). "Beyond the attitude-behaviour gap: Novel perspectives in consumer ethics": Introduction to the thematic symposium. *Journal of Business Ethics,* 1–4. Retrieved from http://link.springer.com/article/10.1007/s10551-014-2444-9.

Chatzidakis, A., Maclaran, P., & Bradshaw, A. (2012). Heterotopian space and the utopics of ethical and green consumption. *Journal of Marketing Management, 28*(3–4), 494–515.

Daily, B. F., Bishop, J. W., & Govindarajulu, N. (2009). A conceptual model for organizational citizenship behavior directed toward the environment. *Business & Society, 48*(2), 243–256.

Davis, I. (2013). How (not) to market socially responsible products: A critical research evaluation. *Journal of Marketing Communications, 19*(2), 136–150.

De Young, R. (2000). New ways to promote proenvironmental behavior: Expanding and evaluating motives for environmentally responsible behavior. *Journal of Social Issues, 56*, 509–526.

DePelsmacker, P., Geuens, M., & Van Den Berg, J. (2013). *Marketing communications: A European perspective* (5th ed.). Upper Saddle River, NJ: Prentice Hall.

Diamantopoulos, A., Schlegelmilch, B. B., Sinkovics, R. R., & Bohlen, G. M. (2003). Can socio-demographics still play a role in profiling green consumers? A review of the evidence and an empirical investigation. *Journal of Business Research, 56*, 465–480.

do Paço, A. F., & Raposo, M. B. (2010). Green consumer market segmentation: Empirical findings from Portugal. *International Journal of Consumer Studies*, *34*(4), 429–436.

Etzioni, A. (1998). Voluntary simplicity: Characterization, select psychological implications, and societal consequences. *Journal of Economic Psychology*, *19*(5), 619–643.

Evans, S. M., Gill, M. E., & Marchant, J. (1996). Schoolchildren as educators: The indirect influence of environmental education in schools on parents' attitudes towards the environment. *Journal of Biological Education*, *30*(4), 243–248.

Fraj, E., & Martinez, E. (2007). Ecological consumer behaviour: An empirical analysis. *International Journal of Consumer Studies*, *31*, 26–33.

Fuentes, C. (2014). Managing green complexities: Consumers' strategies and techniques for greener shopping. *International Journal of Consumer Studies*, *38*(5), 485–492.

Gan, B. C. (2010). *An entrepreneurial theorising of the recycling industry*. Unpublished PhD thesis, Robert Gordon University.

Gentina, E., & Muratore, I. (2012). Environmentalism at home: The process of ecological resocialization by teenagers. *Journal of Consumer Behaviour*, *11*(2), 162–169.

Gentina, E., & Singh, P. (2015). How national culture and parental style affect the process of adolescents' ecological resocialization. *Sustainability*, *7*(6), 7581–7603.

Hamad, C. D., Bettinger, R., Cooper, D., & Semb, G. (1980). Using behavioral procedures to establish an elementary school paper recycling program. *Journal of Environmental Systems*, *10*(2), 149–156.

Higham, J. E. S., Cohen, S. A., & Cavaliere, C. T. (2014). Climate change, discretionary air travel, and the "Flyers' Dilemma". *Journal of Travel Research*, *53*(4), 462–475. doi:10.1177/0047287513500393

Holusha. (1990). Retrieved from http://www.nytimes.com/1990/04/10/business/new-plastic-in-heinz-bottles-to-make-recycling-easier.html. Accessed on April 20, 2015.

Kilbourne, W., McDonagh, P., & Prothero, A. (1997). Sustainable consumption and the quality of life: A macromarketing challenge to the dominant social paradigm. *Journal of Macromarketing*, *17*(1), 4–24.

McDonald, S. (2011). Green behaviour: Differences in recycling behaviour between the home and the workplace. In D. Bartlett (Ed.), *Going green: The psychology of sustainability in the workplace*. Leicester: BPS Publications.

McDonald, S., Aitken, M., & Oates, C. J. (2012). Marketing green energy. *Proceedings of the British Academy of Management Conference*, Cardiff University, September 11–13.

McDonald, S., & Ball, R. (1998). Public participation in plastics recycling schemes. *Resources, Conservation and Recycling*, *22*(3–4), 123–141.

McDonald, S., & Oates, C. J. (2003). Reasons for non-participation in a kerbside recycling scheme. *Resources, Conservation & Recycling*, *39*(4), 369–385.

McDonald, S., & Oates, C. J. (2006). Sustainability: Consumer perceptions and marketing strategies. *Business Strategy and the Environment* (Special issue on Marketing sustainability), *15*(3), 157–170.

McDonald, S., Oates, C. J., Alevizou, P. J., Young, C. W., & Hwang, K. (2012). Individual strategies for sustainable consumption. *Journal of Marketing Management* (Special issue on Re-visiting contemporary issues in green/ethical marketing), *28*(3–4), 445–468.

McDonald, S., Oates, C. J., Thyne, M. A., Alevizou, P. J., & McMorland, L.-A. (2009). Sustainable consumption patterns in different product sectors. *International Journal of Consumer Studies* (Special issue on Sustainable consumption), *33*(2), 137–145.

McDonald, S., Oates, C. J., Young, C. W., & Hwang, K. (2006). Towards sustainable consumption: Researching voluntary simplifiers. *Psychology and Marketing, 23*(6), 515–534.

Miller, D. (1998). *A theory of shopping.* Cambridge: Polity Press.

Moisander, J. (2007). Motivational complexity of green consumerism. *International Journal of Consumer Studies, 31*(4), 404–409.

Moons, I., & De Pelsmacker, P. (2015). An extended decomposed theory of planned behaviour to predict the usage intention of the electric car: A multi-group comparison. *Sustainability, 7,* 6212–6245.

Nelson, M. R., Rademacher, M. A., & Paek, H. J. (2007). Downshifting consumer = upshifting citizen? An examination of a local freecycle community. *The ANNALS of the American Academy of Political and Social Science, 611*(1), 141–156.

Newholm, T., & Shaw, D. (2007). Editorial: Studying the ethical consumer: A review of research. *Journal of Consumer Behaviour, 6,* 253–270.

Oates, C. J., & McDonald, S. (2002). What can marketing do for recycling? *Proceedings of the Academy of Marketing,* Nottingham.

Oates, C. J., & McDonald, S. (2006). Recycling and the domestic division of labour: Is green pink or blue? *Sociology, 40*(3), 417–433.

Oates, C. J., & McDonald, S. (2014). The researcher role in the attitude-behaviour gap. *Annals of Tourism Research, 46,* 168–170.

Oates, C. J., McDonald, S., Blades, M., & Laing, A. (2013). How green is children's television? *Social Business, 3*(1), 37–45.

Oke, A. (2015). Workplace waste recycling behaviour: A meta-analytical review. *Sustainability, 7*(6), 7175–7194.

Ottman, J. (2011). *The new rules of green marketing: Strategies, tools, and inspiration for sustainable branding.* San Francisco, CA: Berrett-Koehler Publishers.

Ottman, J. A. (1993). *Green marketing: Challenges and opportunities for the new marketing age.* Lincolnwood, IL: NTC Business Books.

Peattie, K. (1999). Trappings versus substance in the greening of marketing planning. *Journal of Strategic Marketing, 7,* 131–148.

Peattie, K. (2001). Golden goose or wild goose? The hunt for the green consumer. *Business Strategy and the Environment, 10,* 187–199.

Peattie, K. (2010). Green consumption: Behavior and norms. *Annual Review of Environment and Resources, 35*(8), 8.1–8.34. doi:10.1146/annurev-environ-032609-094328

Perrin, D., & Barton, J. (2001). Issues associated with transforming household attitudes and opinions into materials recovery: A review of two kerbside recycling schemes. *Resources Conservation and Recycling, 33*(1), 61–74.

Pettit, D., & Sheppard, J. P. (1992). It's not easy being green: The limits of green consumerism in light of the logic of collective action. *Queens Quarterly, 99*(3), 328–350.

Potter, J., & Hepburn, A. (2005). Qualitative interviews in psychology: Problems and possibilities. *Qualitative Research in Psychology, 2*(4), 281.

Prillwitz, J., & Barr, S. (2011). Moving towards sustainability? Mobility styles, attitudes and individual travel behaviour. *Journal of Transport Geography, 19*(6), 1590–1600.

Prothero, A. (1990). Green consumerism and the societal marketing concept: Marketing strategies for the 1990s. *Journal of Marketing Management, 6*(2), 87–103.

Redclift, M. (2005). Sustainable development (1987–2005): An oxymoron comes of age. *Sustainable Development, 13*(4), 212–227.

Roberts, J. A., & Bacon, D. R. (1997). Exploring the subtle relationships between environmental concern and ecologically conscious consumer behavior. *Journal of Business Research, 40*(1), 79–89.

Scammell, M. (2003). Citizen consumers: Towards a new marketing of politics? In J. Corner & D. Pels (Eds.), *Media and the restyling of politics: Consumerism, celebrity and cynicism* (pp. 117–136). London: Sage.

Scott, A. (2009). *Understanding sustainable development in households.* Unpublished PhD thesis, University of Sheffield.

Scott, A., Oates, C. J., & Young, C. W. (2015). A conceptual framework of the adoption and practice of environmental actions in households. *Sustainability, 7*(5), 5793–5818.

Shaw, D., & Newholm, T. (2002). Voluntary simplicity and the ethics of consumption. *Psychology and Marketing, 19*(2), 167–185.

Shaw, D., & Shiu, E. (2002). An assessment of ethical obligation and self-identity in ethical consumer decision-making: A structural equation modelling approach. *International Journal of Consumer Studies, 26*(4), 286–293.

Steg, L., & Vlek, C. (2009). Encouraging pro-environmental behaviour: An integrative review and research agenda. *Journal of Environmental Psychology, 29*(3), 309–317.

Straughan, R. D., & Roberts, J. A. (1999). Environmental segmentation alternatives: A look at green consumer behaviour in the new millennium. *Journal of Consumer Marketing, 16*(6), 558–575.

The Roper Organization. (1992). *Environmental behavior, North America: Canada, Mexico, United States.* A report commissioned by S.C. Johnson and Son Inc., New York.

Vining, J., & Ebreo, A. (1990). What makes a recycler? *Environment and Behavior, 22*(1), 55–73.

Wagner, S. A. (1997). *Understanding green consumer behaviour.* London: Routledge.

Wells, P. E. (2010). *The ABS rankings of journal quality: An exercise in delusion.* Discussion paper. Centre for Business Relationships, Accountability, Sustainability and Society, Cardiff.

Young, C. W., Hwang, K., McDonald, S., & Oates, C. J. (2010). Sustainable consumption: Green consumer behaviour when purchasing products. *Sustainable Development Journal, 18*(1), 20–31.

TOWARD PRO-SUSTAINABILITY ACTIONS: A MACRO-BEHAVIORAL PERSPECTIVE

Bipul Kumar and Nikhilesh Dholakia

ABSTRACT

Purpose — *To introduce macro-behavioral perspective for understanding pro-sustainability actions from the perspective of various stakeholders.*

Methodology/approach — *Recent research on sustainability, behavior change, and environmentalism is reviewed to conceptualize a comprehensive macromarketing framework to spawn and diffuse pro-sustainability behaviors.*

Findings — *Provides a comprehensive macromarketing framework that not only explains the behavioral factors from firm's perspective but also explains these factors from the perspective of various stakeholders who are part of the entire value chain.*

Research limitations/implications — *The paper adds to the literature on pro-sustainability behaviors by providing a research framework from macro-marketing point of view.*

Practical implications — *As practical insight, the paper provides some important guidance in terms of better understanding on firm-specific and individual-specific actions which may help in progressing toward sustainability.*

Marketing In and For a Sustainable Society
Review of Marketing Research, Volume 13, 169–192
Copyright © 2016 by Emerald Group Publishing Limited
All rights of reproduction in any form reserved
ISSN: 1548-6435/doi:10.1108/S1548-643520160000013015

Originality/value − *The paper integrates past observations on behavioral aspect of sustainability and develops an important framework to understand pro-sustainability actions.*

Keywords: Sustainability; firm behavior; consumer behavior; co-creation; marketing; macromarketing

SUSTAINABILITY: A COMPLEX QUEST

As the notion of sustainability gains wide public acceptance, it conflicts with a major mainstream belief − the quest for continuous growth. In common political-economic and daily life discourses, the need for growth is seen as fundamental and unquestioned, without taking into account the different anatomies and consequences of growth in a holistic sense. When we discuss the entire fabric of sustainability − comprising of economic, social, and environmental threads − most of the firms and other organizational entities, as well as most consumers, fail to comply with the implied multiple imperatives and multiple responsibilities. Most firms and their main stakeholders normally hold a myopic view of sustainability: viewing it via fractal notions such as efficiency improvement, move toward renewables, or enhancing biodiversity but ignoring the big picture (Kilbourne, McDonagh, & Prothero, 1997). An intriguing question is this: Why do most of us typically understand the peripheral aspects of sustainability as a concept rather than engage with the core of it? The answer lies in understanding the complexity of sustainability as a concept which has, in fact, multifarious dimensions intermingled within it. Several streams of studies, emanating from multiple disciplines, influence sustainability. This necessitates a wide knowledge base to understand, decipher, and implement sustainability in its true holistic sense.

   The genesis of sustainability has its roots in the fundamental approaches of ecocentricism and anthropocentricism. Therefore, various interdisciplinary perspectives based on biology, anthropology, economics, and other subjects form the basis to understand the complex anatomy of sustainability. Sustainability has also been equated with stability, and there are instances where scholars have equated complexity with diversity, which in turn was equated with stability or sustainability (Elton, 1958; Hutchinson, 1959; Tainter, 2006).

Tainter (2006) described sustainability from the viewpoint of social complexity. Tainter's basic premise is that, in terms of social complexity, sustainability entails the creation of resources rather than merely relying upon the existing ones. This, in fact, is the pure notion of the sustainability as a concept: It advocates the maintenance of the resources not only for the current generation but also for the future generations. Tainter's view resonates with the definition of sustainability propounded by Brundtland commission (1987). From a biologist's perspective, Oxford dictionary described sustainability in terms of the bio-goals of supporting life and providing necessities of life (Little, Fowler, Coulson, & Murray, 1955). Adding a multidisciplinary flavor, Barbier (1987) described sustainability as the concept of simultaneously maximizing biological system goals, economic system goals, and social system goals. Pearce, Hamilton, and Atkinson (1996) view sustainability as maintenance and judicious utilization of natural ecosystem and biospheric processes.

Sustainability was also compared and contrasted with resiliency (Moench, 2014) although the basic meanings of the two differ to some extent. Resiliency may denote an attempt to recoup the losses which might take place at any point of time in the system. The idea of sustainability too revolves around recouping the probable losses in the system especially with regard to resources. The recouping and recuperation of resources is an important aspect of achieving sustainability especially to ensure survival for future generations. Such intergenerational, very long-term orientation is typically not a part of resiliency. Taking a leaf from cultural ideology, Costanza, Daly, and Bartholomew (1991) note that within the realm of dynamic economic and ecological systems, development of the human culture needs to take care of the boundary conditions so that diversity, complexity, and ecological life support system are not disturbed. The overall discussion clearly points toward the complex nature of sustainability as a multifaceted concept with very long-term orientation toward problem-solving; the problems to be solved being complex in nature and intertwined with opportunities as well as threats (Tainter, 2006).

The complexity of sustainability was duly acknowledged by US Environmental Protection Agency (EPA). Within the context of environmental sustainability, greenhouse gas (GHG) emission has been classified by EPA into three scopes based on their sources of emissions: (1) direct GHG emissions from the sources owned by an entity; (2) indirect GHG emissions taking place offsite due to purchase and use of electricity and other energy resources by the entity; (3) GHG emissions due to entity's indirect activities such as their vendor's supply chain activities. The US EPA requires an institution or entity to report all three scopes of emissions, and these emission types are monitored by sustainability auditing agencies such as GRI and Dow Jones when they report on sustainability initiatives of firms worldwide.

In the journey to sustainability not only are various complexities involved, at various levels, but *not* embarking on such a journey in earnest is fraught with grave danger. An estimate by the World Business Council in its vision 2050 document for the world stated that humankind would require resources equivalent to 2.3 times the current Earth by the year 2050 if resource extraction continues at the current rate. The report also mentioned that a much reduced resource base would be required if we choose to traverse the path of sustainability, but this requires clear mandates to achieve behavior changes at all levels.

Sustainability has established linkages with behavior, and researchers have identified such linkages (Gardner & Stern, 1996; Press & Arnould, 2009). The successful implementation of sustainability initiatives also depends largely on the institutionalization of the right perspective on behaviors and requires a certain degree of modification in the existing behaviors to accomplish targeted goals (Doppelt, 2003; Steg & Vlek, 2009). Since the issues pertaining to the environment and ecology are intrinsically related to human behaviors (Gardner & Stern, 1996), the success of the sustainability related practices is also very much dependent on the way the different stakeholders perceive and behave in harmonized ways. Non-compliance in terms of behaviors toward sustainability is found equally at the firm level and at the consumer level, and such non-compliance has indeed reduced the degree of benefit which would otherwise have accrued from pro-sustainability initiatives (Midden, Kaiser, & Teddy McCalley, 2007). Since sustainability is complex and multifaceted − involving firms, supply chains, and consumers − a systemic approach, the kind of approach often found in macromarketing literature, is worth exploring.

ADVANTAGES OF A MACROMARKETING APPROACH

Van Dam and Apeldoorn (1996) noted that the rationality of human behavior with respect to environment is bounded by the scale of ecological processes. Humans can deal with ecological processes that are limited in time span, location, and size. Since most ecological activities affect sustainability and take place over a prolonged (often intergenerational) time span and vast (geographic, often global) scale − beyond the perceptual boundaries that humans are conventionally accustomed to – it is difficult to ascertain the impacts of sustainability actions at the micro level. The problems of waste accumulation and disposal, for example, could cause dismay and discomfort at the individual level, but when aggregated at the community, national, or global levels, the waste disposal issues begin to interact with massively complex issues of land use, infectious diseases, global supply chains, cleanliness of water bodies and groundwater, and more. Hardin's (1968) famous "tragedy of the commons" essay noted the struggle between consumers' optimal choices at different points in time resulting in an aggregation of suboptimal results, which are beyond the scope of rationality at the microscopic level (Van Dam & Apeldoorn, 1996). The choice sets pertaining to sustainability are also similar in spirit and nature: they require evaluation and implementation at a more aggregate level rather than at a discrete individual level. The modern business world is replete with examples of individual entities regularly attempting to increase their welfare by passing on the externalities to the ecosystem surrounding them, ultimately causing the overall system to drift toward un-sustainability. Theoretically or tactically, if sustainability is to be practiced in totality, various actors of the entire value chain need to develop conscious macro level orientations and actions toward sustainability goals.

A comprehensive approach to policy measures with regard to sustainable development was laid out in the Brundtland report (1987), which helped to bring the agenda of sustainability to the global forefront. It was probably the first of its kind to integrate the nuances of sustainable development, weaving together the threads like resource utilization, biodiversity, and climate change, and portraying un-sustainability as a crisis affecting the entire ecosystem (Brown, 1995; Dovers, 1996; Myers, 1997). With the change in the scope and definition of sustainability arising from fundamental issues pertaining to energy usage, migration and settlement of population, corruption in the society, and civil wars taking place in various geographies; policy measures to address sustainability have become fluid and need continuous retrospection and amendments, something that policy experts have recognized (Common, 1995; Dovers & Handmer, 1992). Since most of the sustainability problems are temporal (i.e., shows their effects over a long period of time) and spatial (i.e., are not contained by national geographical boundaries; e.g., air pollution) in nature, top-down policy measures will require massive global inter-governmental coordination. In the meanwhile, some progress toward sustainability can be made via proactive efforts to influence bottom-up pro-sustainability behaviors, of institutions and individuals.

In a marketing sense, sustainability qualifies as a megatrend (Mittelstaedt, Shultz, Kilbourne, & Peterson, 2014). In line with arguments of the Development School of thought that marketing has a pivotal role in economic development and societal well-being, issues pertaining to quality of life (Ahuvia & Friedman, 1998; Lee & Sirgy, 2004), socioeconomic development (Dahringer, 1983; Klein & Nason, 2001), socially responsible consumption behavior (Antil, 1984), and sustainable marketing orientation (Mitchell, Wooliscroft, & Higham, 2010) provide some crucial building blocks for a systematic approach toward sustainability. It is apparent that pro-sustainability approaches require systemic thinking that is capable of transcending micro and discrete policy measures. Layton (2011, p. 260) characterizes a marketing system as the "network of individuals, groups, and/or entities embedded in a social matrix linked directly or indirectly through sequential or shared participation in economic exchange which jointly and/or collectively creates economic value with and for customers through the offer of assortments of products, services, experiences, and ideas that emerge in response to or anticipation of customer demand." Therefore, in macromarketing terms, a multi-stakeholder approach on sustainability is needed — an approach that transcends micro and discrete level thinking. In such a macromarketing approach, the behaviors of different stakeholders toward sustainability play pivotal roles in achieving success in the achievement of sustainability goals.

SELECTIVE LITERATURE REVIEW OF SUSTAINABILITY

Scholastic work on sustainability has deepened its root within behavioral science. Marketing scholars like Kilbourne et al. (2009), Prothero, McDonagh, and Dobscha (2010), McDonagh and Brereton (2010), and Kumar (2012) have highlighted the central role of environmentalism with priority at the macro level both for firms and consumers. Stern (2000) commented on human behavior in the context of sustainability with regard to its impact on utilization of natural resources. Considering the behavior toward sustainability as a continuum ranging from direct or proximal behavior (Druckman, Young, & Stern, 1991) to indirect behavior causing changes to the environment (Vayda, 1988), there are a variety of ways in which human behavior may impact the various strands of the fabric of sustainability.

Moving a step forward to understand behavior of consumers toward sustainability, the concept of consumer responsibility may provide some important guidance as discussed in social science disciplines (Bricas, 2008; Wells, Ponting, & Peattie, 2011). In studies involving issues like environmental activism (McAdam, McCarthy, & Zald, 1996) and recycling (Dietz, Stern, & Guagnano, 1998) in the marketing literature, scholars have elaborated on the role of consumer responsibility and its linkage with behavior in the context of sustainability. Some other behavioral issues like behavior related to efficiency enhancement (Black, Stern, & Elworth, 1985; Stern & Gardner, 1981), altruistic behavior leading to financial sacrifice in the domain of environmentalism (Stern, Dietz, Abel, Guagnano, & Kalof, 1999), and emotional attachment toward natural environment (Kals, Schumacher, & Montada, 1999) were also explored in the domain of sustainability.

Although many scholars have dealt with behavioral issues with regard to sustainability at the level of consumers, some broad as well as minute details about determinants of consumers' behavior toward sustainability are yet to be explored. Barring a few studies like consumers' environmental behavior as manifestation of cultural bias (Steg & Sievers, 2000; Stern, 2000) and emotional affinity toward nature (Kals et al., 1999), there is limited research discussing the determinants of pro-sustainability behaviors at the level of consumer.

One important aspect of these studies is their specific focus on "environmentalism" to discuss sustainability, and, as noted, this addresses only one dimension of sustainability, neglecting other dimensions such as social aspects and intergenerational resource aspects.

Expanding the discussion on pro-sustainability behavior at the firm level, it is pertinent to note that behavior of the managers are of significant importance in success of strategic issues like sustainability; indeed, the vision and policies of top managers often drive the strategic aspects of firms, including sustainability stances (Chawla & Kelloway, 2004). Since success of sustainability at the firm level depends highly on institutionalization of appropriate perspectives and behaviors, firms need to instill these through procedures, policies, and organizational culture aimed at attaining the core of sustainability (Doppelt, 2003). Pro-sustainability behaviors at the firm level have to infuse through the complete cycle: from procurement to production to distribution and finally to end consumption.

Scholars like Black et al. (1985), Stern and Oskamp (1987), Gardner and Stern (1996), and Stern et al. (1999) have propounded the value-belief-norm (VBN) theory of environmentalism. This theory provides a snapshot of factors leading to pro-environmental behavior in a causal chain starting from personal values to personal norms. VBN theory holds that personal values such as altruistic, biospheric, or egoistic values lead to formation of beliefs about the deteriorating impacts on the environment due to the actions of human beings, and beliefs regarding the capability of individuals to reduce such adverse impacts of their actions (Stern et al., 1999). It also holds that such beliefs spawn personal norms in the form of obligation to act for the betterment of the environment, ultimately leading to pro-environmental behaviors. Andersson, Shivarajan, and Blau (2005) explored the behavior toward environmental sustainability in the context of multinational firms using VBN theory and found that the behaviors of individuals in an organizational setting are quite different from the behaviors in individual capacity, mainly due to factors like norms, firm's culture, and other pertinent factors acting upon the firm.

Stern (2000) noted categorically the role of contextual factors such as government regulations, legal obligations, and monetary incentives as important determinants of pro-environmental behaviors. Corporate values, beliefs of managers about environment, corporate actions regarding the environment, and norms within the corporation were found by Andersson et al. (2005) as some of the determinants of the pro-environmental behaviors at the firm level.

Both at the firm level as well as at the consumer level, it is interesting to note that much of the attention in the sustainability literature was paid to "environmentalism," which forms an important but only one of the pillars of sustainability. Sustainability literature still lacks rich discussion from the perspective of "triple bottom line" (Elkington, 1998), the concept that visualizes sustainability from the viewpoint of three pillars: environment, society, and economy. Thus, an exclusive attention on environmental dimension provides us only a partial view of the key issues in sustainability, and thus prevents us from the exploration of some relevant but multi-pronged policies.

In this paper, we present a comprehensive framework of pro-sustainability behaviors that could help propel firms, other members of the value chain, and of course consumers toward sustainability. In the proposed framework, the 'triple bottom line' perspective is kept in view as the strategic choice of the firms. We also intend to understand the role of interactions between firms and consumers, as well as firm-firm interactions (especially within linked value-supply-chains), in terms of co-creation efforts toward sustainability.

Mittelstaedt et al. (2014) described markets as the tool for social development and overall well-being of the human society, outlining the importance of issues like co-creation of sustainability and linkages with other factors leading to progress toward sustainability. Since there is scant literature on co-creation of sustainability, this paper also intends to enrich this important aspect, at least conceptually.

SUGGESTED MACROMARKETING FRAMEWORK OF SUSTAINABILITY

To develop the framework, we delved into some important theories such as institutional theory (DiMaggio & Powell, 1983), stakeholder theory (Donaldson & Preston, 1995; Freeman, 1984); transaction cost theory (Williamson, 1979); resource-based view theory (Barney, 1991; Wernerfelt, 1984) and resource dependence theory (Pfeffer & Salancik, 1978). We understand that from a macromarketing standpoint, all key stakeholders — firms, consumers, policymakers, and other stakeholders — have to be brought into the picture. This broader perspective addresses sustainability from a multi-stakeholder stance (Freeman, 1984).

To understand who could be the prospective stakeholders to address the issue of pro-sustainability behavior, we adhered to Freeman (1994, p. 415) describing stakeholders as participants in "the human process of joint value creation." We were also guided by the definition of stakeholder by Hill and Jones (1992, p. 133) who described stakeholders as the "constituents who have a legitimate claim on the firm ... established through the existence of an exchange relationship" who supply "the firm with critical resources (contributions) and in exchange each expects its interests to be satisfied (by inducements)." We further took the guidance from the work by Mitchell, Agle, and Wood (1997) for understanding the attributes of the stakeholders — based on power, legitimacy and urgency — to demarcate them as internal versus external stakeholders and throw light on their behavior toward sustainability, thereby creating a holistic framework to discuss pro-sustainability behaviors at macro level.

As described by Mitchell et al. (1997, p. 869), we adhere to the following definitions of power, legitimacy, and urgency:

> Power is a relationship among social actors in which one social actor, A, can get another social actor, B, to do something that B would not have otherwise done.

> Legitimacy is a generalized perception or assumption that the actions of an entity are desirable, proper, or appropriate within some socially constructed system of norms, values, beliefs, definitions.

Urgency is the degree to which stakeholder claims call for immediate attention. It is further viewed through the lense of time sensitivity and criticality.

We have developed Table 1 based on adaptation from the work by Mithcell et al. (1997). This table describes the types of stakeholders, their basis of classification, relevant examples of types of stakeholders, and the degree of relevance of these for sustainability of the firm. We also attempted to understand the stakeholders in terms of their impact on the decision making process of the firms with regard to goals, expectations, and selection of choices (Cyert & March, 1963). Considering the instrumental aspect (Donaldson & Preston, 1995), the stakeholder theory identifies the linkage between stakeholder management and the achievement of the objectives of the firms such as profitability and growth. It suggests that adherence to the stakeholder management may result in achieving corporate objectives with much better results compared to competitors. The instrumental aspect of stakeholder theory, thus, provides useful guidance as to what should be done to manage relevant stakeholders to achieve desired results. The discussion has important implications in understanding the pro-sustainability behaviors which could be understood with a view of long-term sustained results aligned to corporate objectives. Since the firms have internal as well as external stakeholders, understanding and managing them could have important implications for attaining the objectives of the firms. The normative aspect of the stakeholder theory, on the other hand, is based on the moral and philosophical principles which focus on steps that must be taken to do things correctly (Donaldson & Preston, 1995).

It is obvious that the normative aspect may guide the different activities of the firms to be carried out in an accepted manner commensurate with the achievement of the corporate goals and objectives. Overall, we believe that pro-sustainability behavior itself could be the normative aspect depicting the sustained path to be traversed by the firms in achieving their objectives by understanding and managing their different stakeholders.

We wish to develop a framework based on the macro context which holistically discusses the linkages between the firm and its different stakeholders from the perspective of understanding pro-sustainability behavior.

Table 2 is a more focused version of Table 1 based on which we propose our framework for pro-sustainability behaviors. Depending upon degree of urgency to engage a particular stakeholder to traverse a path of sustainability, we have considered definitive, dominant, dependent, and dangerous category of stakeholders in developing the framework to understanding pro-sustainability behavior.

Table 1. Categories of Stakeholders.

Type of Stakeholder	Basis of Classification	Example	Internal Stakeholder/ External Stakeholder	Degree of Relevance to Engage the Stakeholder with Sustainability of the Firm
Definitive	A stakeholder exhibiting power, legitimacy, and urgency. Salience of the stakeholder will be higher in such scenario	• Managers and employees of the firm	Internal	High
		• Customers of the firm • Suppliers and distributors • Investors of the firm	External	High
Dominant	A stakeholder exhibiting power and legitimacy	Regulators	External	High
Dependent	A stakeholder exhibiting legitimacy and urgency	Different constituents of the society such as local inhabitants	External	Moderate
Dangerous	A stakeholder exhibiting power and urgency	• Social and environmental activist • Competitors	External	Moderate to high
Discretionary	A stakeholder legitimacy only	Institutions/individuals receiving grants/aid from firms as a mean of voluntary philanthropy	External	Low
Dormant	A stakeholder exhibiting power only	For example, a fired employee	External	Low
Demanding	A stakeholder exhibiting urgency only	A standalone entity/individual claiming certain urgency	External	Low

Adapted from Mitchell et al. (1997).

Table 2.　Types of Stakeholders Pertinent to Sustainability.

Type of Stakeholder	Example	Degree of Urgency to Engage the Stakeholder with Sustainability of the Firm	Internal Stakeholder/ External Stakeholder
Definitive	• Managers and employees of the firm	High	Internal
	• Customers of the firm • Suppliers and distributors • Investors of the firm	High	External
Dominant	Regulators	High	
Dependent	Different constituents of the society such as local inhibitants	Moderate	
Dangerous	• Social and Environmental activist • Competitors	Moderate to high	

We start the foundation of the framework with a discussion of pro-sustainability behaviors at the firm level. Firms discussed in this study are all firms like upstream and downstream members of the focal firm in the entire value chain: supplier firms, distributor firms, ancillary firms, and so on. Firms are usually driven by the vision and policies of people at the top like CEOs. The C-suite orientations and behaviors, in fact, play an important role in decisions regarding sustainability initiatives. At the firm level, the success of the initiatives pertaining to sustainability is highly contingent upon institutionalization of complementary behaviors, especially behaviors of the top management (Doppelt, 2003). As discussed earlier, sustainability is a complex decision for the top managements of firms. Such complex organizational decisions are in many ways the result of behavioral factors rather than mechanical processes for achieving optimization in performance outcomes. Such decision making scenarios are influenced by a variety of conflicting goals, options, and even varying levels of aspiration of the individuals involved (Cyert & March, 1963; March & Simon, 1958).

To conceptualize the proposed framework and understand the pro-sustainability behaviors at the firm level, we have adapted some of the theoretical underpinnings from Upper Echelon Theory by Hambrick and Mason (1984). This theory has been verified in a variety of situations such as changes in corporate strategy (Wiersema & Bantel, 1992), top management team's gender diversity interaction with firm's culture and performance (Dwyer, Richard, & Chadwick, 2003), and firm's innovation culture and outcomes (Bantel & Jackson, 1989). As per this theory, the upper echelon characteristics comprise of the cognitive bases and values of the top management in the firms. These upper echelon characteristics ultimately form a basis for the strategic choices within the firms and these choices themselves are manifestation of the values and cognitive abstraction of the people who take important decisions at the level of top management. Hambrick and Mason (1984) discussed the suitability of the behavioral factors in decision making scenarios in complex and strategic matters in firms. Sustainability – being a complex phenomenon and becoming increasingly strategic in the current business world – could find some new directions using this theory. The theory describes strategic choices in the context of the firms as the function of the decision maker's cognitive bases. These covers knowledge about the future, knowledge about the alternatives, and knowledge about the consequences arising from the alternatives considered. Upper Echelon theory also suggests that decision makers' values are also reflected in considering and sequencing of various alternatives.

Hambrick and Mason (1984) noted that the top management, in a given scenario, provides cognitive bases and value judgements that act as screens between the situation at hand and the perception of the situation by the firm; thus equipping the firm and its leaders to take some important strategic decisions. Since a firm passes through many dynamic situations, which are acted upon by several internal and external stimuli, a manager or even a team of managers cannot comprehend every single event. Hence, they selectively grasp some important key elements, which again are filtered through the cognitive base and values of the top managers. These value-filtered perceptions undergird the groundrules for making the strategic choices within the firm on important issues. The values of the decision maker here act to modify the perceptions formed as well as affect the strategic choices directly. In terms of sustainability, it is apparent that product innovations, process innovations, adoption of renewable energy, recycling of resources, emphasis on social responsibility projects, emphasis on environmental upgradation projects, and corporate governance could qualify as some of the salient elements belonging to the set of strategic choices in the context of sustainability. These strategic choices are affected by the objective situational factors which might arise internally such as the quest for growth in a sustainable manner. Strategic choices also entail various balancing acts such as developing the right mix of corporate social responsibility actions and sustainability initiatives, while paying close attention to external factors such as regulatory requirements, cultural issues, action of activists, and legal aspects.

The Upper Echelon theory also emphasizes the important role of obser-
vable managerial characteristics such as age, experience in a particular role,
socioeconomic roots, and financial position. These are often important
determinants of strategic choices made. In the context of strategic choices
made to achieve progress toward sustainability, these dynamic and complex
forces might act in tandem or separately.

Apart from including firm level behaviors toward sustainability in the
overall schema of pro-sustainability framework, it is equally important to
understand and discuss the individual level behavior directed toward sustainability such as behaviors of consumers (Gardner & Stern, 1996). Even
if the firm level behaviors are aligned with sustainability, the non-alignment
at the level of consumer behaviors could undercut the core of sustainability
efforts (Midden et al., 2007). Hence, it is equally worthwhile to understand
pro-sustainability behaviors at the consumer end, the corporate end, and at
other stakeholders' ends (linked firms or individuals), so that the overall
macro level framework is robust.

Fig. 1 depicts different stakeholders, as identified in Tables 1 and 2, who
either have a direct relationship with the focal firm or those who directly or
indirectly influence the pro-sustainability behaviors. Those stakeholders
having direct relationship may even reciprocate in creation of sustainability
such as co-creation of sustainability by the interaction of firm and
consumers.

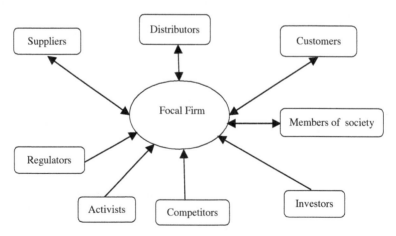

Fig. 1. Schematic Diagram Depicting the Firm and Its Stakeholders for
Considering Pro-Sustainable Behaviors.

To extend the proposed framework on pro-sustainability behaviors, we have taken some important guidance from value-belief-norm (VBN) theory propounded by Stern (2000) and others to understand the behaviors at the individual level. VBN links different threads of value theory, norm-activation theory, and the New Environmental Paradigm leading to pro-environmental behaviors. The basic premise of the theory revolves around the causal chain that propagates from personality and belief structure of the individual to a more dedicated and focused belief about the human-environment linkage. It states that the personal norms to take pro-environmental initiatives are guided by the belief that deteriorating environmental conditions pose a threat to the individual's values and that the individual has the capability to descale the degree of such a threat. These norms also in a way have direct correlation with the pro-environmental intentions.

We propose that the perceived personal values for environment and society lead to personal beliefs about the ability to reduce threats to the environment and society. Personal values – such as pro-environment values – have been found to have limited direct implication on the pro-environmental behaviors, which is evident from several studies exploring these relationships and getting mixed results (Stern, Dietz, & Guagnano, 1995; Thogersen & Grunert-Beckmann, 1997). Altruistic values, which represent one form of personal values suggested by Schwartz (1973), along with personal norms and moral obligations, have been found to support similar results in many relevant studies pertaining to pro-environmental behaviors ranging from recycling (Nielsen & Ellington, 1983) to energy saving (Black et al., 1985).

Overall, personal values for environment and society are not found to directly affect the pro-environmental behaviors in all instances. Rather, there are some mediating steps which help in reaching the desired behavioral ends. Dunlap, Van Liere, Mertig, and Jones (2000) noted that individuals with a caring attitude toward the environment are more likely to engage in pro-environmental behaviors. There is an emerging view from several studies that those with personal beliefs about their own capability to reduce threats to the environment and society – developed because of perceived personal values for environment and society – are more likely to engage in pro-environmental behaviors than those who lack such beliefs (Andersson et al., 2005; Cordano, Frieze, & Ellis, 2004; Stern, 2000; Stern et al., 1999). This is also in line with the social dilemma discussed by Stern (1976) who found that the individuals' information about the long-term consequences of their irresponsible actions is closely aligned to pro-environmental behaviors. On the whole, pro-sustainability personal behaviors seem to depend on the perceived beliefs about the individual ability to reduce the threat to the environment and society, especially when people are informed about the long-term negative consequences of irresponsible behaviors.

Norms are usually related to the individual's self-expectations (Schwartz, 1977). As per Schwartz's norm activation model (1970), individuals' beliefs about consequences of their actions toward betterment of environment and society are the prime drivers of personal norms, leading in turn to pro-environmental behaviors. The role of such beliefs has been studied well and reported to influence pro-environment behaviors (Dunlap & Van Liere, 1978; Stern, Dietz, & Black, 1985). If we consider the social part of the personal norms, more precisely social norms, this social aspect collectively acts in favor of aggregate outcomes to help others from side effects of the negative actions (Biel, Eek, & Gärling, 1999; Coleman, 1990). Social norms also have direct implications for pro-social behaviors, which is an important part of sustainability. Thus, collectively we may infer that pro-environmental and pro-social personal norms have the ability to drive pro-sustainability behaviors at the consumer level. Equipped with the personal belief about the ability to reduce the threat to environment and society, consumers are able to visualize the long-term impacts of their consumption choices and progress toward sustainability.

Indeed, we are rapidly transitioning into an era where many firms are acting in pro-sustainable ways, as are increasing (but still relatively small) segments of socially conscious consumers. The joint participation of consumers and firms in sustainability activities can potentially create new ways of co-creation and co-extraction of values by consumers and firms, spawning new win-win situation for both entities (Prahalad & Ramaswamy, 2004). Within the context of pro-sustainability behaviors, we propose that co-creation could prove to be an important tool helping consumers as well as firms to progress toward sustainability by bringing them together on a single platform (Kania & Kramer, 2011). In the proposed framework, we have depicted the important role of co-creation in progress toward sustainability to illustrate the complementarity of roles played by different stakeholders at multiple levels. We also believe that co-creation provides an avenue for customers to understand the nuances of sustainability and its impact on the marketing mix elements such as higher cost (hence higher prices), at least initially, for the products in some of the cases. Such co-creation relationship experience between firm and the customer actually may lower the adoption barriers and may eventually shift consumers toward adopting more sustainable products. In the era of social media, such experiences by the consumers could propagate salutary stories of sustainable consumption behaviors at much faster pace.

Fig. 2 is a detailed framework showing internal as well as external factors affecting pro-sustainability behavior at the firm level, behavioral factors at the individual level, and an interaction of behavior at firm and individual levels for co-creation of sustainability. The interaction of behaviors or more precisely the co-creation may also take place between two or more firms in business-to-business contexts such as between a focal firm and supplier firms.

It is important to note that the scope and meaning of sustainability are ever changing. Hence it is vital to understand that both top down influences such as government regulations as well as bottom-up changes at the firm level affect sustainability. It is also important to note that such dynamic behaviors may also be explained with the concept of isomorphism. DiMaggio and Powell (1983) described isomorphism, in discussions of Institutional Theory, as the process by which one unit in a population tries to resemble other units facing similar environmental conditions. The concept of isomorphism is very important in the context of pro-sustainable behaviors since it may create mimicking and then homogenization of such behaviors. Isomorphism has two types – competitive and institutional. The institutional part has greater relevance in the context of modern firms (DiMaggio & Powell, 1983). Institutions strive for resources, customers, institutional legitimacy, social, and economic power; hence, within the given constraints, the concept of isomorphism explains the way by which all firms compete to gain their fair share. This clearly throws some light on the dynamic nature of the proposed framework wherein each entity in the value chain continuously makes efforts to attain higher levels of sustainability.

CONCLUDING COMMENTS ON ACHIEVING SUSTAINABILITY

It is true that sustainability requires substantial behavior changes at various levels in the entire value chain. It is important therefore to understand the determinants of pro-sustainability behaviors at all levels – the firm level, the consumer level, and at the level of interaction of the firm and the consumer. In this paper, we have offered a framework for pro-sustainability

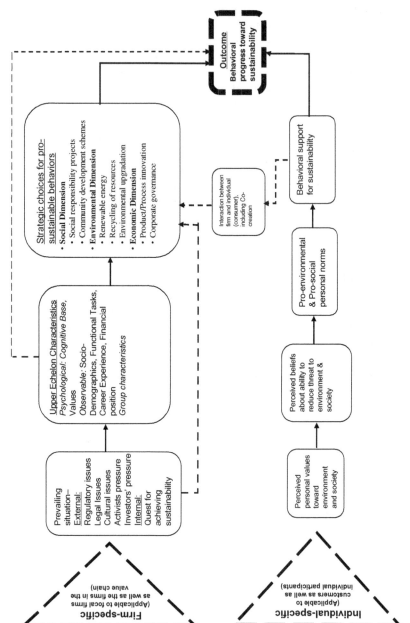

Fig. 2. Proposed Macromarketing Framework for Pro-Sustainability Behaviors (at Firm Level and Individual Level).

behaviors at the level of different stakeholders, to illustrate that achieving sustainability is a multi-actor and multidimensional process. At the firm level, Upper Echelon Theory provides some guidance regarding how, via top management cognitive bases and values, a firm can progress toward sustainability. Even though managers in the firms are faced with a variety of challenging situations on a regular basis, their ultimate quest lies in creating value for their firms as well as for other stakeholders. If we look at the Upper Echelon Theory, the cognitive bases and values act as filters for the managers in a decision making scenario in strategic circumstances. Clubbed with the observational factors like age, career experience, and socioeconomic roots, the cognitive bases and values provide a platform for a focused approach for strategic thinking about sustainability. For firms aspiring to perform high on sustainability, a practical implication is to hire top managers who have career experience in areas like waste reduction and environmental stewardship. Firms can shape their corporate governance to emphasize economic aspects of sustainability as well as social aspect of sustainability. In many instances, the socioeconomic and demographic roots of the managers could also play significant roles in steering the firm toward social sustainability; in essence, managers whose life experiences have been pro-social are likely to enact policies that are pro-sustainability.

At the level of consumers, VBN theory provides an approach to motivate individual consumers to proceed toward sustainability. A stepwise approach starting from personal values, linking to personal beliefs, and ultimately connecting to personal norms can motivate individual behaviors toward sustainability. The VBN side of the framework also has some important practical implications. Marketers could undertake communication efforts that instil a sense of can-do confidence, a belief by the consumers that their actions have the capability to reduce the threat to environmental and social degradation. Of course, such communications have to be perceived as utterly earnest, and not as efforts at "greenwashing." If such efforts are matched with the personal values of even a small but dedicated and proactive segment of consumers, the result may be the creation of a conducive atmosphere for the consumers to feel a sense of urgency to act for the sake of the environment and society. Marketers may get some useful cues from this theoretical approach in terms of communications strategy as well as guidance for the design and offering of suitable products and services.

The framework also provides some guidance for the co-creation of sustainability in the entire value chain. If likeminded firms and consumers join hands on such issues, there could be manifold benefits. Products and services could be co-designed by firms and proactive consumers toward the larger goal of achieving sustainability, and the resulting market offerings could provide greater consumer satisfaction and cement loyalty to brands and firms seen as "pro-sustainable."

Based on strategic choices for the firm toward pro-environmental behaviors, policymakers could think of regulatory actions — especially incentives — for firms to adopt product and process innovations, recycling methods, social responsibility projects, and related pro-sustainability business practices. Policymakers may even design communication programs to guide consumers on environmental issues in order to create a sense of belief in them about the visibility and tangibility of sustainable results of their actions.

REFERENCES

Ahuvia, A. C., & Friedman, D. C. (1998). Income, consumption, and subjective well-being: Toward a composite macromarketing model. *Journal of Macromarketing, 18*(2), 153−168.

Andersson, L., Shivarajan, S., & Blau, G. (2005). Enacting ecological sustainability in the MNC: A test of an adapted value-belief-norm framework. *Journal of Business Ethics, 59*(3), 295−305.

Antil, J. H. (1984). Conceptualization and operationalization of involvement. *Advances in Consumer Research, 11*(1), 203−209.

Bantel, K. A., & Jackson, S. E. (1989). Top management and innovations in banking: Does the composition of the top team make a difference? *Strategic Management Journal, 10*(S1), 107−124.

Barbier, E. B. (1987). The concept of sustainable economic development. *Environmental Conservation, 14*(02), 101−110.

Barney, J. (1991). Firm resources and sustained competitive advantage. *Journal of Management, 17*(1), 99−120.

Biel, A., Eek, D., & Gärling, T. (1999). The importance of fairness for cooperation in public-goods dilemmas. *Judgment and Decision Making: Neo Brunswikian and Process Tracing Approaches* (pp. 245−259). Mahwah, NJ: Erlbaum.

Black, J. S., Stern, P. C., & Elworth, J. T. (1985). Personal and contextual influences on house-hold energy adaptations. *Journal of Applied Psychology, 70*(1), 3.

Bricas, N. (2008). Attentes et responsabilité des consommateurs [Consumer expectations and responsibility]. *OCL Oleagineux Corps Gras Lipides, 15*(2), 142−144.

Brown, J. H. (1995). *Macroecology*. Chicago, IL: University of Chicago Press.

Brundtland, G. H. (1987). Report of the World Commission on *Environment and Development: "Our Common Future."* United Nations.

Chawla, A., & Kelloway, E. K. (2004). Predicting openness and commitment to change. *Leadership & Organization Development Journal, 25*(6), 485−498.

Coleman, J. S. (1990). *Foundations of social theory*. Cambridge, MA: Belnkamp.

Common, M. (1995). *Sustainability and policy: Limits to economics.* Cambridge: Cambridge University Press.

Cordano, M., Frieze, I. H., & Ellis, K. M. (2004). Entangled affiliations and attitudes: An analysis of the influences on environmental policy stakeholders' behavioral intentions. *Journal of Business Ethics, 49*(1), 27−40.

Costanza, R., Daly, H. E., & Bartholomew, J. A. (1991). Goals, agenda, and policy recommendations for ecological economics. In *Ecological economics: The science and management of sustainability* (pp. 1−20). New York, NY: Columbia University Press.

Cyert, R. M., & March, J. G. (1963). *A behavioral theory of the firm* (p. 2). Englewood Cliffs, NJ: Prentice-Hall.

Dahringer, L. D. (1983). Public policy implications of reverse channel mapping for Lesotho. *Journal of Macromarketing, 3*(1), 69−75.

Dietz, T., Stexrn, P. C., & Guagnano, G. A. (1998). Social structural and social psychological bases of environmental concern. *Environment and Behavior, 30*(4), 450−471.

DiMaggio, P., & Powell, W. W. (1983). The iron cage revisited: Institutional isomorphism and collective rationality in organizational fields. *American Sociological Review, 48,* 147–160.

Donaldson, T., & Preston, L. E. (1995). The stakeholder theory of the corporation: Concepts, evidence, and implications. *Academy of Management Review, 20*(1), 65−91.

Doppelt, B. (2003). *Leading change toward sustainability: A change-management guide for business, government and civil society.* Sheffield: Greenleaf Publishing.

Dovers, S. R. (1996). Sustainability: Demands on policy. *Journal of Public Policy, 16*(3), 303−318.

Dovers, S. R., & Handmer, J. W. (1992). Uncertainty, sustainability and change. *Global Environmental Change, 2*(4), 262−276.

Druckman, D., Young, O. R., & Stern, P. C. (Eds.). (1991). *Global environmental change: Understanding the human dimensions.* Washington, DC: National Academies Press.

Dunlap, R. E., & Van Liere, K. D. (1978). The "new environmental paradigm". *The Journal of Environmental Education, 9*(4), 10−19.

Dunlap, R. E., Van Liere, K. D., Mertig, A. G., & Jones, R. E. (2000). New trends in measuring environmental attitudes: Measuring endorsement of the new ecological paradigm: A revised NEP scale. *Journal of Social Issues, 56*(3), 425−442.

Dwyer, S., Richard, O. C., & Chadwick, K. (2003). Gender diversity in management and firm performance: The influence of growth orientation and organizational culture. *Journal of Business Research, 56*(12), 1009−1019.

Elkington, J. (1998). Partnerships from cannibals with forks: The triple bottom line of 21st-century business. *Environmental Quality Management, 8*(1), 37−51.

Elton, C. S. (1958). *The ecology of invasions by plants and animals* (p. 18). London: Methuen.

Freeman, R. E. (1984). *Strategic management: A stakeholder approach.* Englewood Cliffs, NJ: Prentice Hall.

Freeman, R. E. (1994). The politics of stakeholder theory: Some future directions. *Business Ethics Quarterly, 4*(04), 409–421.

Gardner, G. T., & Stern, P. C. (1996). *Environmental problems and human behavior.* Boston, MA: Allyn & Bacon.

Hambrick, D. C., & Mason, P. A. (1984). Upper echelons: The organization as a reflection of its top managers. *Academy of Management Review, 9*(2), 193−206.

Hardin, G. (1968). The tragedy of the commons. *Science, 162*(3859), 1243−1248.

Hill, C. W., & Jones, T. M. (1992). Stakeholder-agency theory. *Journal of Management Studies, 29*(2), 131–154.

Hutchinson, G. E. (1959). Homage to Santa Rosalia or why are there so many kinds of animals? *American Naturalist, 93*, 145–159.

Kals, E., Schumacher, D., & Montada, L. (1999). Emotional affinity toward nature as a motivational basis to protect nature. *Environment and Behavior, 31*(2), 178–202.

Kania, J., & Kramer, M. (2011). Collective impact. *Stanford Social Innovation Review, 9*(1), 36–41.

Kilbourne, W., McDonagh, P., & Prothero, A. (1997). Sustainable consumption and the quality of life: A macromarketing challenge to the dominant social paradigm. *Journal of Macromarketing, 17*(1), 4–24.

Kilbourne, W. E., Dorsch, M. J., McDonagh, P., Urien, B., Prothero, A., Grünhagen, M., ... Bradshaw, A. (2009). The institutional foundations of materialism in western societies a conceptualization and empirical test. *Journal of Macromarketing, 29*(3), 259–278.

Klein, T. A., & Nason, R. W. (2001). Marketing and development: Macromarketing perspectives. *Handbook of Marketing and Society* (pp. 263–297). Thousand Oaks, CA: Sage.

Kumar, B. (2012). *Theory of planned behaviour approach to understand the purchasing behaviour for environmentally sustainable products*. Working Paper No. 2012-12-08, Indian Institute of Management, Ahmedabad.

Layton, R. A. (2011). Towards a theory of marketing systems. *European Journal of Marketing, 45*(1–2), 259–276.

Lee, D., & Sirgy, M. J. (2004). Quality-of-life (QOL) marketing: Proposed antecedents and consequences. *Journal of Macromarketing, 24*(1), 44–58.

Little, W., Fowler, H. W., Coulson, J. S., & Murray, J. A. H. (1955). In C. T. Onions (Ed.), *The Oxford universal dictionary on historical principles*. Oxford: Clarendon Press.

March, J. G., & Simon, H. A. (1958). *Organizations*. New York, NY: Wiley.

McAdam, D., McCarthy, J. D., & Zald, M. N. (Eds.). (1996). *Comparative perspectives on social movements: Political opportunities, mobilizing structures, and cultural framings*. Cambridge: Cambridge University Press.

McDonagh, P., & Brereton, P. (2010). Screening not greening: An ecological reading of the greatest business movies. *Journal of Macromarketing, 30*(2), 133–146.

Midden, C. J., Kaiser, F. G., & Teddy McCalley, L. (2007). Technology's four roles in understanding individuals' conservation of natural resources. *Journal of Social Issues, 63*(1), 155–174.

Mitchell, R. K., Agle, B. R., & Wood, D. J. (1997). Toward a theory of stakeholder identification and salience: Defining the principle of who and what really counts. *Academy of Management Review, 22*(4), 853–886.

Mitchell, R. W., Wooliscroft, B., & Higham, J. (2010). Sustainable market orientation: A new approach to managing marketing strategy. *Journal of Macromarketing, 30*(2), 160–170.

Mittelstaedt, J. D., Shultz, C. J., Kilbourne, W. E., & Peterson, M. (2014). Sustainability as megatrend two schools of macromarketing thought. *Journal of Macromarketing, 34*(3), 253–264.

Moench, M. (2014). Experiences applying the climate resilience framework: Linking theory with practice. *Development in Practice, 24*(4), 447–464.

Myers, N. (1997). *The world's forests and their ecosystem services* (pp. 215–235). Washington, DC: Island Press.

Nielsen, J. M., & Ellington, B. L. (1983). Social processes and resource conservation: A case-study in low technology recycling. In N. R. Fiemer & E. S. Geller (Eds.), *Environmental psychology: Directions and perspectives* (pp. 288–311). New York, NY: Praeger.

Pearce, D., Hamilton, K., & Atkinson, G. (1996). Measuring sustainable development: Progress on indicators. *Environment and Development Economics, 1*(1), 85–101.

Pfeffer, J., & Salancik, G. R. (1978). *The external control of organizations: A resource dependence approach.* New York, NY: Harper and Row Publishers.

Prahalad, C. K., & Ramaswamy, V. (2004). Co-creation experiences: The next practice in value creation. *Journal of Interactive Marketing, 18*(3), 5–14.

Press, M., & Arnould, E. J. (2009). Constraints on sustainable energy consumption: Market system and public policy challenges and opportunities. *Journal of Public Policy & Marketing, 28*(1), 102–113.

Prothero, A., McDonagh, P., & Dobscha, S. (2010). Is green the new Black? Reflections on a green commodity discourse. *Journal of Macromarketing, 30*(2), 147–159.

Schwartz, S. H. (1970). Elicitation of moral obligation and self-sacrificing behavior: An experimental study of volunteering to be a bone marrow donor. *Journal of Personality and Social Psychology, 15*(4), 283.

Schwartz, S. H. (1973). Normative explanations of helping behavior: A critique, proposal, and empirical test. *Journal of Experimental Social Psychology, 9*(4), 349–364.

Schwartz, S. H. (1977). Normative influences on altruism. *Advances in Experimental Social Psychology, 10*, 221–279.

Steg, L., & Sievers, I. (2000). Cultural theory and individual perceptions of environmental risks. *Environment and Behavior, 32*(2), 250–269.

Steg, L., & Vlek, C. (2009). Encouraging pro-environmental behavior: An integrative review and research agenda. *Journal of Environmental Psychology, 29*(3), 309–317.

Stern, P. C. (1976). Effect of incentives and education on resource conservation decisions in a simulated common dilemma. *Journal of Personality and Social Psychology, 34*(6), 1285.

Stern, P. C. (2000). New environmental theories: toward a coherent theory of environmentally significant behavior. *Journal of Social Issues, 56*(3), 407–424.

Stern, P. C., Dietz, T., Abel, T., Guagnano, G. A., & Kalof, L. (1999). A value-belief-norm theory of support for social movements: The case of environmentalism. *Human Ecology Review, 6*(2), 81–98.

Stern, P. C., Dietz, T., & Black, J. S. (1985). Support for environmental protection: The role of moral norms. *Population and Environment, 8*(3–4), 204–222.

Stern, P. C., Dietz, T., & Guagnano, G. A. (1995). The new ecological paradigm in social-psychological context. *Environment and Behavior, 27*(6), 723–743.

Stern, P. C., & Gardner, G. T. (1981). Psychological research and energy policy. *American Psychologist, 36*(4), 329.

Stern, P. C., & Oskamp, S. (1987). Managing scarce environmental resources. *Handbook of Environmental Psychology, 2*, 1043–1088.

Tainter, J. A. (2006). Social complexity and sustainability. *Ecological Complexity, 3*(2), 91–103.

Thogersen, J., & Grunert-Beckmann, S. C. (1997). Values and attitude formation towards emerging attitude objects: From recycling to general, waste minimizing behavior. *Advances in Consumer Research, 24*(1), 182–189.

Van Dam, Y. K., & Apeldoorn, P. A. C. (1996). Sustainable marketing. *Journal of Macromarketing, 16*(2), 45–56.

Vayda, A. P. (1988). Actions and consequences as objects of explanation in human ecology. In R. J. Borden, J. Jacobs, & G. L. Young (Eds.), *Human ecology: Research and applications* (pp. 9–18). College Park, MD: Society for Human Ecology.

Wells, V. K., Ponting, C. A., & Peattie, K. (2011). Behaviour and climate change: Consumer perceptions of responsibility. *Journal of Marketing Management, 27*(7–8), 808–833.

Wernerfelt, B. (1984). A resource-based view of the firm. *Strategic Management Journal, 5*(2), 171–180.

Wiersema, M. F., & Bantel, K. A. (1992). Top management team demography and corporate strategic change. *Academy of Management Journal, 35*(1), 91–121.

Williamson, O. E. (1979). Transaction-cost economics: The governance of contractual relations. *Journal of Law and Economics, 22*, 233–261.

REDUCING THE ATTITUDE-BEHAVIOR GAP IN SUSTAINABLE CONSUMPTION: A THEORETICAL PROPOSITION AND THE AMERICAN ELECTRIC VEHICLE MARKET

Diane M. Martin and Terhi Väistö

ABSTRACT

Purpose — *The purpose of this paper is to re-evaluate the sustainable attitude-behavior gap by reconsidering the cognitive-rational aspects of consumer purchase behavior. We aim to show how companies can benefit from focusing on hedonic aspects of consumption in their marketing of sustainable products. We claim that consumer culture research needs to examine the link between hedonic, aesthetic, and cognitive-rational aspects of sustainable consumption.*

Methodology/approach — *We use the electric vehicle marketing strategy in the United States as an example of an approach to bridge the attitude-behavior gap. More specifically, we focus on the car manufacturer Tesla as an example of marketing a sustainable product.*

Marketing In and For a Sustainable Society
Review of Marketing Research, Volume 13, 193–213
ISSN: 1548-6435/doi:10.1108/S1548-643520160000013016

Findings – *We find that Tesla's marketing strategy focuses on aesthetics and hedonics-ludic performance. Similarly to other luxury cars, Tesla markets itself with a full compliment of consumer benefits. Compared to economical electric vehicles, sustainability is not the primary focus of Tesla's marketing communication strategy.*

Research limitations/implications – *Sustainable consumption theory benefits from examining the interlinking of hedonic, aesthetic and cognitive-rational aspects product purchasing and use. Future research in the development of sustainable consumption theory in additional complex product categories is needed.*

Practical implications – *Greater regard for consumer experience in sustainable consumption offers the potential for additional strategies to bridge the attitude-behavior gap and marketing of sustainable goods.*

Originality/value – *We move beyond the attitude-behavior gap by not only focusing on expressed attitudes of sustainability, but also focusing on the hedonic aspects at play in sustainable consumption.*

Keywords: Attitude-behavior gap; electric vehicles; hedonic; aesthetic; automotive consumption

INTRODUCTION

The complications of moving toward sustainability are many and varied. As Schaefer and Crane (2005) concisely argue "a change toward more sustainable consumption, depending on a change of values and behavior by a majority of individual consumers … raises quite fundamental problems and tensions in contemporary society that make such prospects unlikely" (p. 89). This pronouncement underscores one particularly vexing problem when it comes to marketing and consumption of sustainable products: why do consumers say they will buy sustainable products and then fail to do so? This discrepancy between avowed attitude and actual buying behavior has been conceptualized as the attitude-behavior gap. Multiple reasons have been given for this gap including a lack of marketplace options, distrust, and high prices for sustainable products. The focus of most research has been the consumer; consumer attitudes and behaviors don't align and thus consumers are confused, uncertain, or may be just plain lying when asked about their attitudes regarding sustainability and fall under the halo effect in their desire to give attitude researchers the "correct" answers. But blaming consumers masks more useful possibilities for reducing the gap between attitude and behavior and moving toward sustainability.

Marketers of green products often focused on performativity and sustainability product benefits, relying on rational arguments of product competency and moral superiority over conventional marketplace options (Schaefer & Crane, 2005). However, consumers buy for a plethora of reasons. We propose consideration of the appeal of pleasure, the pleasure of ownership and use, provides important insights into sustainable consumption. Although the cognitive-rational appeal speaks to the reasoning capacities of the consumer, the aesthetic and hedonic influences focus on consumers embodied consumption experience (Küpers, 2000; Sherry, 1998). While it may be difficult to imagine hardcore environmentalists ceding to the notion that hedonics have a part to play in sustainability (Schaefer & Crane, 2005), we propose that a focus on the hedonic and aesthetic aspects of consumption, in concert with the more commonly examined cognitive-rational aspects, moves consumers toward sustainable consumption. We offer this theoretical proposition with the purpose of bridging the attitude-behavior gap. This proposition, exemplified in electric vehicle (EV) industry, helps us begin to understand the nature of consumers' experience with sustainable products. Focusing on EVs and in particular the automaker Tesla as an example of marketing a sustainable luxury brand, we show how companies can draw on hedonics and aesthetics, along with rational-cognitive influences to move consumers toward consumption of sustainable products.

A Problem of Focus

In 1960 Theodore Levitt famously coined the term "marketing myopia" to describe being so focused on one aspect of business as to miss important industry developments: technical, social, and competitive. He exemplified the resulting likely economic malaise with the railroads that considered themselves to be in the railroad business rather than the transportation business and thereby missed opportunities for growth in the face of competition from cars, trucks, and planes. In Levitt's view, marketing myopia kept firms and entire industries from correctly assessing possibilities brought about through technological change, competitor innovation, and consumer needs and desires (1960). It's fair to say that early efforts to market ecologically sustainable products, particularly organic food and personal care products suffered mightily from what Ottman, Stafford, and Hartman (2006) call green marketing myopia: privileging either environmental qualities or customer satisfaction to the determent of the other.

The history of sustainable products in the American marketplace is rife with green marketing myopia missteps. Early efforts to create and market sustainable products resulted in items that failed to fulfill even the most basic needs. Household cleaners didn't get surfaces as clean as conventional products, natural clothing didn't hold dyes and shape, and any five-year-old could tell you carob never really tasted like chocolate. In short, products privileged sustainability at the expense of utility and function. Early product offerings within the sustainable category were marketed first as "green" products and second as products to fulfill a consumer need. This created an uphill battle for legitimacy as new products emerged in the sustainable market segment. In fact even consumers who identify as sustainably minded fail to choose the more sustainable product. Currently, American consumer attitudes toward sustainability are generally supportive (Bonnell, 2015); however, the reality of consumption behavior demonstrates the gap between rhetoric and reality, in short the attitude-behavior gap.

THE ATTITUDE-BEHAVIOR GAP: FAILING TO WALK THE TALK

Many theories have been devised to explain sustainable consumption practices. For example, anti-consumption, voluntary simplicity, moral imperatives have all found ideological footing among consumers who hold strong attitudes and beliefs at the intersection of sustainability and personal behavior (for an overview see McDonagh & Prothero, 2014). Consumption and sustainability also intersect in the downshifting and slow food movements (Parkins & Craig, 2006; Schor, 1998). Izberk-Bilgin (2010) argues that anti-consumption theories of resistance fall into paradigms of "manipulation and enslavement" or "agency and empowerment" discourses, each one relating to a different perspective of the power of consumption in contemporary society. Those who choose what Leonard-Barton (1981) describes as voluntary simplicity demonstrate "the degree to which an individual selects a lifestyle intended to maximize his/her direct control over daily activities and to minimize his/her consumption and dependency" (p. 244). Balancing consumption with sustainability can also be found among "consumers [who] activate a moral choice calculus that enables them to maintain an overall positively balanced sense of a good self should they choose to deviate from the moral ideal" (Beruchashvili, Gentry, & Price, 2006, p. 303). Sustainability attitudes and beliefs are inherent in each of these perspectives. While each of these theorizing efforts adds to our understanding of consumer sustainability projects, they fail to explain the gap between avowed attitudes and actual buying behavior.

The attitude-behavior gap has been investigated through social, psychological, and educational lenses (Chawla, 1999; Gupta & Ogden, 2009; Vermeir & Verbeke, 2006). Scholars have also studied the firm's role in encouraging attitude-behavior congruence (Boulstridge & Carrigan, 2000; Joy, Sherry, Venkatesh, Wang, & Chan, 2012). Kilbourne, McDonagh, and Prothero (1997) argue that nothing short of a wholesale change in the dominant social paradigm (DSP) is needed to bring about truly sustainable societies. Still, there are a number of ways consumers stray from their ideals of sustainable consumption. For instance, among voluntary simplifiers, pursing anti-consumption goals often means actually using more resources and consuming more products (Craig-Lees & Hill, 2002). Other research shows how lack of awareness, negative perceptions, distrust, high prices and low availability are all barriers to sustainable consumption (Bonini & Oppenheim, 2008; Schaefer & Crane, 2005). Gupta and Ogden (2009) employ reference group theory in their argument that individual characteristics including "trust, in-group identity, expectation of others' cooperation and perceived efficacy were significant in differentiating between "non-green" and "green" buyers" (p. 376). In their study the attitude-behavior gap is framed as a social dilemma wherein the expectations of others cooperation, the collective rather than the individual gain, is the strongest factor in determining sustainable consumption. Chawla (1999) notes sources of environmental awareness changes during different stages of human development. Families were most influential during childhood; education and friends dominate influences during adolescence and early adulthood; pro-environmental organizations were most influential during adulthood. While these results are not surprising, it is important to note how environmental awareness is influential at each life stage and yet the attitude-behavior gap remains intransigent.

Kollmuss and Agyeman (2002) map out 30 years of psychological and sociological research to explore why people act in a pro-environmental manner and what are the barriers to pro-environmental behavior. They examine "linear progression models; altruism, empathy and prosocial behavior models; and finally, sociological models" (p. 240). They find flaws in the underlying rationale for the relationships between the theories used to try to explain the gap and the research methods and measurements, and claim that "the biggest positive influence on pro-environmental behavior ... is achieved when internal [personal values] and external [social and cultural] factors act synergistically" (Kollmuss & Agyeman, 2002, p. 257). In order to avoid what they see as the problematic direct relationship between attitudes and behaviors, they offer a complex and yet untested model of values, knowledge and attitudes that they name the "pro-environmental consciousness."

While Gupta and Ogden (2009) situate their work at the intersection of micro and meso-level analysis, Kilbourne et al. (1997) argued that only macro-level approaches can examine the relationship between "... sustainable consumption and the quality of life critically because the essence of the relationship lies in the dominant social paradigm (DPS)" (p. 4). However, without wholesale cultural change and the political will to regulate and enforce for sustainability, macro-level approaches, relying on culturally appropriate moralizing while and arguing for ethical behavior won't result in more sustainable consumer behavior (Holt, 2012; Martin & Schouten, 2012). Focusing on consumers is just part of the story. Marketers are also making efforts to reduce the gap.

Producers and marketing managers with sustainable sensibilities look for discrete, pragmatic options for increasing sustainable product and service purchases. Companies work to build good corporate reputations to keep consumers buying their products (Boulstridge & Carrigan, 2000). However, there is no evidence that consumers' purchase behavior relates to this form of responsible marketing. Moreover, Joy et al. (2012) found consumers were concerned about environmental and social implications of their purchasing decisions, but this did not translate to their consumption behavior. Among these consumers of fast fashion, few talked about the devastating ecological and human capitol effects. Attitude-behavior gap research has thoroughly identified the dilemma but so far has failed to determine how to move the behavioral needle.

Barriers to Sustainable Consumption

The gap between avowed desire to purchase sustainable products and actual purchase behavior is attributed to multiple barriers. Blake (1999) characterized obstacles to sustainable action broadly as individuality, responsibility, and practicality. More recent research found impediments including lack of awareness, negative perceptions, distrust, high prices, and low availability (Bonini & Oppenheim, 2008). Although Schwartz (1973) argued that environmentalism is a collective good, which motivates consumers through common goals, sustainable consumption behavior doesn't necessarily follow. Even in the face of increased interest in sustainability and positive attitudes of consumers toward it, behavioral patterns are inconsistent with these attitudes (Vermeir & Verbeke, 2006). Knowledge and sophistication in sustainability does not necessarily translate into ethical and wise buying practices (Carrigan & Attalla, 2001). In short, consumers do not necessarily purchase ethical products despite positive attitudes. For consumers who do not want to be inconvenienced, ethical purchasing will only take place when there are no costs to the consumer in terms of added price, loss of quality or having to "shop around" (Carrigan & Attalla, 2001).

This continued gap between green attitudes and consumption behavior also causes great consternation for activists and theorists: Even though "numerous theoretical frameworks have been developed to explain the gap between the possession of environmental knowledge and environmental awareness, and displaying pro-environmental behavior. Although many hundreds of studies have been done, no definitive answers have been found" (Kollmuss & Agyeman, 2002, p. 239). Given the number of factors and arbitrary nature of the factors needed to produce a workable model, it's difficult to determine all the factors needed for a conclusive model to the point that some theorists seem to have given up. They summarize this frustration: "… the question of what shapes pro-environmental behavior is such a complex one that it cannot be visualized in one single framework or diagram" (p. 239). Developing sustainable consumer behavior models require unambiguous and clear factor boundaries. For those attempting to close the attitude-behavior gap with ethical, moralistic, and rational arguments, this effort has brought little success. We propose additional factors, in particular, hedonic and aesthetic appeals are needed to engage consumers in sustainable products.

HEDONIC, AESTHETIC, AND CONSUMPTION

A primary focus on cognitive-rational aspects of sustainable consumption has left the field with a new sort of myopia, one that fails to see the importance of fun, excitement, pleasure and joy, in short the embodied consumption experience (Holbrook & Hirschman,1982; Carù & Cova, 2003; Lanier & Rader, 2015 for reviews).

Holbrook and Hirschman (1982) define hedonic consumption as the "facets of consumer behavior that relate to the multisensory, fantasy and emotive aspects of one's experience with products" (p. 92). They state that the criteria as to whether a product is successful or not is aesthetic in nature. Askegaard (2010) notes that early studies of hedonic and aesthetics in consumer behavior led to the distinction between utilitarian product categories that were investigated using positivists research methods and hedonic and experiential consumption methods examining arts and popular culture consumption. Subsequently, consumer culture research has begun to focus on hedonism and fantasies that can be found in consumption of utilitarian goods. Carù and Cova (2005) argue that "consumers are feelers as well as thinkers" and thus attention must be paid to the emotional experience of buying and owning. Early work addressing consumer behavior focused on the hedonic aspects of the shopping process as well as the utilitarian outcomes (Babin, Darden, & Griffin, 1994; Woodruffe, 1997). Kozinets et al. (2004) show how consumer competence, among other attributes is "part of the very deeply intertwined viewpoints, interests, and constructions of consumers and producers" of hedonic-ludic outcomes at the ESPN zone (p. 660). Belk (2000) focuses on the possibly more sinister side of ludic public consumption environments, with his investigation of casino gambling, noting that management efforts to provide fun have "the effect of bombarding, overwhelming, and coercing consumers" (in Kozinets et al., 2004). Even re-experiencing consumption, such as re-reading a book or seeing a movie more than once can provide hedonic outcomes (Russell & Levy, 2012).

Soper (2007) speaks directly to pleasure in consumption while also living in a sustainable way with her concept of "alternative hedonism" which "points ... to the way in which affluent consumption may itself prompt revisions in thinking about the 'good life' as a result of its less enjoyable by-products (noise, pollution, danger, stress, health risks, excessive waste and aesthetic impact on the environment)" (p. 211). In short, privileging one's citizenship role over one's consumer role means consumption commences from a perspective of concern for the public good. While this perspective opens the door to bridging the schism between one's citizen concerns about the environment and consumer needs, it demands a re-evaluation of what is meant by "the good life." Developing a shift in one's definition of hedonic and the good life may prove difficult particularly with respect to the dominate social paradigm (Kilbourne et al., 1997). Efforts toward even greater consumer responsibilization (Giesler & Veresiu, 2014) may also prove difficult. The hedonic and aesthetic appeals in the proposition at hand are less reliant on what Soper (2007) calls "pleasure in committing to a more socially accountable mode of consuming" (p. 213) and more reliant on pleasurable experiential consumption inherent in sustainable product consumption. Rather than revising the notion of hedonism as the alternative of a meaning of the "the good life" the proposition at hand suggests that hedonic experience is possibly inherent in the sustainable goods and services already in the marketplace.

Consumer research has recently provided additional compelling evidence for the importance of aesthetics in consumer decision making by demonstrating that consumers attend to aesthetics both beyond the margin of their decision processes and within product categories that are not purely aesthetic (Hagtvedt & Patrick, 2008a; Reimann, Zaichkowsky, Neuhaus, Bender, & Weber, 2010). For instance, aesthetics may not always be enjoyed in and of itself alone, but also appreciated through its influence on other product-related dimensions, including the placement of artwork on a product or package changes the perceived luxury of the brand. Perceptions of luxury and the pleasure that results may prompt consumers to be more prone to be more accepting of the brand (Hagtvedt & Patrick, 2008b, 2009; Park, Milberg, & Lawson, 1991).

Specific conceptualizations of the hedonic are nuanced, yet Alba and Williams (2013) promote a lay definition that provides the most broadly encompassing approach. They state that the vital component of hedonic consumption is whether the experience of consuming the product or event is pleasurable. Sources and determinants are sorted into two categories: first, the product or event and its inherent qualities and second, the consumer's personal interpretation or experience of the product or event. Pleasure in the product can stem from style and care put into a product's basic essence with regard for its purity and authenticity. Pleasure in the product can be divided into three categories: aesthetic and design, having versus doing, and essences. Alba and Williams's (2013) conceptualization of hedonic dovetails with Le Bel and Dubé (1998) description of three sources of pleasure: sensorial pleasure, social pleasures, and psychological pleasures. These multiple sources of pleasure can underlie a single hedonic experience. First, the aesthetic and design viewpoint takes a design-based perspective to pleasure. In this work consumer research has mainly focused on the consequences rather than determinants of hedonic consumption. Second, having versus doing studies examine the nature of consumption itself. This approach is interested in, for example, whether consumers derive more happiness from possessions or experiences. Finally, the approach focusing on essences builds on the idea that the pleasure consumers feel due to a hedonic event is determined by the meaning they associate with it (Alba & Williams, 2013). Pleasure from product-person interaction considers consumers as moderators of pleasure in their experience of products. This pleasure is divided into consumer's expectations of the product and consumer's engagement with the product. Expectations guide consumer's choices but they also determine consumer's enjoyment of the consumption outcomes. Expectations can influence pleasure before, during and after the consumption occurs. Pleasure can achieved through engagement with the product. Specialized knowledge can make consumption more enjoyable to an expert consumer than to the novice (Alba & Williams, 2013)

The difference between hedonic and aesthetic consumption is nuanced, yet the two concepts are connected (Charters, 2006). Hedonic consumption is about pleasure, of which aesthetic appreciation can be an element. Aesthetic appreciation leads to hedonic response, but they are not identical. Charters (2006) suggests that aesthetic experience is a type of hedonic consumption, but other non-aesthetic forms of hedonic consumption exist as well. Parsing out the differences between hedonic and aesthetic consumption may be warranted particularly in the study of aesthetic cultural products, however, for the purpose of building a theoretical proposition for sustainable product consumption we are less concerned about these nuances that the inclusion of hedonic and aesthetic influences in general. In the context of automotive consumption, the embodied experiences of driving and riding allows for conflation of the hedonic and aesthetic.

The concept of luxury is also closely related to hedonics, aesthetics, and pleasure. Rather than privileging alternative consumption, rejecting consumerism or embracing voluntary simplicity (Martin & Schouten, 2012), luxury consumers look for a brand that expresses markers of prestige including luxury appointments, high performance standards and technological advancements. Patrick and Hagtvedt (2009) conceptualize a luxury brand as "one that is at the top of its category in terms of premiumness and connects with consumers on an emotional level, providing pleasure as a central benefit" (p. 5). Among luxury automotive brands, pleasure comes from a combination of consumer touch points of fit and finish, performance, and technological advancement.

MARKETING THE LUXURY EV: FOCUSING ON HEDONIC AND AESTHETIC APPROACHES

Automotive marketing has long relied on a combination of aesthetic, hedonic, and cognitive-rational approaches. Manufacturers refresh design elements for each new car model year. Zero to 60 times and technical advancements are touted to offer potential drivers an even more exciting motoring experience. However, when the industry turned to promoting electric and hybrid vehicles, marketers fell into the familiar green myopia (Ottman et al., 2006) that hampered other sustainable products marketing efforts. Rather than selling the entire benefit package to likely electric vehicle consumers, manufacturers have relied on the attitudes of sustainably minded consumers to respond to cognitive-rational arguments. Bill Destler, President of the Rochester Institute of Technology, details the performance specifics at the heart of most initial electric vehicle (EV) marketing efforts:

Efficiency: 75% vs. 25% for gasoline;

Emissions: zero carbon with renewable power;

Versatility: Multiple and local energy sources;

Infrastructure: Existing power distribution system;

Range: Americans drive < 40 miles (64 km) per day;

Inevitability: Next-gen technologies (e.g., fuel cells) require electric drive trains (Energy Overviews).

EV marketers failed to be mindful of attitude-behavior gap; they forgot that drivers love their cars and that love is a combination of beauty, fun, and power. When Toyota first launched the Prius in Los Angeles, the company proudly presented a quirky aesthetic and "greenness" which provided an odd cocktail of functional and design features befitting its unique position in the Mecca of American automotive consciousness and soon embraced by celebrity owners. However fascinating the Hollywood set found the early Prius, the car was not designed to win beauty contests or promote a pleasurable driving experience.

In the context of the automotive industry, aesthetics are part of the consumer embodied consumption experience (Küpers, 2000; Sherry, 1998). The confines of a well-designed automobile passenger compartment offers the hedonic-ludic experience of quiet and comfort. Driving is both a personal and private experience and a very public consumption behavior. The gaze of public spectators and the experiences of the driver co-create the particular hedonic-ludic level of the vehicle. Automotive marketing communication is designed to convey particular sorts of hedonic experiences possible with particular brands and models. In general, EV marketers in the United States seem to have forgotten this. In a departure from other sustainable products cognitive-rational appeals, the electric car company

Tesla adopted conventional automotive marketing strategy, promoting first illuminating aesthetic, hedonic-ludic aspects of their car, followed by cognitive-rational appeals. Rather than focusing primarily on the green aspects of the product, Tesla promotes aesthetic and hedonic luxury, experiences that are then followed by the sustainability benefits of ownership:

> With the All Glass Panoramic Roof, Model S is the only sedan capable of delivering a convertible-like drive experience every day. It's more than a sunroof: the entire roof is constructed from lightweight safety glass. With a simple swipe of the Touchscreen, it opens wider than any other sedan's panoramic roof ... Scan the streamlined body panels and you'll discover that Model S lacks a fuel door. Approach the driver's side taillight holding a connector, press the button, and something surprising happens: a triangle opens to reveal a small charge port. (Tesla Motors)

Tesla's marketing strategy privileges aesthetics and hedonics-ludic performance. In sharp contrast to moralistic appeals for sustainable consumption choices, Tesla provides an EV driving experience that is a gain, not a sacrifice. Owners experience the thrill of acceleration, precision handling and the admiring gaze. Like other cars in its luxury comparative set, Tesla markets itself with a full compliment of consumer benefits. However, unlike its more modest electric vehicle counterparts, the sustainable benefit of Tesla is far down the list. The marketing messages position the products as luxury automobiles that also happen to be electric, and therefore a more sustainable choice than gas-powered competitors in the luxury category.

Experiential consumption in the automotive industry is related to vehicle performance:

> Introducing a car so advanced it sets the new standard for premium performance .... Performance Plus takes one of the world's best sedans into supercar handling territory, while also improving the ride quality and range .... Model S epitomizes efficiency, embodying the grace and performance of a world-class athlete. Its sculpted form expresses a constant state of speed and motion. (Tesla Motors)

Speaking directly to the hedonic-ludic desires of the target market situates Tesla in a prime position among the consideration set. The metaphor of "world-class athlete" provides an apt vision of beauty and performance possibilities. Consumers are invited to fill in the imagery with their preferred vision.

Technology provides consumers with increasingly pleasurable and sophisticated experiences:

> Behind the wheel, you'll notice that Tesla has combined meticulous noise engineering with Tesla's uniquely quiet powertrain to obtain the sound dynamics of a recording studio. The gem of the interior is the 17″ touchscreen. It puts rich content at your

fingertips and provides mobile connectivity .... Model S comes equipped with two USB ports that enable passengers to charge devices while on the go. Equipped with high-speed connectivity, the Touchscreen accesses a vast supply of music, maps, and the web. (Tesla Motors)

The technological messaging focuses first and foremost on consumer touch points and sensations. Luxury cars have long pushed the boundaries of lavishness bringing personal comfort to ever-higher levels. The technological advances that make the Tesla possible don't intermingle with the luxury technologies. They come later.

When the automaker does promote its sustainability credentials it's done with a vision of inclusion, liberation, and consumer choice. Sustainability for Tesla is less about giving up something valued, that is, motoring freedom traditionally provided by gas-powered vehicles, and more about adding value in the form of more sustainable electric power. Tesla's power sources are free standing Supercharger charging stations that now span the United States and are "incredibly fast and always free" (Tesla Motors). The idea of power (gas) stations from sea to shining sea is not innovative, but development of an infrastructure for a single power plant is a new idea. This could be seen as yet another form of exclusivity for luxury consumers; however, Tesla actually democratized its charging stations (TechTimes, 2015) and other innovations when the company made its technical specifications available to all comers:

"... it's the goal of Tesla to accelerate the advent of sustainable transport, and I'd rather the other manufacturers would go fully electric as soon as possible .... Open sourcing the patents does have the advantage of making Tesla a more attractive place for the world's best engineers to work." considers (founder Eldon) Musk .... "And it builds goodwill, which I believe will be important ...." (French-Constant, 2014)

In another clear departure from other EV brands, Tesla's sustainability message links liberation for owners directly to geopolitical issues of continued oil and gas consumption:

With no tailpipe to spew harmful emissions, Tesla vehicles liberate their owners from the petroleum-burning paradigm .... Petroleum is a limited resource and a vexing source of price spikes, geopolitical instability, and environmental disasters of epic proportions. Petroleum currently fuels 95% of the United States transportation sector, a sector that demands nearly 28% of total energy usage. Globally, demand for personal transportation is increasing while reserves are decreasing. Not only is petroleum a diminishing resource, but it is also a significant source of greenhouse gas emissions .... Fortunately, reducing the use of oil for transportation can quickly increase independence and reduce emissions. Tesla vehicles are seminal to developing a cleaner, more independent transportation paradigm. (Tesla Motors)

Although the deepest of "green" consumers characterized as True Greens (Hanes, 2007) among Mintel's segmentation of sustainable consumers would likely take issue with the source of electric power, citing electricity produced from burning coal as a particularly problematic concern, EV manufacturers sidestep this issue with the promotion of renewable power including wind and solar sources. Tesla's cleaner transportation message takes a decidedly libertarian stance:

> Gasoline-powered vehicles and hybrids burn refined petroleum. Tesla vehicles can use electricity however it is produced, be it from coal, solar, hydro, geothermal, or wind power. As the grid shifts to increasingly efficient technologies, Tesla owners reap the efficiency benefits .... If you're looking to reduce your driving emissions even further, consider installing solar panels at your home. You'll produce renewable energy to power your home and your car. Model S becomes truly zero emissions. (Tesla Motors)

Producing power becomes a personal issue. Tesla suggests one build a solar panel at home to be as sustainable as possible, but also concedes the need for broader societal and governmental efforts. Tesla provides the car of the future, and then implores owners to decide if their attitude toward sustainability takes them farther down the road and eventually off the grid.

The Highest Form of Flattery

Since Tesla established greater demand for luxury sustainable automobiles, competitors in the segment have found the EV market to be enticing. BMW and Cadillac rolled out electric versions of their popular models. And other luxury carmakers are not far behind, Porsche, Mercedes, and Audi "are all readying electric cars to respond to the success of the Californian newcomer Tesla with its Model S" (Freitag, 2014). True to the conventions of marketing to high-end consumers, these brands tout their familiar luxury brand position first, and sustainability as a secondary benefit.

Economy entrants to the EV market have also increased. For a short time in the early 1990s the General Motors EV1 was the only electric option on the American highway. The demise of the model was famously profiled in the 2006 film, *Who Killed the Electric Car?* Toyota forged new EV ground with the Prius, followed by Chevrolet Volt, Nissan Leaf, Ford Focus, and others. The Light Greens consumer segment (Hanes, 2007) now has an increasing number of electric options. However, marketing of economy EVs addresses consumer need by primarily focusing on cognitive-rational appeals. For example, Chevrolet makes only a brief mention of design while focusing primarily on efficiency and combating range anxiety:

> The next-generation 2016 Chevrolet Volt hybrid-electric car combines stunning design and incredible efficiency, offering up to 53 pure electric miles on a single charge. With a range of up to 420 miles with a full charge and full tank of gas, Chevrolet expects owners will drive 1,000 miles between fill-ups by charging regularly. Voted 2016 Green Car of the Year by Green Car Journal, Volt is an award-winning way to go green. (Chevrolet Volt homepage)

Subsequent messages on the Chevy Volt homepage explain the logic of the car's power system, battery charging and ease of ownership. Nissan's marketing message leads with a comparison of Leaf models according to price, mile range and kilowatts of each model's lithium battery (Nissan Leaf homepage). With the Focus, Ford is:

> Charging ahead ... avoiding the gas station is fun in the 2016 Focus Electric. With zero gas, zero oil changes and zero CO2 emissions, it delivers a 100 percent electrifying driving experience. What's more, you have the choice of charging options – the standard 120-volt/30-amp convenience charge cord or the available 240-volt/30-amp home charging station. (Ford Focus homepage)

These economy models mention "design," "fun," and the "100 percent electrifying driving experience" in their opening messages while still putting the bulk of their effort into the economic, sustainable and ease of use appeals. Highlighting cost savings suits the psychographic needs of economy car buyers. They also take the issues of range anxiety and ease of charging up head-on. In short, the economic appeal of the vehicles feature more than the sustainability appeal.

A long-held focus on the attitude-behavior gap to promote sustainable products with cognitive-rational appeals concerning broad, societal, and environmental basis has left researchers puzzled as to why consumers don't walk their talk. However, the automotive industry focus on hedonics and aesthetics among luxury brands, and savings and ease of use among economy brands suggests a strategy for focusing less on trying to appeal to consumers through sustainability as a primary attitude and more on selling to the consumer in her entirety. Providing fun, beauty, and positive embodied consumption experience along with sustainable benefits brings the joy of purchasing and owning into focus.

MARKETING TO BRIDGE THE ATTITUDE-BEHAVIOR GAP?

In many ways Tesla's marketing efforts are not a major departure from traditions in the automotive industry. Touching automotive consumers with a combination of hedonic, aesthetic, and cognitive-rational approaches is commonplace. Tesla's efforts point to a more nuanced ideological perspective. Rather than assuming a need to first segment the marketing along the lines of sustainable ideology, Tesla sells the hedonic and aesthetic aspects of the vehicle, which also happens to be electric. The company's mission: "to accelerate the advent of sustainable transport by bringing compelling mass market electric cars to market as soon as possible" (Tesla) takes sustainability as a given, not an unusual and suspect pretender to conventional transport that would require particular consumer attitudes for adoption. By marketing their products in manner of conventional vehicles, Tesla privileges Holbrook and Hirschman's (1982) three facets of experiential consumption "multisensory, fantasy and emotive aspects of one's experience with products" (p. 92).

Tesla's marketing strategy is an example of how supposedly incongruent market ideologies can combine for more sustainable outcomes. The technologically advanced, luxury car is an unabashedly political active green machine. Under the head-turning design, lies a powerful statement of future possibilities, emblematic of systemic approaches to sustainable consumption. Marketing theorists can learn something from the aesthetic, hedonic, libertarian sustainable mix that is Tesla. A focus on linear information processing and other reductionist efforts impedes innovative multidisciplinary theory development needed to overcome the attitude-behavior gap conundrum.

ADDITIONAL PROPOSITIONAL POSSIBILITIES

Scholars in a wide variety of disciplines are taking up sustainable consumption and arguing for more inclusive theorizing. Cultural and contextual macro perspectives provide opportunities for theorizing. For instance Spaargaren (2003) argues that:

> Environmental sociologists need to conceptualize sustainable consumption behavior, lifestyles, and daily routines in such a way as to avoid the pitfalls of many of the so called micro-approaches that have been developed to date. We argue for a contextual approach to sustainable consumption and for that purpose try to develop a conceptual model that combines a focus on the central role of human agency with proper treatment of the equally important role of social structure. (p. 687)

Sanne (2002) suggest that structural issues inherent in working life conditions underpin the work-to-spend consumption behaviors even more than urban living or corporate marketing efforts. Any policy to move toward limited consumption also needs to address work-life balance. Thorpe (2010) entreats designers to consider if design sensibilities can "move from being a cog in the wheel of consumerism to having a substantial role in supporting sustainable consumption" (p. 3). McDonald, Oates, Alevizou, Young, and Hwang (2012) argue for flexibility in theorizing, finding that "even the same green consumer will not use the same information sources or decision-making criteria, consider the same options or focus on the same industry actors" (p. 445). Kollmuss and Agyeman (2002) note many of theories begin with absolutist dualism. By their very structure these theories failed to provide holistic approaches to understanding difference between consumers' reported sustainability attitudes and actual buying behavior. Consumer culture theorizing offers alternative perspective for understanding and shaping sustainable consumption practices. Central to these theories are concepts of ideology in cultural discourses, materiality and semiotics. Expecting calls for ethical behavior alone to move the needle of sustainable consumption is unreasonable. Addressing consumers through aesthetic, hedonic experiences before any mention of sustainability may be the best hope yet for a sustainable future. In her conceptual work, Sheller (2004) argues for theoretical links of "social, material and affective dimensions" in car culture, refuting the primacy of rationale choice in automotive consumption (p. 2). She calls for qualitative research of "emotional geographies" (p. 3) derived from a combination of individual psychological and collective cultural patterns which allows for "an emotional sociology of automobility [that] can contribute an invaluable theorization of the connections between the micro-level preferences of individual drivers, the meso-level aggregation of specifically located car cultures, and the macro-level patterns of regional, national, and transnational emotional/cultural/material geographies" (p. 3).

Holt (2012) offers an alternative to the wholesale effort to shift contemporary consumer society from the dominant social paradigm (Kilbourne et al., 1997) or from what he calls the "ideological lock-in" to more sustainable practices. He presents this approach as an "alternative sustainability strategy [that] requires effective market-facing social movements. And since the transformation process must aim at specific market ideologies, institutions, and practices, effective strategies must proceed market by market, rather than pursue an overarching shift in consumer society" (Holt, 2012, p. 253). Bettany and Kerrane's (2011) examination of urban stock-keeping offers a pathway to challenge dualism of consumption/anti-consumption and consumer resistance/domination as organizing constructs. This research also moves well beyond reductionist typologies generally found in attitude-behavior gap literature. And finally McDonagh and Prothero (2014) pinpoint the problem with marketing theorizing about sustainability to date calling "for theoretical and managerial reflections which tackle broader systemic and institutional issues within the discipline" (p. 1186).

The case of Tesla's marketing strategy is just one demonstration of the value of multi-faceted approaches possible for sustainable product and service providers. Research encompassing greater regard for consumer experience in sustainable consumption offers potential for additional strategies to bridge the gap. Consumer culture research needs to examine the interlinking of hedonic, aesthetic, and cognitive-rational aspect of sustainable consumption and consumer behavior. Moving beyond the attitude-behavior gap means, in part, rethinking the role of other aspects of consumer behavior, avoiding the myopia of focusing only on expressed attitudes and not forgetting in the importance of fun.

REFERENCES

Alba, J. W., & Williams, E. F. (2013). Pleasure principles: A review of research on hedonic consumption. *Journal of Consumer Psychology*, 23(1), 2−18.
Askegaard, S. (2010). Experience economy in the making: Hedonism, play and coolhunting in automotive song lyrics. *Consumption, Markets and Culture*, 13(4), 351−371.
Babin, B. J., Darden, W. R., & Griffin, M. (1994). Work and/or fun: Measuring hedonic and utilitarian shopping value. *Journal of Consumer Research*, 20, 644−656.
Belk, R. (2000). May the farce be with you: On Las Vegas and consumer infantilization. *Consumption, Markets and Culture*, 4(2), 101−123.
Beruchashvili, M., Gentry, J., & Price, L. (2006). Striving to be good: Moral balance in consumer choice. *European Advances in Consumer Research*, 7, 303−308.
Bettany, S., & Kerrane, B. (2011). The (post-human) consumer, the (post-avian) chicken and the (post-object) Eglu: Towards a material-semiotics of anti-consumption. *European Journal of Marketing*, 45(11−12), 1746−1756.
Blake, J. (1999). Overcoming the 'value−action gap' in environmental policy: Tensions between national policy and local experience. *Local Environment*, 4(3), 257−278.
Bonini, S., & Oppenheim, J. (2008). Cultivating the green consumer. *Stanford Social Innovation Review*, 6(4), 56−61.
Bonnell, A. (2015). Sustainability in America: Consumer attitudes toward green brands reach all-time high. *MarketResearch.com*. Retrieved from http://blog.marketresearch.com/sustainability-in-america-consumer-attitudes-toward-green-brands-reach-all-time-high
Boulstridge, E., & Carrigan, M. (2000). Do consumers really care about corporate responsibility? Highlighting the attitude-behaviour gap. *Journal of Communication Management*, 4(4), 355−368.
Carrigan, M., & Attalla, A. (2001). The myth of the ethical consumer-do ethics matter in purchase behaviour? *Journal of Consumer Marketing*, 18(7), 560−578.

Carù, A., & Cova, B. (2003). Revisiting consumption experience a more humble but complete view of the concept. *Marketing Theory, 3*(2), 267–286.

Carú, A., & Cova, B. (2005). The impact of service elements on the artistic experience: The case of classical music concerts. *International Journal of Arts Management, January*(1), 39–54.

Chevrolet Volt homepage. Retrieved from http://www.chevrolet.com/volt-electric-car.html. Accessed on November 25, 2015.

Charters, S. (2006). Aesthetic products and aesthetic consumption: A review. *Consumption, Markets and Culture, 9*(3), 235–255.

Chawla, L. (1999). Life paths into effective environmental action. *The Journal of Environmental Education, 31*(1), 15–26.

Craig-Lees, M., & Hill, C. (2002). Understanding voluntary simplifiers. *Psychology & Marketing, 19*(2), 187–210.

Energy Overviews. (2014). Retrieved from http://epoverviews.com/articles/visitor.php?page = 327&start_date = 1900-01-01&end_date = 2011-06-07&keyword = AT

Ford Focus homepage. Retrieved from http://www.ford.com/cars/focus/trim/electric/. Accessed on November 25, 2015.

Freitag, M. (2014). *Porsche, Mercedes und Audi planen Tesla-Fighter.* Retrieved from http://arstechnica.com/cars/

French-Constant, A. (2014). *Elon Musk talks Tesla. GQ Magazine.* Retrieved from http://www.gq-magazine.co.uk/entertainment/articles/2014-11/25/elon-musk-interview-tesla-p85dmars?utm_content = buffer7091f&utm_medium = social&utm_source = facebook. com&utm_campaign = buffer

Giesler, M., & Veresiu, E. (2014). Creating the responsible consumer: Moralistic governance regimes and consumer subjectivity. *Journal of Consumer Research, 41*(3), 840–857.

Gupta, S., & Ogden, D. T. (2009). To buy or not to buy? A social dilemma perspective on green buying. *Journal of Consumer Marketing, 26*(6), 376–391.

Hagtvedt, H., & Patrick, V. M. (2008a). Art infusion: The influence of visual art on the perception and evaluation of consumer products. *Journal of Marketing Research, 45*(3), 379–389.

Hagtvedt, H., & Patrick, V. M. (2008b). Art and the brand: The role of visual art in enhancing brand extendibility. *Journal of Consumer Psychology, 18*, 212–222.

Hagtvedt, H., & Patrick, V. M. (2009). The broad embrace of luxury: Hedonic potential as a driver of brand extendibility. *Journal of Consumer Psychology, 19*, 608–618.

Hanes, J. (2007). A world gone green. *Advertising Age,* June 8.

Holbrook, M., & Hirschman, E. (1982). The experiential aspects of consumption: Consumer fantasies, feelings, and fun. *Journal of Consumer Research, 9*(2), 132–140.

Holt, D. (2012). Constructing sustainable consumption: From ethical values to the cultural transformation of unsustainable markets. *The ANNALS of the American Academy of Political and Social Science, 644*(1), 236–255.

Izberk-Bilgin, E. (2010). An interdisciplinary review of resistance to consumption, some marketing interpretations, and future research suggestions. *Consumption, Markets and Culture, 13*(3), 299–323.

Joy, A., Sherry, J. F., Jr., Venkatesh, A., Wang, J., & Chan, R. (2012). Fast fashion, sustainability, and the ethical appeal of luxury brands. *Fashion Theory, 16*(3), 273–295.

Kilbourne, W., McDonagh, P., & Prothero, A. (1997). Sustainable consumption and the quality of life: A macromarketing challenge to the dominant social paradigm. *Journal of Macromarketing, 17*(1), 4–24.

Kollmuss, A., & Agyeman, J. (2002). Mind the gap: Why do people act environmentally and what are the barriers to pro-environmental behavior? *Environmental Education Research, 8*(3), 239–260.

Kozinets, R. V., Sherry, J. F., Storm, D., Duhachek, A., Nuttavuthisit, K., & DeBerry-Spence, B. (2004). Ludic agency and retail spectacle. *Journal of Consumer Research, 31*(3), 658–672.

Küpers, W. (2000). Embodied emotional and symbolic 'Pro-Sumption': Phenomenological perspectives for an interpretative consumer research. In S. C. Beckmann & R. H. Elliott (Eds.), *Interpretive consumer research* (pp. 293–317). Copenhagen: Copenhagen Business School Press.

Lanier, C. D., & Rader, C. S. (2015). Consumption experience: An expanded view. *Marketing Theory, 15*(4), 1–22.

Le Bel, J. L., & Dubé, L. (1998). Understanding pleasures: Source, experience, and remembrances. *Advances in Consumer Research, 25*(1), 176–180.

Leonard-Barton, D. (1981). Voluntary simplicity lifestyles and energy conservation. *Journal of Consumer Research, 8*, 243–252.

Levitt, T. (1960). Marketing myopia. *Harvard Business Review, 38*(4), 24–47.

Martin, D. M., & Schouten, J. W. (2012). *Sustainable marketing.* Upper Saddle River, NJ: Pearson Prentice Hall.

McDonagh, P., & Prothero, A. (2014). Sustainability marketing research: Past, present and future. *Journal of Marketing Management, 30*(11–12), 1186–1219.

McDonald, S., Oates, C. J., Alevizou, P. J., Young, C. W., & Hwang, K. (2012). Individual strategies for sustainable consumption. *Journal of Marketing Management, 28*(3–4), 445–468.

Nissan Leaf homepage. Retrieved from http://www.nissanusa.com/electric-cars/leaf/. Accessed on November 25, 2015.

Ottman, J. A., Stafford, E. R., & Hartman, C. L. (2006). Avoiding green marketing myopia: Ways to improve consumer appeal for environmentally preferable products. *Environment: Science and Policy for Sustainable Development, 48*(5), 22–36.

Park, C. W., Milberg, S., & Lawson, R. (1991). Evaluation of brand extensions: The role of product feature similarity and brand concept consistency. *Journal of Consumer Research, September*, 185–193.

Parkins, W., & Craig, G. (2006). *Slow living.* Oxford: Berg.

Patrick, V. M., & Hagtvedt, H. (2009). Luxury branding. In *The handbook of brand relationships* (pp. 267–280). New York, NY: Society for Consumer Psychology.

Reimann, M., Zaichkowsky, J., Neuhaus, C., Bender, T., & Weber, B. (2010). Aesthetic package design: A behavioral, neural, and psychological investigation. *Journal of Consumer Psychology, 20*(4), 431–441.

Russell, C. A., & Levy, S. J. (2012). The temporal and focal dynamics of volitional reconsumption: A phenomenological investigation of repeated hedonic experiences. *Journal of Consumer Research, 39*(2), 341–359.

Sanne, C. (2002). Willing consumers – or locked-in? Policies for a sustainable consumption. *Ecological Economics, 42*(1), 273–287.

Schaefer, A., & Crane, A. (2005). Addressing sustainability and consumption. *Journal of Macromarketing, 25*(1), 76–92.

Schor, J. B. (1998). *The overspent American: Downshifting and the new consumer.* New York, NY: Basic Books.

Schwartz, S. H. (1973). Normative explanations of helping behavior: A critique, proposal, and empirical test. *Journal of Experimental Social Psychology, 9*(4), 349–364.

Sheller, M. (2004). Automotive emotions: Feeling the car. *Theory, Culture & Society, 21*(4–5), 221–242.

Sherry, J. F. (1998). The soul of the company store: Nike Town Chicago and the emplaced brandscape. In J. F. Sherry (Ed.), *Servicescapes: The concept of place in contemporary markets* (pp. 109–150). Lincolnwood, IL: NTC Business Books.

Soper, K. (2007). Re-thinking the good life. The citizenship dimension of consumer disaffection with consumerism. *Journal of Consumer Culture, 7*(2), 205–229.

Spaargaren, G. (2003). Sustainable consumption: A theoretical and environmental policy perspective. *Society & Natural Resources, 16*(8), 687–701.

Tech Times. (2015). *Elon Musk 'Totally Cool' with rivals using Tesla's supercharger network.* Retrieved from http://www.techtimes.com/articles/89313/20150929/elon-musk-totally-cool-with-rivals-using-teslas-supercharger-network.htm. Accessed on November 24, 2015.

Tesla Motors. Retrieved from http://www.teslamotors.com/. Accessed on November 25, 2015.

Thorpe, A. (2010). Design's role in sustainable consumption. *Design Issues, 26*(2), 3–16.

Vermeir, I., & Verbeke, W. (2006). Sustainable food consumption: Exploring the consumer "Attitude–Behavioral Intention" gap. *Journal of Agricultural and Environmental Ethics, 19*(2), 169–194.

Woodruffe, H. (1997). Compensatory consumption: Why women go shopping when they're fed up and other stories. *Marketing Intelligence and Planning, 15*(7), 325–334.

PREVIOUS VOLUME CONTENTS

REVIEW OF MARKETING RESEARCH: VOLUME 1

REVIEW OF MARKETING RESEARCH: VOLUME 2

EDITOR: *Naresh K. Malhotra*

REVIEW OF MARKETING RESEARCH: VOLUME 3

EDITOR: *Naresh K. Malhotra*

REVIEW OF MARKETING RESEARCH: VOLUME 4

EDITOR: *Naresh K. Malhotra*

REVIEW OF MARKETING RESEARCH: VOLUME 5

REVIEW OF MARKETING RESEARCH: VOLUME 6

EDITOR: *Naresh K. Malhotra*

REVIEW OF MARKETING RESEARCH: VOLUME 8

EDITOR: *Naresh K. Malhotra*

REVIEW OF MARKETING RESEARCH: VOLUME 9

REVIEW OF MARKETING RESEARCH: VOLUME 10

EDITOR: *Naresh K. Malhotra*

REVIEW OF MARKETING RESEARCH: VOLUME 11

EDITOR: *Naresh K. Malhotra*

REVIEW OF MARKETING RESEARCH: VOLUME 12

EDITOR: *Naresh K. Malhotra*